APHORISMS ON

THE GOSPEL OF DIVINE LOVE

OR

NĀRADA BHAKTI SŪTRAS

with Sanskrit text, word-by-word meaning, English rendering of the text and elaborate explanatory and critical Notes

BY

SWĀMĪ TYĀGĪŚĀNANDA

SRI RAMAKRISHNA MATH
MADRAS–600 004 : : INDIA

Published by :
The President
Sri Ramakrishna Math
Mylapore, Chennai - 4

XII-1M 1C-4-2005
ISBN 81-7120-329-9

Printed in India at
Sri Ramakrishna Math Printing Press
Mylapore, Chennai - 4

PREFACE

In February 1940, the present work, appearing for about a couple of years as a serial in *The Vedanta Kesari*, was completed. Since then there has been continuous call for it in book form. After considerable revision, a provisional edition of it is now issued to meet this demand. As it is, the book now comprises two parts. The original aphorisms, as constituted from four previous editions, are printed first in Devanāgarī alphabet, chapter by chapter, along with their word-by-word meaning and English rendering which aims to be faithful to the spirit of the original rather than to the letter. The division into five chapters is also based on the editions consulted for deriving the text. All the variant readings too noticed in them are indicated in the body of the book itself within brackets. It has been intentionally made so to make the book welcome to the lay reader who has not the equipment to penetrate to the important arguments of the Sanskrit text through the hurdle of exegetical appurtenances.

The Notes which come as the second part run over fifty-thousand words and constitute the major portion of the book. Attempt has been made, in this part, to elucidate the text from all possible viewpoints, to note down the syntactic sequence, to canvas the sense of the various significant expressions, to evaluate the doctrine in the light of allied literature, and to answer the doubts and objections which are likely to arise in connection with the various points discussed. One may modestly say that this division of the publication is a mine of information on almost all matters connected with religion and spiritual life. The writer has spared no pains to make the explanations specially useful to the intelligent modern spiritual aspirant who cannot insulate himself from the scientific atmosphere in which he is brought up, and who, besides, is not prejudiced against religion so as to flout its authority simply because it partly rests on tradition. The explanations are therefore made, as far as possible, rational, in line with possible experience, and copiously documented. Under the circumstance a large number of extracts from Sanskrit scriptures and mystical writings of other religions had to be incorporated. These citations show, by the way, the universality of the religious experience itself in all its levels, and reassure the aspirants of all classes about the reality of their quest. One may find a few repetitions and some divagations here and there. They are intentionally retained to stress some of the important points from different bearings and fresh settings, as well as to dispel the doubts that are likely to assault the novitiate in spiritual life while pondering over the various problems discussed under each aphorism. Remembering all these specific features this part may be considered a distinct work.

It is a matter of regret that we were handicapped in various ways in dealing with all the references in a uniform manner. One would have wished very much to reproduce all of them in full along with the translation of all the Sanskrit passages. This could not be done in this edition owing to certain difficulties. Nevertheless most of the quotations of an illustrative character have been printed in full with translation or the substance of the original in English, preceding or following the extracted texts. Only a few such texts and translations are left out without the corresponding translations or text, or both. It is hoped that this irregularity will be removed in the next issue. The deficiency of an index and sectional headings are also to some extent made good by different head-lines on each page referring to the leading idea below. To facilitate frequent reference to the text the number of the aphorisms are given in the upper inside corner of each page.

It is superfluous to state here anything about this sacred text itself, except perhaps that this precious gem of a tract is a complete and thorough guide book, an indispensable companion, for all sincere seekers after God and the divine life, from the start of their spiritual ascent to the very summit of it. Srī Rāmakṛṣṇaparamahaṁsa has stressed again and again that for Kaliyuga the Path of Devotion as described by Nārada is indeed, the best and the easiest. This is but an echo of the experience and verdict of innumerable saints and holy men who have preceded him.

The aphoristic statements of Nārada are likely to appear to the superficial reader a group of eighty-four recondite devotional sayings. The fact is quite different. For, one will find on examination that all of them fall within a scheme with perfect inner coherence, if one reads bearing in mind the relation subsisting between the various aspects of Divine Love.

Supreme Divine Love, together with the steps leading to it, is called Bhakti. The phenomenon of Bhakti therefore has a pre-mature stage, designated as Aparabhakti and a mature stage of subjective experience known as Parabhakti. Mature Divine Love may be viewed again subjectively and objectively. The transcendental aspect of it is an uncharacterizable, incommunicable, and ineffable experience of unsurpassed bliss and illumination always equated with Self-realization or God-realization. It is also called Liberation-in-Life, or Perfect Gnosis. The marks that may be observed in a person who possesses this perfect realization, when that realization expresses through his moods, thoughts, words, and deeds, are called the objective aspect of Parabhakti. The first chapter of the book describes these various aspects of Parabhakti in twentyfour solemn and lucid aphorisms. In the second chapter this Parabhakti is extolled as superior to all spiritual disciplines, and all who are aspiring after liberation are exhorted to seek after that and that alone.

Aparabhakti, or the pre-mature stage of Divine Love, is further subdivided into Gauṇabhakti and Mukhyabhakti styled as Vaidhabhakti and Rāgānugabhakti by Srī Rāmakṛṣṇa. The former division of this classification refers to a preparatory stage of discipline, and the latter to the most advanced stage resulting from the practice of that preparatory discipline; but both are only means to the highest realization. While Parabhakti is of the nature of the actual realization of the goal itself, or the full maturation of the whole endeavour, Aparabhakti is a stage prior to the attainment of that maturation; and therefore it involves effort and gradual achievement; it is a process. The most advanced stage of Aparabhakti, called Mukhyabhakti or Ekānta-bhakti, supervenes upon the fulfilment of the duties enjoined on the novitiate in the disciplinary Path of Devotion, as a result of Divine grace which then naturally flows into the devotee's heart. This stage prepares the mind of the devotee fully and perfectly for the final realization; and God then blesses him with divine illumination instantaneously. The third chapter sets forth at length with much psychological insight the moral rules and spiritual discipline of Vaidhabhakti which the aspirant ought to practise with meticulous care, unflagging zeal, and unbroken continuity. The fourth chapter characterizes the behaviour of the aspirant who, as a result of the above discipline, has come to have Rāga-Bhakti in which God-realization is immediate and inevitable. The closing chapter, which is the fifth, depicts how the Mukhya-Bhakta lives in the world, how he satisfies all beings, what blessings society derives from him, and how God reveals Himself to him as his most Beloved Self and how the Mukhya-bhakti transforms itself into the Parabhakti.

From the above synopsis the logical sequence underlying the aphorisms is evident. The Divine sage Nārada declares to the entire humanity through his auspious gospel, with the anxiety of a great saviour, the existence of Immortal Divine Bliss as the birthright of all; admonishes ignorant man to strive for it, leaving aside all allurements of sense life; instructs the seeking aspirant about the methods by which he may attain to the Goal; heartens the seekers after the Divine with the shining example of the perfect devotees; and assures and gladdens all by his own experience and example how the Master and Lord of all the universe is ever eager to confer upon the earnest and one-pointed lover of God His unconditioned Grace, by the power of which he attains freedom from Saṁsāra and eternal Bliss. May Nārada's Gospel of Divine Love in this setting be helpful to many to reach that goal of life.

PUBLISHER.

ABBREVIATIONS

Adhr(a)(m).	Adhyātmarāmāyaṇa
Atharv.	Atharvaveda
Bg.	Bhagavadgītā
Bhāg.	Bhāgavata
Brahmāṇdp.	Brahmāṇḍapurāṇa
Brahp.	Brahmapurāṇa
Brahvaip.	Brahmavaivartapurāṇa
Bṛh.	Brhadāraṇyakopaniṣad
Bsū.	Brahmasūtras
Chan(d).	Chāndogyopaniṣad
Devibhāg.	Devībhāgavata
Garuḍap.	Garuḍapuraṇa
Hv.	Harivaṁśa
Jsū.	Jaiminisūtras
Kaṭh.	Kaṭhopaniṣad
Ken.	Kenopaniṣad
Kūrmap.	Kūrmapurāṇa
Kauṣ.	Kauṣītakyupaniṣad
Māṇd.	Māṇḍūkyopaniṣad
Mātsp.	Matsyapurāṇa
Muṇḍ.	Muṇḍakopanisad
Mnu.	Manusmrtī
Mbh.	Mahābhārata
Npāñ.	Nāradapāñcarātra
Nṛsiṁhap.	Nṛsiṁhapurāṇa
Pad(m)p.	Padmapurāṇa

Rgv.	Rgveda
Sāmv.	Sāmaveda
Sivap.	Sivapurāṇa
Skdr.	Sabdakalpadruma
Skp.	Skåndapurāṇa
Ssū.	Sāṇdilyasūtra
Sū.	Sūtra
Sūs.	Sūtras
Sve.	Svetāśvataropaniṣad
Tait.	Taittiríyopaniṣad
Upd.	Upaniṣad
Vp.	Viṣṇupurāṇa
Yājsmṛti.	Yājñavalkyasmṛti
Yājñ.	do
Ysū.	Yogasūtras of Patañjali
Yvā. (or *Yogv.*)	Yogavāsīṣṭha

नारदभक्तिसूत्राणि

प्रथमोऽध्यायः — परभक्तिस्वरूपम् ।

हरिः ॐ ॥ १ अथातो भक्तिं व्याख्यास्यामः ।

अथ now अतः therefore भक्तिम् the religion of Divine Love व्याख्यास्यामः we shall expound.

1. Now, therefore, we shall expound the religion of Divine Love.

२. सा त्वस्मिन् पर(म)प्रेमरूपा ।

सा that (i.e., Bhakti) तु but अस्मिन् in This परम-प्रेम-रूपा of the nature of Supreme Love (भवति is).

2. That, verily, is of the nature of supreme Love of God.

३. अमृतस्वरूपा च ।

(सा that भक्तिः Divine Love) अमृत-स्वरूपा having the essential form of Amṛta च also (भवति is).

3. And in its own intrinsic nature, Divine Love is nothing less than the immortal bliss of freedom (Mukti) itself, which comes unsolicited by the grace of God and by self-sacrifice.

४. यल्लब्ध्वा पुमान् सिद्धो भवति, अमृतो भवति, तृप्तो भवति ।

यत् which लब्ध्वा having gained पुमान् a person सिद्धः perfect भवति becomes, अमृतः Divine भवति becomes, तृप्तः contented भवति becomes.

4. Gaining that, man realizes his perfection and divinity and becomes thoroughly contented.

५. यत् प्राप्य न किञ्चिद वाञ्छति, न शोचति, न द्वेष्टि, न रमते, नोत्साही भवति ।

यत् which प्राप्य having attained (पुमान् a person) किञ्चित् anything न not वाञ्छति desires, न not शोचति grieves, न not द्वेष्टि feels enmity, न not रमते rejoices, उत्साही one who is active (in one's own interest) न भवति is not.

5. Attaining that, man has no more desire for anything; he is free from grief and hatred; he does not rejoice over anything; he does not exert himself in furtherance of self-interest.

६. यत् ज्ञात्वा मत्तो भवति, स्तब्धो भवति. आत्मारामो भवति ।

यत् which ज्ञात्वा having known (पुमान् a person) मत्तः intoxicated (इव as it were) भवति becomes. स्तब्धः stiff or fascinated (इव as it were) भवति becomes. (यतः because) आत्मारामः one continually enjoying the Bliss of the Atman भवति becomes.

6. Realizing that, man becomes intoxicated and fascinated, as it were, because he is completely immersed in the enjoyment of the Bliss of the Atman, the truest and highest self.

७. सा न कामयमाना, निरोधरूपत्वात् ।

सा that (i.e., Bhakti described as Paramaprema in Sūtra 2) कामयमाना of the nature of lust न not (भवति is); निरोध-रूपत्वात् being of the form of renunciation.

7. Bhakti (described before as Paramaprema or Supreme Love) is not of the nature of lust, because it is a form of renunciation.

८. निरोधस्तु लोकवेदव्यापारन्यासः ।

निरोधः renunciation (referred to in the previous Sūtra as an invariable characteristic of Supreme Love) तु now लोक-वेद-व्यापार-न्यासः consecration (Nyāsa) of secular and sacred activities (भवति is).

8. Now this renunciation (which is referred to in the last Sūtra as an invariable characteristic of Parābhakti) is only a consecration of all activities, sacred as well as secular.

९ तस्मिन्ननन्यता तद्विरोधिषूदासीनता च ।

तस्मिन् in that (i.e., Nyāsa) अनन्यता identification, complete unification तद्-विरोधिषु in respect of what is opposed to it उदासीनता indifference च and (जायते is engendered).

9. In such renunciation by consecration, there is complete unification, and indifference towards everything opposed to it.

१०. अन्याश्रयाणां त्यागोऽनन्यता ।

अन्य-आश्रयाणाम् of all other supports त्यागः rejection अनन्यता unification.

10. 'Unification' means the abandonment of all other support.

११. लोकवेदेषु तदनुकूलाचरणं तद्विरोधिषूदासीनता ।

लोक-वेदेषु regarding secular and sacred activities तद्-अनुकूल-आचरणम् practices only favourable to it तद्

विरोधिषु in respect of what are hostile to it उदासीनता indifference (एव alone).

11. 'Indifference to factors hostile to devotion' means performance of such secular and sacred activities as are favourable to devotion.

१२ भवतु निश्चयदार्ढ्यादूर्ध्वं शास्त्ररक्षणम् ।

निश्चयदार्ढ्याद्-ऊर्ध्वम् after realization becoming firmly established (अपि even) शास्त्र-रक्षणम् protection or care for scriptural ordinances भवतु let there be.

12. Let a man have care for the Scriptural teachings even after his spiritual realization becomes well established.

१३. अन्यथा पातित्य(ा)शङ्कया ।

अन्यथा otherwise पातित्य-शङ्कया peril of a fall (भवितव्यम् is likely).

13. For, otherwise there is the risk of fall.

१४. लोकोऽपि तावदेव ; भोजनादिव्यापारस्त्वाशरीर-धारणावधि ।

लोक: social practices अपि too तावत् that much एव only; भोजन-आदि-व्यापार: activities such as taking food तु but आ-शरीर-धारण-अवधि to the extent of keeping bodily fitness till the body falls off in the natural course (भवतु let there be).

14. Social customs and practices also may be followed, in like manner, to that extent only; but activities, like taking food, may be continued to the measure necessary for the preservation of the health of the body until it falls off in its natural course.

१५. तल्लक्षणानि वाच्यन्ते नानामतभेदात् ।

तत्-लक्षणानि its characteristics मत-भेदात् owing to difference in view-points नाना variously वाच्यन्ते are being described.

15. The characteristics of Bhakti are described variously on account of difference in view-points.

१६. पूजादिष्वनुराग इति पाराशर्यः ।

पूजा-आदिषु in acts of worship etc., अनुरागः devotion इति thus पाराशर्यः son of the sage Parāśara, i.e., Vyāsa (मन्यते holds).

16. Vyāsa, the son of Parāśara, is of the opinion that Bhakti expresses itself in devotion to acts of worship and the like.

१७. कथादिष्विति गर्गः ।

कथा-आदिषु in holy talk and the like (अनुरागः devotion) इति thus गर्गः sage Garga (मन्यते holds).

17. The sage Garga thinks that it expresses itself in devotion to 'sacred talk' and the like.

१८. आत्मरत्यविरोधेनेति शाण्डिल्यः ।

आत्मरति-अविरोधेन without prejudice to delight in the Atman इति thus शाण्डिल्यः sage Sāṇḍilya (मन्यते thinks).

18. The sage Sāṇḍilya holds that it must be without prejudice to the delight in the Atman.

१९. नारदस्तु तदर्पिताखिलाचारता तद्विस्मरणे परमव्याकुलतेति (च) ।

नारदः sage Nārada तु in distinction from others तद्-अर्पित-अखिल-आचार-ता (तस्मिन् अर्पितः आचारः येन सः, तस्य

भाव:) the state of one who has consecrated all activities to Him through self-surrender तद्-विस्मरणे in the event of forgetting Him परम extreme व्याकुलता anguish (च and परभक्ति: Supreme Devotion) इति thus (मन्यते holds).

19. But Nārada is of the opinion that the essential characteristics of Bhakti are the consecration of all activities, by complete self-surrender to Him, and extreme anguish if He were to be forgotten.

२०. अस्त्येवमेवम् ।

एवम् एवम् thus and thus (उदाहरणम् example) अस्ति there is.

20. Examples do exist, of such perfect expression of Bhakti.

२१. यथा व्रजगोपिकानाम् ।

यथा for instance व्रज-गोपिकानाम् of the Gopis of Vraja (उदाहरणम् example).

21. Such indeed was the Bhakti of the Gopis of Vraja.

२२. तत्रापि न माहात्म्यज्ञानविस्मृत्यपवादः ।

तत्र there i.e., in respect of the example of the Gopis. अपि even माहात्म्य-ज्ञान-विस्मृति-अपवाद: (माहात्म्यस्य ज्ञानम्, तस्य विस्मृति:, स एव अपवाद:) the blame or contradiction of not recognizing or forgetting, the glory and greatness the Lord न not (अस्ति exists).

22. Even here, the charge that they did not recognize the divine glory of the Lord, does not hold good.

२३. तद्विहीनं जाराणामिव ।

तत् (=महात्म्यज्ञानम्) विहीनम् bereft of the knowledge of that (glory of the Lord) (प्रेम love) जाराणाम् of couples indulging in unlawful love इव like.

23. Had they lacked this knowledge of the Divinity of the object of their love, their love would have been similar to the base passion of a mistress for her paramour.

२४. नास्त्येव तस्मिन् तत्सुखसुखित्वम् ।

तस्मिन् in that (profane love) तत्-सुखसुखित्वम् तस्यसुख तत्सुखं, तस्मिन् सुखं यस्य स तत्सुखसुखी, तस्य भावः) happiness in the happiness of the other न not अस्ति is एव assuredly.

24. There, i.e., in that profane love of the mistress for her paramour, her happiness does not at all consist in the happiness of the other.

द्वितीयोऽध्यायः — परंभक्तिमहत्त्वम् ।

२५. सा तु कर्मज्ञानयोगेभ्योऽप्यधिकतरा ।

सा that Parābhakti तु in distinction from others कर्मज्ञान-योगेभ्यः than spiritual work, Self-knowledge and disciplined contemplation अपि even अधिकतरा superior, greater.

25. But the Supreme Divine Love described before is also something more than Karma, Jñāna, and Yoga.

२६. फलरूपत्वात् ।

फल-रूपत्वात् because of its being of the nature of the result (of all the three methods mentioned above).

26. For, it is of the nature of the fruit or result of all these.

२७. ईश्वरस्याप्यभिमान(नि)द्वेषित्वात् दैन्यप्रियत्वात् च ।

ईश्वरस्य in reference to the Lord अपि also अभिमान-द्वेषित्वात् dislike for conceit or egoism दैन्यप्रियत्वात् liking for the feeling of distress च and (हेतो: because भक्ति: love for God एव alone अधिकतरा superior).

27. And also because God dislikes the reliance on one's own unaided self-effort, and likes the complete feeling of misery due to the consciousness of one's helplessness in independently working out one's salvation, Bhakti is greater.

२८. तस्या: ज्ञानमेव साधनमित्येके ।

तस्या: of that Supreme Love ज्ञानम् knowledge एव alone साधनम् means इति thus एके some (आचार्या: teachers मन्यन्ते think).

28. In the view of some, knowledge alone is the means to attain it.

२९ अन्योन्याश्रयत्वमित्यन्ये ।

अन्योन्य-आश्रयत्वम् mutual dependence इति thus अन्ये others (मन्यन्ते deem).

29. Others think that these various means or faculties are inter-dependent.

३० स्वयं फलरूपतेति ब्रह्मकुमार(1): ।

स्वयम्-फल-रूपता the fact of a thing (Bhakti) being its own fruit इति thus ब्रह्मकुमार: son of Brahmā, i.e., Nārada (मन्यते thinks).

30. But Nārada says that the spiritual realization is its own fruit.

३१ राजगृहभोजनादिषु तथैव दृष्टत्वात् ।

राज-गृह-भोजन-आदिषु in the case of the king, home, and dinner तथा in similar manner एव only दृष्टत्वात् because it has been seen.

31. For it is seen only thus in the case of the king, home and dinner.

३२. न तेन राजा परितोषः क्षु(धाशा)च्छान्तिर्वा ।

तेन by that राजा king परितोषः satisfaction क्षुत्-शान्तिः appeasement of hunger वा or न, not (दृष्टः is seen).

32. Not as a result of that does the king become king, nor the wayfarer derive satisfaction, nor the hungry man feel appeased.

३३. तस्मात् सैव ग्राह्या मुमुक्षुभिः ।

तस्मात् hence मुमुक्षुभिः by seekers of Liberation सा that (Supreme Love) एव alone ग्राह्या worthy of being accepted (as the goal).

33. Therefore that highest spiritual realization alone is worthy of being accepted as the goal by people who are desirous of permanent release from all bondage.

तृतीयोऽध्यायः — भक्तिसाधनानि ।

३४. तस्याः साधनानि गायन्त्याचार्याः ।

तस्याः of that Supreme Love साधनानि means आचार्याः teachers गायन्ति sing.

34. Teachers describe in hymns and songs (i.e., Vedas, Epics, and the rest) the following as the means of spiritual realization.

३५. तत् तु विषयत्यागात् सङ्गत्यागात् च ।

तत् that (Prema referred to before) तु now विषय-त्यागात् by rejecting the objective (reality of the world as it appears to an ego-centric intellect) सङ्ग-त्यागात् by renunciation of attachment च and (सम्भवति is possible).

35. But that state of Supreme Love and Immortality is made possible only by giving up the objective reality of the world as it appears to the ego-centric intellect and senses, and the consequent renunciation of attachment.

३६. अव्यावृत्त(त)भजनात् ।

अव्यावृत्त-भजनात् by uninterrupted loving service.

36. By uninterrupted loving service.

३७. लोकेऽपि भगवद्गुणश्रवणकीर्तनात् ।

लोके while engaged in the ordinary activities of life अपि even भगवद्-गुण-श्रवण-कीर्तनात् by hearing and singing the glories of the Lord.

37. By hearing and singing the glory of the Lord, even while engaged in the ordinary activities of life.

३८. मुख्यतस्तु महत्कृपयैव भगवत्कृपालेशाद् वा ।

मुख्यत: chiefly तु but महत्-कृपया through the grace of great men भगवत्-कृपा-लेशात् through a slight measure of the grace of the Lord वा or (सम्भवति is possible).

38. Primarily, it is got only through the grace of great souls, or through a slight measure of Divine grace.

३९. महत्सङ्गस्तु दुर्लभोऽगम्योऽमोघश्च ।

महत्-सङ्ग: company of the great तु then दुर्लभ: difficult to obtain अगम्य: subtle and incomprehensible अमोघ: infallible, unerringly effective च and (भवति is).

39. But it is extremely difficult to come into contact with a great soul and to be benefited by his company; the influence of such a one is subtle, incomprehensible, and unerringly infallible in its effect.

४०. लभ्यतेऽपि तत्कृपयैव ।

अपि nevertheless लभ्यते is attained तत्-कृपया by their grace एव only.

40. Nevertheless it is attainable by the grace of God and Godmen alone.

४१. तस्मिंस्तज्जने भेदाभावात् ।

तस्मिन् in Him तत्-जने in His creatures भेद-अभावात् because of the absence of difference.

41. Because in God and in His devotees there is no sense of difference between any two objects of the universe.

४२. तदेव साध्यतां तदेव साध्यताम् ।

तत् that (i.e., aids to Love of God referred to in Sū. 35-37) एव alone साध्यताम् be adopted.

42. Such practices as would enable us to take advantage of their grace alone are to be adopted.

४३. दुस्सङ्गः सर्वथैव त्याज्यः ।

दुःसङ्ग: evil company सर्वथा by every means त्याज्य: to be shunned एव only.

43. Evil company, however, is fit only to be shunned by all means.

४४. कामक्रोधमोहस्मृतिभ्रंशबुद्धिनाश(सर्वनाश)कारणत्वात्

काम-क्रोध-मोह-स्मृति-भ्रंश-बुद्धि-नाश-सर्व-नाश-कारण-त्वात् being the cause of lust, anger, delusion, loss of remembrance as well as discrimination and utter ruin.

44. For it leads to the rousing up of desire, anger, and delusion, to loss of memory, to loss of discrimination, and to utter ruin in the end.

४५. तरङ्गायिता अपीमे सङ्गात् समुद्रायन्ते(न्ति) ।

इमे these तरङ्गायिता: acting as ripples अपि though सङ्गात् by (evil) association समुद्रायन्ते become like an ocean.

45. Though they rise only in the form of ripples in the beginning, they become like a veritable sea as a result of evil company.

४६. कस्तरति कस्तरति मायाम्? यः सङ्गं(ङ्गान्)त्यजति, यो महानुभावं सेवते, निर्ममो भवति ।

कः who तरति goes across; कः who मायाम् the world of senses (with all contingent troubles) तरति crosses? यः he who सङ्गम् contact त्यजति gives up; यः who महानुभावम् a great spiritual man सेवते resorts to and serves: निर्ममः free from the sense of possession भवति becomes.

46. Who crosses, who crosses the Māyā? He who avoids all contact with such objects of senses as are likely to inflame passions, resorts to spiritually great souls, serves them, and gets rid of all possessions in the service of the needy.

४७. यो विविक्तस्थानं सेवते, यो लोकबन्धमुन्मूलयति, (यो) निस्त्रैगुण्यो भवति, (यो) योगक्षेमं त्यजति ।

यः who विविक्त स्थानम् a lone and holy place सेवते resorts to. यः who लोकबन्धम् bondage to the rewards of the three worlds उन्मूलयति roots out; निस्त्रैगुण्यः free from the effects of the three modes of Nature भवति becomes; योगक्षेमम् acquisition and preservation त्यजति abandons.

47. He who resorts to a solitary and pure place, roots out his bondage to the pleasures of the three worlds, gets free from the effects of the three Guṇas, and gives up all ideas of acquisition and preservation;

४८. यः कर्मफलं त्यजति, कर्माणि सन्न्यस्यति, ततो निर्द्वन्द्वो भवति ।

यः who कर्मफलम् results of work त्यजति gives up कर्माणि selfish work सन्न्यस्यति renounces, ततः thereby निर्द्वन्द्वः free from pairs of opposites such as pleasure and pain भवति becomes.

48. He who gives up the fruits of all work, renounces all selfish activities and passes beyond all pairs of opposites such as pleasure and pain;

४९. (यो) वेदानपि सन्न्यस्यति ; केवलमविच्छिन्नानुरागं लभते ।

यः who वेदान् the duties enjoined by the Vedas अपि even सन्न्यस्यति renounces; केवलम् unalloyed अविच्छिन्न-अनुरागम् unintermittent love लभते attains.

49. He who gives up even the rites and ceremonies prescribed by the Vedas and obtains unintermittent hankering for God;

५०. स तरति स तरति, स लोकांस्तारयति ।

सः he तरति crosses; सः he तरति crosses; लोकान् all the world सः he तारयति carries across.

50. He crosses indeed, he crosses this Māyā and carries also the world across it.

चतुर्थोऽध्यायः — प्रेमनिर्वचनम् ।

५१. अनिर्वचनीयं प्रेमस्वरूपम् ।

प्रेम-स्वरूपम् the intrinsic nature of love अनिर्वचनीयम् (is) incapable of being described precisely.

51. The intrinsic nature of devotion defies exact and precise analysis, definition, or description.

५२. मूकास्वादनवत् ।

मूक-आस्वादन-वत् like the dumb man's experience of delightful taste.

52. It is like the experience of joy which a dumb man has when he tastes something sweet.

५३. प्रकाश(श्य)ते क्वापि पात्रे ।

(तत् that love) क्व-अपि at any place and time पात्रे in a fit recipient प्रकाशते is manifested.

53. The devotion, nevertheless, manifests itself, in one,—whosoever it be—when one has made oneself fit for such manifestation by constant Sādhanā.

५४. गुणरहितं कामनारहितं प्रतिक्षणवर्धमानं अविच्छिन्नं सूक्ष्मतरं अनुभवरूपम् ।

गुण-रहितम् devoid of all attributes कामना-रहितम् devoid of characteristic tendencies to selfish action प्रतिक्षण-

वर्धमानम् expanding every moment अविच्छिन्नम् homogeneous and integral सूक्ष्मतरम् extremely subtle अनुभवरूपम् of the nature of an inner experience.

54. Devoid of all attributes and free from all characteristic tendencies to selfish action, it is of the nature of a homogeneous and integral subjective experience, subtler than the subtlest, manifesting itself automatically in the wake of the fulfilment of certain conditions, and expanding every moment.

५५. तत् प्राप्य तदेवावलोकयति, तदेव शृणोति, (तदेव भाषयति), तदेव चिन्तयति ।

तत् that प्राप्य having attained तत् that एव alone अवलोकयति sees; तत् that एव alone शृणोति hears; तत् that एव alone भाषयति speaks; तत् that एव alone चिन्तयति ponders over.

55. Attaining that, one sees and hears only that, talks and thinks only that.

५६ गौणी त्रिधा, गुणभेदाद् आर्तादिभेदाद् वा ।

गौणी secondary (Bhakti) त्रिधा threefold (भवति is)—गुण-भेदात् according to the difference in the dispositions of Nature (i.e., Sattva, Rajas, and Tamas) आर्त-आदि-भेदात् according to the division of the distressed and the rest (given in the *Bg.* VII. 16) वा or.

56. Secondary devotion is of three kinds, according to the qualities of the mind of the person in whom it manifests itself; either it may be classified as Sāttvika, Rājasika, and Tāmasika; or it may be divided as Ārta, Jijñāsu, and Arthārthin as per statement in the *Bg.* VII. 16.

५७. उत्तरस्मादुत्तरस्मात् पूर्वपूर्वा श्रेयाय भवति ।

उत्तरस्मात् उत्तरस्मात् than each succeeding one पूर्व-पूर्वा each preceding one श्रेयाय for the sake of the highest good भवति is.

57. Each preceding one conduces better to the highest good than the one succeeding.

५८. अन्यस्मात् सौलभ्यं भक्तौ ।

भक्तौ with respect to Divine Love अन्यस्मात् than others सौलभ्यं easy recognizability.

58. This devotion is more easily attained and recognized than Parābhakti.

५९. प्रमाणान्तरस्यानपेक्षत्वात् स्वयं प्रमाणत्वात् (च) ।

प्रमाण-अन्तरस्य of any proof other than itself अनपेक्षत्वात् because of non-dependence स्वयम् in itself प्रमाणत्वात् being the nature of a proof.

59. Because it does not depend on any other proof; and it is self-evident.

६०. शान्तिरूपात् परमानन्दरूपाच्च ।

शान्ति-रूपात् because of its being of the form of peace of mind परम-आनन्द-रूपात् because of its being of the form of supreme happiness च and.

60. Because it is of the form of complete peace of mind and supreme joy.

६१. लोकहानौ चिन्ता न कार्या ; निवेदितात्मलोकवेद-(शील) त्वात् ।

लोकहानौ with regard to the miseries of the world चिन्ता anxiety न not कार्या (is) to be entertained—

निवेदित-आत्म-लोक-वेद-त्वात् on account of (his) having surrendered (to the Lord his own) self, the worlds, and the Vedas.

61. The Bhakta has no cause to worry himself over the miseries of the world; for he has surrendered his own self, the world as well as the Vedas to the Lord.

६२. न त(द)त्सिद्धौ लोकव्यवहारो हेयः, किन्तु फलत्यागः तत्साधनं च (कार्यमेव)।

तत्-सिद्धौ for or on attaining it लोक-व्यवहारः social life न not हेयः to be forsaken; किन्तु but फल-त्यागः renunciation of (the desire for the) fruits of actions तत्-साधनम् means helpful to it च and कार्यम् must be performed एव certainly.

62. On the attainment of Bhakti, or even for the attainment of it, life in society need not be shunned; but only the fruits of all social activities are to be surrendered to the Lord; while all such activities, naturally righteous and so bearing noble fruit, may be continued.

६३. स्त्रीधननास्तिक(वैरि)चरित्रं न श्रवणीयम् ।

स्त्री-धन-नास्तिक-चरित्रम् descriptions of the behaviour of women and ungodly persons as well as of wealth न श्रवणीयम् should not be listened to.

63. Stories or descriptions of women, wealth, or atheists should not be listened to.

६४. अभिमानदम्भादिकं त्याज्यम् ।

अभिमान-दम्भ-आदिकम् pride, vanity and other vices त्याज्यम् must be cast out.

64. Pride, vanity and other vices should be given up.

६५. तदर्पिताखिलाचारः सन् कामक्रोधाभिमानादिकं तस्मिन्नेव करणीयम् ।

तद्-अर्पित-अखिल-आचारः one who has dedicated all activities to Him सन् being काम-क्रोध-अभिमान-आदिकम् desire, anger, pride, etc. तस्मिन् with reference to Him एव alone करणीयम् should be employed.

65. Dedicating all activities to Him, desire, anger, pride, etc., should be directed only towards Him, or employed only in the exercise of Bhakti towards Him.

६६. त्रिरूपभङ्गपूर्वकं नित्यदास्य(स)नित्यकान्ताभजनात्मकं प्रेम कार्यं प्रेमैव कार्यम् ।

त्रि-रूप-भङ्गपूर्वकम् transcending the triple form नित्य-दास्य-नित्य-कान्ता-भजन-आत्मकम् consisting of constant loving service such as that of a devoted servant or wife प्रेम love कार्यम् should be practised प्रेम love एव alone कार्यम् should be cultivated.

66. Love and love alone such as that of a devoted servant or a wife, which transcends the three forms mentioned in Sūtra 56, should be practised.

पञ्चमोऽध्यायः — मुख्याभक्तमहिमा ।

६७. भक्ता एकान्तिनो मुख्याः ।

एकान्तिनः those who possess one-pointed love of the Lord for His own sake भक्ताः devotees मुख्याः are primary.

67. Those are primary devotees who have one-pointed love of God foı His·own sake.

६८. कण्ठावरोधरोमाञ्चाश्रुभिः परस्परं लपमानाः पावयन्ति कुलानि पृथिवीं च ।

कण्ठ-अवरोध-रोमाञ्च-अश्रुभिः with choking of voice hair standing on end, and tears (flowing from the eyes) परस्परम् with one another लपमानाः conversing कुलानि clans पृथिवीम् the earth च and पावयन्ति purify.

68. Conversing with one another with choking voice, tearful eyes, and thrilled body, they purify not only their families but the land which gave birth to them.

६९. तीर्थीकुर्वन्ति तीर्थानि, सुकर्मीकुर्वन्ति कर्माणि, सच्छास्त्रीकुर्वन्ति शास्त्राणि ।

(ते they) तीर्थानि holy places तीर्थीकुर्वन्ति make holy कर्माणि deeds सुकर्मीकुर्वन्ति make good and righteous शास्त्राणि scriptures सच्छास्त्रीकुर्वन्ति make authoritative.

69. They impart sanctity to places of pilgrimage, render actions righteous and good, and give spiritual authority to Scriptures.

७०. तन्मयाः ।

(यतः for ते they) तत्-मयाः filled with that (spirit of holiness).

70. Every one of those, mentioned in the last Sūtra, is filled with the spirit of the saints and through that with the spirit of God Himself.

७१. मोदन्ते पितरो, नृत्यन्ति देवताः, सनाथा चेयं भूर्भवति ।

पितरः fathers मोदन्ते rejoice, देवताः gods नृत्यन्ति dance in joy, इयम् this भूः earth सनाथा possessing a saviour च and भवति becomes.

71. The fathers rejoice, the gods dance in joy, and this earth gets a saviour.

७२. नास्ति तेषु जातिविद्यारूपकुलधनक्रियादिभेदः ।

तेषु among them जाति-विद्या-रूप-कुल-धन-क्रिया-आदि-भेदः distinction based on caste, learning, beauty, family, wealth, profession, and the rest न not अस्ति there is.

72. In them there is no distinction based on caste or culture, beauty or birth, wealth or profession, and the like.

७३. यतस्तदीयाः ।

यतः because तदीयाः His own.

73. Because they are His own.

७४. वादो नावलम्ब्यः ।

वादः dispute न not अवलम्ब्यः deserve to be entered into.

74. It is not proper for one to enter into a controversy about God, or other spiritual truths, or about comparative merits of different devotees.

७५. बाहुल्यावकाशत्वाद् अनिय(न्त्रि)तत्वाच्च ।

बाहुल्य-अवकाशत्वात् as there is room for diversity in views अनियतत्वात् as no (view based on mere) reason is conclusive च and.

75. For there is plenty of room for diversity in views, and no one view, based upon mere reason, is conclusive in itself.

७६ भक्तिशास्त्राणि मननीयानि तदुद्बोधककर्माणि करणीयानि ।

भक्ति-शास्त्राणि scriptural teachings of devotion मननीयानि should be reflected upon तत्-उद्बोधक-कर्माणि practices that rouse devotion करणीयानि must be performed.

76. The teachings of Scriptures dealing with love and devotion for God may still be discussed and meditated upon, and spiritual practices which rouse devotion, may still be undertaken.

७७. सुखदु:खेच्छालाभादित्यक्ते काले प्रती(क्ष्य)क्षमाणे क्षणार्धमपि व्यर्थं न नेयम् ।

सुख-दु:ख-इच्छा-लाभ-आदि-त्यक्ते freed from pleasure, pain, desire, gain, etc. काले time प्रतीक्ष्यमाणे when expectantly waited upon क्षणार्धम् half a moment अपि even व्यर्थम् to no purpose न not नेयम् should be spent.

77. Time becoming available to him because of his freedom from pleasure and pain, desire and gain, etc., it behoves him not to waste even half a second.

७८. अहिंसासत्यशौचदयास्तिक्यादिचारित्र्याणि परिपालनीयानि ।

अहिंसा-सत्य-शौच-दया-आस्तिक्य-आदि-चारित्र्याणि virtues like non-violence, truthfulness, purity, compassion, faith in spiritual realities परिपालनीयानि should be cultivated and preserved.

78. He should cultivate and preserve virtues such as non-violence, truth, purity, compassion, faith in higher spiritual realities, and the like.

७९ सर्वदा सर्वभावेन निश्चिन्तैः(न्तितैः) भगवानेव भजनीयः ।

सर्वदा always सर्व-भावेन through every aspect of life निश्चिन्तै: by people free from all cares भगवान् the blessed Lord एव alone भजनीय: is to be adored and worshipped.

79. It is the Lord alone, Who is the repository of all the blessed qualities, that is to be worshipped always by him free from all cares and worries, in every aspect of his life.

८०. स कीर्त्यमानः(कीर्तनीयः)शीघ्रमेवाविर्भवत्यनुभावयति (च) भक्तान् ।

कीर्त्यमान: being glorified स: He शीघ्रम् speedily आविर्भवति manifests Himself भक्तान् devotees अनुभावयति makes realize.

80. Being thus glorified, He, the Lord, manifests Himself and blesses His devotees with realization.

८१. त्रिसत्यस्य भक्तिरेव गरीयसी, भक्तिरेव गरीयसी ।

त्रि-सत्यस्य of the absolute, eternal truth भक्ति: Divine Love एव alone गरीयसी is greater भक्ति: Divine Love एव indeed गरीयसी is greater.

81. Only love of the absolute, eternal Truth is the greatest; this love, indeed is the greatest.

८२. गुणमाहात्म्यासक्ति-रूपासक्ति-पूजासक्ति-स्मरणासक्ति-दास्यासक्ति-सख्यासक्ति - वात्सल्यासक्ति - कान्तासक्ति -आत्मनिवेदनासक्ति-तन्मयतासक्ति-परमविरहासक्ति - रूपा एकधा अपि एकादशधा भवति ।

(भक्तिः Divine Love) एकधा of one way अपि even गुण-माहात्म्य-आसक्ति love for glorifying the Divine qualities and attributes रूप-आसक्ति love of Divine beauty पूजा-आसक्ति love of worship स्मरण-आसक्ति love of remembering दास्य-आसक्ति love of service सख्य-आसक्ति love (of God) as a friend वात्सल्य-आसक्ति love (of God) as a child कान्ता-आसक्ति love (of God) as that of a wife आत्म-निवेदन-आसक्ति love of self-surrender तन्मयता-आसक्ति love of complete absorption in Him परम-विरह-आसक्ति love of the pain of separation from Him रूपा in the form एकादशधा of eleven forms भवति is.

82. Bhakti, or Divine Love, though in itself one only, manifests itself in the following eleven different forms: (*a*) Love of the glorification of the Lord's blessed qualities, (*b*) Love of His enchanting beauty, (*c*) Love of worship, (*d*) Love of constant remembrance, (*e*) Love of service, (*f*) Love of Him as a friend, (*g*) Love of Him as a son, (*h*) Love for Him as that of a wife for her husband, (*i*) Love of self-surrender to Him, (*j*) Love of complete absorption in Him, (*k*) Love of the pain of separation from Him.

८३. इत्येवं वदन्ति जनजल्पनिर्भयाः एकमताः कुमार-व्यास-शुक-शाण्डिल्य-गर्ग-विष्णु-कौण्डिन्य-शेषोद्धवारुणि-बलि-हनुमद्-विभीषणादयो भक्त्याचार्याः ।

इति एवम् in the manner described above जन-जल्प-निर्भयाः fearless of the prattle of people एकमताः of unanimous opinion कुमार...विभीषणादयः Kumāra, Vyāsa, Suka, Sāṇḍilya, Garga, Viṣṇu, Kauṇḍinya, Seṣa,

Uddhava, Aruṇi, Bali, Hanumān, Vibhīṣaṇa, etc., भक्ति-आचार्या: teachers of Divine Love वदन्ति declare.

83. Thus the teachers of Bhakti unanimously declare, without being in the least afraid of public criticism—the great teachers: Kumāra, Vyāsa, Suka, Sāṇḍilya, Garga, Viṣṇu, Kauṇḍinya, Seṣa, Uddhava, Aruṇi, Bali, Hanumān, Vibhīṣaṇa and others.

८४. य इदं नारदप्रोक्तं शिवानुशासनं विश्वसिति श्रद्धते, स भक्तिमान् भवति, सः प्रेष्ठं लभते सः प्रेष्ठं लभते ॥ॐ तत् सत्॥

य: who इदम् this नारद-प्रोक्तम् reported by Nārada शिव-अनुशासनम् auspicious teaching विश्वसिति believes श्रद्धते practises with faith, स: he भक्तिमान् endued with love of God भवति becomes स: he प्रेष्ठम् the most beloved Lord लभते realizes; स: he प्रेष्ठम् the dearest Lord लभते attains; इति thus ॐ तत् सत् ॥

84. Whosoever amongst us believes in this auspicious Gospel of Nārada and has faith in it, becomes a lover of God, and attains the highest Beatitude and Goal of life.

NOTES

NOTES

Introduction. Nārada's *Book of Aphorisms on Divine Love* and Śāṇḍilya's *Enquiry into Divine Love* form the classical authority on the philosophy of Bhakti. The Sūtra literature is generally obscure and ambiguous because of the laconic expressions and elliptical contructions employed in its composition; for this reason Sūtras have given room for many interpretations, even mutually opposed. Almost as a solitary exception, Nārada's *Book of Aphorisms* stands apart for its clarity of thought and simplicity of language. The chief reason for this perspicuity must be that the work is a transcript from the author's own life. What is presented here is not an intellectually spun-out system of thought, but a simple record of spiritual experience and a course of conduct to aid spiritual realization of the most exalted type. Nārada must have felt the influence of, or received help from, godmen who preceded him, and some of his contemporaries or predecessors are clearly mentioned by name. Such citations are, however, only for corroborating his own realizations in the field, or for recording where his experiences have compelled him to differ from them. Nowhere is any attempt made to refute or criticize views and experiences which he does not endorse. The aspirant, who studies these aphorisms for guidance in spiritual life, is therefore left free to make his own choice from the methods and realizations described here. This is a distinct and admirable feature of this Gospel of Divine Love.

In Sanskrit literature we come across four works attributed to Nārada, besides several philosophical and mystical disquisitions like the Anusmṛti in the S'āntiparva. It is impossible to ascertain whether these four works, *Nāradabhaktisūtra*, *Nāradasmṛti*, *Nāradīyas'ikṣā* and *Saṅgītamakaranda*, have come from the same author; probably we owe them to different authors. Three other works, *Nāradaparivrājakopaniṣat*, *Nāradīyapurāṇa*, and *Nāradapāñcarātra* are also associated with the name of Nārada, not as the author, but as the inspirer. There is nothing in the present work to prove that it is not the composition of a great divine sage; on the other hand, a careful perusal of the Sūtras, keeping in mind the life and character of the sage Nārada, would convince anyone that the ideas presented therein very well deserve to have come from one of his eminence. The view that the work could not have been composed before the twelfth century A.D, and that it was written by an unknown author, who chose to disguise his identity under the weighty name of Nārada, may have reference only to the language in which the Sūtras are couched. It is therefore safe to hold on to the traditional opinion regarding the authorship of the teachings of these aphorisms.

Nārada, the divine sage, is a reputed figure in the religious literature of India. From a study of his life as depicted in ancient works we can see, as shown below, that the doctrines taught in the aphorisms are made alive in his character and behaviour. It may be gathered from the account given in *Bhāg.* I. 5. 23—31; I. 6. 5—36; and VII. 15. 69—73 that he was the son of a servant maid, who, through the grace of some great souls, became a godman. We know of one Nārada, earliest, as the seer of a hymn, *Ṛgv.* VIII. 13. In the nineteenth verse of this hymn the devotional strain is explicit: स्तोता यत् ते अनुव्रतः, उक्थान्यृतुथा दधे, शुचिः पावक उच्यते सो अद्भुतः—'This divine minstrel devoted to Thee offer Thee hymn oblations in season. O Lord wonderfully glorious, Thou art holy and Thou makest all holy—so I declare.' Two other hymns (*Ṛgv.* IX. 104 and 105) also are sometimes attributed to Nārada in combination with Parvata. This union of the two sages Nārada and Parvata is noted in *Mbh.* XII. 28, where Nārada is referred to as the maternal uncle of Parvata. That this sage was specially associated with the Sāmaveda is evident from the reference that he was the Udgāta among the Ṛtviks in some sacrifices, *Hv.* II. 169. Purāṇas contain many references to him as the heavenly melodist; and the invention of the lute (Viṇā) is laid to his credit. 'He rejoices himself by playing on his divine viṇa; and singing the glories of the Lord he delights the afflicted world', *Bhāg.* I. 7. 38, 39. Nārada's Divine Love is equalled by his divine wisdom acquired through austerities and contact with Sanatkumāra. He admits to Sanatkumāra that vast erudition in the Vedas, its auxiliaries, and secular sciences like mathematics, physics, medicine, chronology, polity, archery, logic, and the rest could not remove the burden of sorrow; and then the latter illumines him about the infinite Bliss, Bhūmā, *Chān*. VII. 1. 2. *Mbh*. XII. 194-195 describes what great zeal he had for realizing the Truth, how he contemplated for a hundred years under ascetic discipline, how he arrived at the Infinite in the form of S'rī Kṛṣṇa sporting in the Vraja, and how he was taught by the Lord the need of unswerving devotion. It is also stated (*Mbh*. XII. 190) that he performed great austerities by the side of a Hymālayan lake for a long period and got first a vision of Sāvitrī and then of Lord Viṣṇu. In the view of ancient hagiographers his greatness exceeded all this. He is one of the ten spiritual sons of Brahmā, *Man*. I. 34, 35. He is the third incarnation in the 21 renowned Avatāras of Viṣṇu, *Bhāg*. I. 3. 8.

Nārada is the divine messenger in the Purāṇas, nay, the friend, philosopher, guide and consoler of all—gods, men and demons—the intermediary between God and his creation. The name is explained thus—नारम् परमात्मविषयकं ज्ञानम ददाति इति नारदः (*Skdr.*) This is the exalted role of the Divine Sage. There is, however, not so exalted an explanation too : नारं नरसमूहं कलहेन द्यति खण्डयतीति ; here the sage is pictured as a fomenter of quarrels *Hv*. II. 169, *Vp*. V. 16. 20, etc. Though Nārada is thus known also as 'Kalipriya', we are never left in the dark as to his real motive which is nothing but the good of the persons concerned. He advises the demon Andhaka to try the potency of Siva's boon on himself ; he manages to get Rāvaṇa entangled on the tail of Bāli ; he counsels Kaṁsa to kill Devakī's children ; he acts as messenger to Indra from Kṛṣṇa to remove his pride by depriving him of the Pārijāta; these and other similar acts of his, apparently contradictory in a sage, are really from unselfish motives and for the good of the world. When the Devas, who got ambrosia after churning the ocean, with the new power gained therefrom, were about to exterminate the Asuras, Nārada advises them to desist from the ruthless act, *Bhāg.* VIII. 12. 43; again when Hiraṇya went away to Mandara mountain for Tapas and the Asura women were oppressed by the Devas, he takes into his care Hiraṇya's wife who was then carrying Prahlāda, and makes Prahlāda what he was, through spiritual contact. These incidents reveal the greatness of his character. The *Padp.* says: 'Glory to the son of Brahmā—the abode of all good—a single word from whom has brought salvation to Prahlāda, and through whose grace Dhruva was enthroned permanently in his celestial station. Reverence to him'—जयति जगति मायां यस्य कायाधवस्ते वचनरचनमेकं केवलं चाकलय्य। ध्रुवपदमपि यातो यत्कृपातो ध्रुवोऽयं सकलकुशलपात्रं ब्रह्मपुत्रं नतोऽस्मि। It appears that Nārada also, like S'rī Rāmakṛṣṇa, holds the view that the first and foremost duty of a creature is to realize the Divine Truth and then only should he enter upon the worldly life. *Bhāg.* IV. 8; IV. 25; VI. 5., and *Vp.* I. 15 recite incidents to this purpose. At the beginning of creation, Dakṣa procreated 10000 children in his wife Asiknī, daughter of Pāñcajanya, with a view to populate the whole world. These children of Dakṣa called Haryas'vas, who were on a pilgrimage at Nārāyaṇasaras and were intent on Tapas to carry out their father's behests, were advised by the Divine Sage to know the

Self, God, and Nature and to seek the highest goal of life, viz. salvation. They became Sannyāsins and never returned to the worldly life. Infuriated Dakṣa was somehow consoled by Brahmā, and he again procreated another 10000 called S'abalās'vas. They too went to Nārāyaṇasaras where their elders had attained perfection. Through the spiritual counsel of Nārada, they too became absorbed in God and never returned. Depressed at this frustration, Dakṣa cursed Nārada by the force of which Nārada is ever an itinerant without a permanent abode—स्वरब्रह्मणि निर्भातहृषीकेशपदाम्बुजे। अखण्डं चित्तमावेश्य लोकाननुचरन् मुनिः। He wanders over all the world as a sage with his individuality entirely merged in the Lotus-feet of the Lord realized through Nādabrahman, *Bhāg.* VI. 5. 22. Dazzling with vast spiritual splendour, bereft of all sin, and immersed in austerities, from time to time, Nārada wandered over all the worlds, *Mbh.* XII. 213-5. —ब्रह्मेवामितदीप्तौजाः शान्तपाप्मा महातपाः। विचचार यथा कालं त्रिषु लोकेषु नारदः॥ That Nārada is one of the wisest among the sages and one ever engaged in austerities is most significantly borne out by the great sage Vālmīki in the opening verse of his mellifluous poem—तपःस्वाध्यायनिरतं, वाग्विदां वरम्. It is also worth remembering in this connection that it was through his inspiration that the 'first poet' made up his mind to compose the great epic, *Rāmāyaṇa*, and Vyāsa achieved self-fulfilment through the composition of ***Srī Bhāgavata***, the greatest devotional scripture. In *Mbh.* XII. 215 Bhīṣma tells Yudhiṣṭhira that Nārada is a perfect ideal personality and cites the words of S'rī Kṛṣṇa to Ugrasena:—

कुकुराधिप यान् मन्ये शृणु तान् मे विवक्षतः । नारदस्य गुणान् साधून् संक्षेपेण नराधिप ॥ न चारित्रनिमित्तोऽस्याहङ्कारो देहपातनः । अहीनश्रुतचारित्रः तस्मात् सर्वत्र पूजितः ॥ तेजसा यशसा बुध्या नयेन विनयेन च । जन्मना तपसा वृद्धः तस्मात् सर्वत्र पूजितः ॥ अरतिः क्रोधचापल्ये भयं नैतानि नारदे । अदीर्घसूत्रः शूरश्च तस्मात् सर्वत्र पूजितः । उपास्यो नारदो बाढं वाचि नास्य व्यतिक्रमः । कामाद् वा यदि वा लोभात् तस्मात् सर्वत्र पूजितः ॥ अध्यात्मविधितत्वज्ञः क्षान्तः शान्तो जितेन्द्रियः । ऋजुश्च सत्यवादी च तस्मात् सर्वत्र पूजितः ॥ दृढभक्तिरदीनात्मा श्रुतवानानृशंस्यवान् । वीतसम्मोहदोषश्च तस्मात् सर्वत्र पूजितः ॥ सुशीलः सुखसंवेशः सुतेजाः स्वादरः शुचिः । सुवाक्यश्चाप्यनीर्ष्यश्च तस्मात् सर्वत्र पूजितः ॥ कल्याणं कुरुते बाढं पापमस्मिन् न विद्यते । न प्रीयते परानर्थैः तस्मात् सर्वत्र पूजितः ॥ वेदश्रुतिभिराख्यानैरर्थानभिजिगीषते । तितिक्षुरनवज्ञश्च तस्मात् सर्वत्र पूजितः ॥ समत्वाद् हि प्रियो नास्ति नाप्रियश्च कथञ्चन । मनोनुकूलवादी च तस्मात् सर्वत्र पूजितः ॥ बहुश्रुतश्चित्रकथः पण्डितोऽनलसोऽशाठः । अदीनोऽक्रोधनोऽलुब्धः तस्मात् सर्वत्र पूजितः ॥ समाधिर्नास्य मानार्थं नात्मानं स्तौति कर्हिचित । अनीर्ष्युर्मृदुसम्भाषः तस्मात् सर्वत्र पूजितः ॥ लोकस्य विविधं वृत्तं प्रेक्षते चाप्यकुत्सयन् । संसर्गविद्याकुशलः तस्मात् सर्वत्रपूजितः ॥ असक्तः सर्वभूतेषु सक्तात्मेव च लक्ष्यते । अदीर्घसंशयो वाग्मी तस्मात् सर्वत्र पूजितः ॥ नासूयत्यागमं कञ्चित् स्वनयेनोपजीवति । अवन्ध्यकालो वश्यात्मा तस्मात् सर्वत्र पूजितः ॥ कृतश्रमः कृतप्रज्ञो ज्ञानतृप्तः समाहितः । नित्ययुक्तोऽप्रमत्तश्च तस्मात् सर्वत्र पूजितः ॥ सापत्रपश्च युक्तश्च विनेयः श्रेयसे परैः । अभेत्ता परगुह्यानां तस्मात् सर्वत्र पूजितः ॥ न हृष्यत्यर्थलाभेषु नालाभेषु व्यथत्यपि । स्थिरबुद्धिरसक्तात्मा तस्मात् सर्वत्र पूजितः ॥ तं सर्वगुणसम्पन्नं दक्षं शुचिमनाकुलं । कालज्ञं च नयज्ञं च कः प्रियं न करिष्यति ॥—'O King, I shall briefly recount the noble traits of Nārada's character. The deadly pride of having a high character never enters his mind, although he possesses sacred learning and noble conduct to perfection. He is honoured everywhere because he possesses a full measure of spiritual dignity, glory, intellectual penetration, tact, humility, noble birth, austerity, and heroism; and he is free from discontent, anger, unsteadiness, and procrastination. Assuredly he deserves worship, for he never deviates from his word moved by lust or greed. High honour is paid to Nārada everywhere, because he is possessed of true Self-knowledge, forbearance, tranquillity, sense-control, straightforwardness, truthfulness in speech, firm love for God, high spirit, holy wisdom, compassion, an undeluded mind, and shining manners. He can be easily accommodated, for he is gifted with dignity, sweet decorum, purity, and power of good speech, and has no envy. Certainly he is doing what is auspicious and no sin stains him. He never finds pleasure in other's perils; he secures his ends with the aid of scriptural wisdom and knowledge of past events. Meek and equitable to all, he despises none; hence also he neither likes nor dislikes anyone specially. He is vastly learned and endowed with the wonderful gift of diverse speech, and is never lazy or stubborn. He practises meditation not for securing esteem from others; he is leagues away from self-praise and speaks always softly. He observes the diverse behaviour of men without despising anyone; and he is a master in the art of reconciling others; so he is honoured everywhere. Though not attached to anyone, he is found to be deeply interested in all. He never keeps a doubt in suspense for long and is a good speaker. He is not regardless of other faiths, but lives according to his own. He never wastes a moment and ever remains a master of himself. He has striven hard for perfection and has attained supreme wisdom. He is ever contented with Self-realization, and with great zeal he is ever absorbed in that realization. He is not without the sense of shame and, is always open to instruction from others if that would add to his perfection. Never does he divulge the secrets of others, for his mind is always detached, intellect firm, and he is not affected agreeably or disagreeably by the obtainment or deprivation of objects of desire. Who would not make this paragon of virtue—efficient, holy, provident, and tactful—a beloved friend? It is impossible to give weight to the vulgar disparagement of Nārada after this brilliant encomium of Sri Kṛṣṇa himself, reported by none other than the great Bhiṣma.

From what we have mentioned about Nārada's greatness as a seer of Vedic Mantras, as a divine minstrel, as a great ascetic, as one who rose from a low position to the highest spiritual glory through divine grace and self-effort, as a knower of Brahman, as a saviour of men and reformer of their manners, it may easily be seen how he lived and exemplified the truths taught in the Sūtras. Indeed he is one of those commissioned with a divine mission—an आधिकारिकपुरुष referred to in *Bsū.* III. 3. 32—who is gracious enough to retain a little ego to teach souls engulfed in Saṁsāra. This group of enlightend souls place themselves in the hands of God as willing instruments for the service of man ; they prefer to enjoy the Divine play and company to becoming merged in Him for ever. And so Nārada is the typical Jñānin, Yogin, and Bhakta in one. He however prefers to deal with Bhakti as being the easiest and most efficient of all paths, which is available for all irrespective of caste, creed, or sex. In their full maturity, Bhakti, Jñāna, and Karma merge into one another; but in the early stages they appear to be different methods of approach to the one unity of spiritual experience. All the Yogas aim at the purity of the mind, the sole condition of knowing God. Jesus Christ puts this great truth in his oft-quoted words: Blessed are the pure in heart, for they shall see God. The three functions of the mind—intellect, emotion, and will—have to be purified of the dirt of the ego; and the three Yogas aim at achieving this. Jñānayoga purifies the intellect, Bhaktiyoga the emotions, and Karmayoga the will, and man is free to adopt any one among these paths in preference to the others. But the seeker would do well to attempt a synthesis of all these paths as it would be very helpful to achieve the end more speedily. Those who are by nature more intellectual, or emotional, or dynamic may prefer to adopt only one of the paths as suits their nature. However, the mind being homogeneous in nature, any single path, strenuously pursued, must necessarily result in the purity of the whole mind, as physical exercise, though confined to particular organs, such as the arms or the legs, necessarily results in the health of the whole organism. While choosing to write a book on Divine Love, Nārada does not lose sight of the other paths, but accepts them all as aids to achieve the final goal. We thus find in these aphorisms a happy synthesis of all the Yogas as attempted before by Bhagavān S'rī Kṛṣṇa, the Yoges'vara, in the *Bg.* If the *Bsū.* of Vyāsa aims at the knowledge of God and man, and the Dharmasūtras aim at the service of God and man, the Bhaktisūtras aim at nothing more than completing the scheme by advocating a way for purifying the emotions so as to provide a proper background and motive for the service of God and man.

Sutra 1. अथ (now) in this aphorism expresses अधिकार (capacity, competence); *i.e.* the best possible condition under which an exposition of the religion of Love is likely to appeal to a spiritual aspirant. In other words, it refers to the proper recipient or Adhikārin. A study of any subject will appeal only to one who has an intense desire (आर्थित्व) for knowing the subject; it is likely to profit only one who has the capacity (शक्तत्व) to understand; and it is readily practised only by one who is free from disabilities and possesses the opportunity (अपर्युदस्तत्व). Vide S'rī S'aṅkara's com. on *Tait.* II. 1. In order that one may not be excluded from the study and practice, one should possess deep interest in the study, and sufficient faith in the capacity of the teacher and scripture whose help he seeks with reverence and trust; otherwise he is not likely to profit by such study. So S'raddhā is very much needed. These are, however, only general qualifications for taking up the study and practice of any subject. Each scripture, laying down a particular path to spiritual attainment, insists upon certain specific qualifications also. For example, as the necessary qualifications of a Vedāntin or seeker of the knowledge of Brahman, S'rī S'aṅkara insists on the four-fold aid to Brahmajñāna (साधनचतुष्टय), namely, Viveka or discrimination between the eternal and the transient, Vairāgya or the spirit of renunciation, moral discipline resulting in the control of the body and the senses, and a yearning for liberation ; the Mīmāṁsakas (those devoted to Vedic liturgy) insist on a study of the entire Veda as a prerequisite to the enquiry into the Sūtras of Jaimini. Both these again go to the length of saying that such study and practices are to be confined to the aspirants of the first three castes only, all others being ineligible. The Scriptures of Bhakti are more liberal in this respect as they declare the path of Divine Love open to all. A belief in the grace of God and in the possibility of escape from the round of birth and death with the help of God is the only qualification for the study of the Bhakti-sūtras and the practice of Divine Love. Even illiteracy is no bar, nor a previous record of a vicious life. On this point there are the following authorities : First of all we have the declaration of Bhagavān S'rī Kṛṣṇa in the *Bhagavad-gītā*, IX. 30, 31, and 32. 'Even a hard-baked sinner, if he comes to have unswerving love for the Lord, must be regarded as righteous, for he has decided aright. He soon becomes righteous and obtains lasting peace. Proclaim it boldly, O Arjuna, that My devotee never perishes. For those who take refuge and abide in Me—women, Vais'yas, S'ūdras, nay, even those on whom their past deeds have imposed the very worst of births—attain to the highest goal.' Sage S'āṇḍilya lays down :

आनिन्द्ययोनि अधिक्रियते पारम्पर्यात सामान्यवत्, सू. ७८—'Every one, to the lowest-born, is eligible to follow the path of devotion; this is borne out by the long line of devotees; besides, virtues like non-violence and truthfulness and love for God are common to all'. S'rī S'uka salutes the Lord: 'I bow to the Almighty Lord, by adoring even whose devotees people like the Kirātas, Huns, Āndhras Pulindas, Pulkasas, Ābhīras, Kaṅkas, Yavanas, Khas'as, as well as those who are sinners, purify themselves'—किरातहूणान्ध्रपुलिन्दपुल्कसा आभीरकङ्का यवना खशादयः। येऽन्ये च पापा यदुपाश्रयाश्रयाः शुध्यन्ति तस्मै प्रभविष्णवे नमः। *Bhāg*. II. 4. 18.

Untouchable saints like Nanda, Cokamela, Ravidās, Kaṇṇappa, Tiruppāṇālvār, and Tirumaṅgaiālvār, and female devotees like Mīrābāī, Avvayār, and Āndāl and some of the Nāyanārs have thus graced this land to bear witness to the catholicity of the path of devotion. Moral wrecks like Ajāmila, Ratnākara, Tondaradippodiālvār, Nārāyaṇa-bhatta, (the author of the famous *Nārāyaṇīya*), and Vilvamaṅgal are all shining examples of what the religion of Divine Love can do for redeeming even the worst sinners, however low they might have had fallen. Saints like Kabīr, Nānāk, Tukārām and others prove to the hilt that the religion of Divine Love does not stand in need even of book-learning. There is no doubt, however, that if the seeker on the path of devotion has equipped himself properly before he takes to it, the greater is his profit The previous qualifications mentioned by S'rī Rāmanuja are: 1. Viveka or discrimination in food, 2. Vimoka or freedom from desires, 3. Abhyāsa or practice, 4. Kriyā or doing good to others, 5. Kalyāṇa or purity consisting of truthfulness, straight-forwardness, kindness, non-violences, charity, etc., 6. Anavasāda or cheerfulness, 7. Anuddharṣa or absence of excessive hilarity. The word अतः (therefore) in this Sūtra refers to the reasons that prompted Nārada to write on Bhakti in preference to Jñāna or Karma. His reasons might be that 1. Bhakti by itself leads to God-realization and escape from Saṁsāra; 2. that it is the easiest of all paths; 3. that it is the only path available to all creatures; 4. that it is a help even to those who aspire for Jñāna; 5. that even Jñānins, after realization, sometimes take to Bhakti for the sake of the sweetness of loving relationship with God; 6. and that he himself, above all, is eager to share his bliss of Love with others. व्याख्यास्यामः (shall expound) literally means 'shall comment upon.' But the work under consideration is not at all a commentary in the ordinary sense of the word either in matter or in form. The present work does not purport to be an original composition, but assumes only the humble role of a व्याख्यान (commentary). What the author perhaps means is that Bhakti-śāstra is a commentary on the actual experiences of the devotees, and not a mere speculative philosophy based only on reason. Nor is it only second-hand knowledge interpreted by a mere scholar. For the exposition is based upon the author's own personal experiences, supported by those of others, as recorded in the Scriptures. Such an interpretation by a man of realization is necessary, as otherwise people may be carried away by the stories of miracles and supernatural incidents connected with the lives of the saints, and may neglect to put into practice the true spiritual principles illustrated in their lives.

Sutra 2. Diviṇe Love may be viewed from the standpoint of an aspirant who is following the path of Bhakti, or one who has realized the goal of that path. As a path it is designated Apara- or Gauṇa-Bhakti ; but when it expresses itself in one who has achived the result, i.e. one who has realized the goal, it is called Parabhakti. In this *Sū*. a description of the latter is given so that one may judge the tree by its mature and ripe fruit ; moreover it is also helpful to identify the highest and best form of Love by noting its similarities and dissimilarities with other ordinary known phenomena. तु (but) in the *Sū*. is meant to draw attention to the fact that true Bhakti as a means of God-realization, or in the form of the blissful divine experience, is far removed from the crude notion of worship of spirits, gods, etc, out of fear or desire for favours. This adversative particle also emphasizes the author's disagreement with the view of some that emotions like fear, hatred, and lust also may be considered as helps to salvation equally as devotion towards God. Apparently such a view is attributed to Nārada himself in *Bhāg*. VII. 1. 22—32. यथा वैरानुबन्धेन मर्त्यस्तन्मयतामियात् । न तथा भक्तियोगेन इति मे निश्चिता मतिः— In this verse, Nārada expresses a diametrically opposed view ; namely, that one is not so deeply absorbed in God through Bhaktiyoga as through continued dislike, *Bhāg*. VII. 1. 26. A similar theory is put forth in *Bhāg*. III. 2. 24 ; X. 29. 15 ; and XI. 9. 22 also. However, the contradiction between the *Bhāg*. statements and the

Sū. is only superficial. In the fourth verse immediately following the one we have cited from the *Bhāg.* Nārada clearly differentiates Bhakti from lust, fear, hatred and kinship. In the thirty-first verse, the problem that has occupied the centere of attention is plainly put : Somehow to fix the mind on God !—तस्मात् केनाप्युपायेन मनः कृष्णे निवेशयेत् । The controversial stanza only asserts that the deepest kind of absorption is possible through hatred. The purpose is not an advocacy of hatred, but the glorification of love. Nārada, while speaking of S'is'upāla, in the context referred to, takes care also to point out that the latter was not an ordinary sinner, but that he was formerly a devotee and servant of the Lord, and that his hatred towards God was the result of a particular curse and a special promise of redemption through hatred. Even the hatred was preferred to love because of the intensity of love which could not bear separation for a long time. Thus, in S'is'upāla's case, the hatred was specially chosen because of intense love; hence it is only a form of love. The attitude of hatred which his mind took at birth was only a temporary aberration from its real nature. What brought liberation to him was the submerged love, and not the hatred, which only helped him in securing the necessary concentration. That the mention of hatred and the rest in the *Bhāg.* to realize God is only to stress the excellence of Bhakti is learned from direct statements also :— उक्तं पुरस्तादेतत् ते चैद्यः सिद्धिं यथा गतः । द्विषन्नपि हि गोविन्दं किमुताधोक्षजप्रियाः ॥ (S'uka to Parīkṣit) ' I have told you before how Caidya attained perfection even though he was hating the Lord; *a fortiori* how easily would those who love Him reach that end', *Bhāg*. X. 29. 13. वैरेण यं नृपतय: शिशुपालपौण्ड्रसाल्वादयो गतिविलासविलोकनाद्यै:। ध्यायन्त आकृतधिय: शयनासनादौ तत्साम्यमापुरनुरक्तधियां पुन: किम्?—'Even rulers like S'is'upāla, Pauṇḍra, and Sālva, who, lying down, sitting up, or in any other state, thought of Him only with feeling of hatred, had their mind transformed into Kṛṣṇa, as they remembered His gait, His winning deportment, glances and the rest, attained to Him. Should it be then averred that those who are full of love for Him would reach Him?' *Bhāg*. XI. 5. 4. 8. The whole question is discussed in a masterly way by S'rī Madhvācārya in his Bhāṣya on *Bg*. IX. 12. *Vide* also Jayatīrtha's sub-commentary thereon. Thus the Purāṇa only shows how much easier it would be to obtain salvation through Bhakti when God is so gracious as to save even those who hate him. This is reinforced by the following statement also, attributed by Svapnes'vara to the *Atri-smṛti*: विद्वेषादपि गोविन्दं दमघोषात्मज: स्मरन्। शिशुपालो गत: स्वर्गं किं पुनस्तत्परायण:।—'Remembering Govinda even through hatred, S'is'upāla the son of Damaghoṣa attained Heaven. What to say of those who are devoted to Him!' Sāṇḍilya also makes the point clear thus: 'Devotion is of the nature of love only, because it is the opposite of hatred, and because it is expressed by the word 'रस' in *Tait*. II. 7', *S'sū*. 6. Moreover in *Bg*. XVI. 16 it is specifically mentioned that all those who hate God go in for spiritual ruin. It is clearly stated in the Nārāyaṇīya section of the *Mbh*. that those who hate God send even their fathers to eternal hell, and that it is impossible to hate God who is one's own Self—मज्जन्ति पितरस्तस्य नरके शाश्वती समा: । यो द्विष्याद विबुधश्रेष्ठं देवं नारायणं हरिम् ॥ कथं नाम भवेद् द्वेष्य आत्मा लोकस्य कस्यचित् । आत्मा हि पुरुषव्याघ्र ज्ञेयो विष्णुरिति श्रुतिः ॥ Another reason for the Bhakti scriptures giving these illustrations of S'is'upāla and others is to show that, if at all anger has to be shown, it is better to sublimate it by directing it to God, for then in the long run there is at least a chance of remembering Him. It is with this view that Nārada himself refers to it in *Sū.* 65.

That Bhakti is firm love is the opinion of all authorities from early days. The following citations are instructive :—अनन्यममता विष्णौ ममता प्रेमसङ्गता । भक्तिरित्युच्यते भीष्म प्रह्लादोद्धवनारदैः—Prahlāda, Uddhava, and Nārada declare that Bhakti is a loving sense of possession—a feeling that the Lord is one's own, *Npañ*; सर्वोपाधिविनिर्मुक्तं तत्परत्वेन निर्मलम् । हृषीकेण हृषीकेशसेवनं भक्तिरुच्यते—What is called Bhakti is nothing but the enjoyment of the Lord, the Master of the senses, with the senses themselves purified by intentness on Him, without laying any condition whatsoever; भक्तिरस्य भजनं ; एतदिहामुत्रोपाधिनैराश्येनामुष्मिन् मनःकल्पनम्—Bhakti is adoring service of Him that implies centering of the mind on Him, expecting no other gain here or hereafter, *Gopālapūrvatāpinī Upd.* 2. 1; मनोगतिरविच्छिन्ना हरौ प्रेमपरिप्लुता । अभिसन्धिविनिर्मुक्ता भक्तिर्विष्णुवशंकरी—The constant flow of mind, brimming with love, towards the Lord, without any selfish desire, is Bhakti; and the Lord is attracted by it, *Npañ*; या प्रीतिरस्ति विषयेष्वविवेकभाजां, सेवाच्युते भवति भक्तिपदाभिधेया । भक्तिस्तु काम इव

तत्कमनीयरूपे, तस्मान्मुनेरजनि कामुकत्वाक्यभङ्गी—The fondness which indiscriminating people have for sense pleasures, if it is diverted to the Lord, is called Bhakti ; it is like lust for the object of one's love ; hence the sage got the name of 'lover' by way of a figure of speech, *Dramidopaniṣatsārasaṅgati* of Maṇavālamāmuni : अन्याभिलषिताशून्यं ज्ञानकर्माद्यनावृतम् । आनूकूल्येन कृष्णानुशीलना भक्तिरुत्तमा—Loving contemplation of Kṛṣṇa without break or motive of gain—free from the overpowering influence of Jñāna and Karma—is the highest Bhakti, *Bhaktirasāmṛtasindhu* ; इष्टे स्वारसिको रागः परमाविष्टता भवेत् । तन्मयी या भवेत् भक्तिः सात्र रागात्मिका स्मृता—One's own natural affection for one's Chosen Ideal will mature into extreme love : the absorbed state of mind then noticeable is called Bhakti, and its essence is love, *Ibid.* ; द्रुतस्य भगवद्धर्मात् धारावाहिकतां गता । सर्वेशे मनसो वृत्तिः भक्तिरित्यभिधीयते—What is called Bhakti is a state of mind in which, being melted by the force of spiritual discipline, the mind constantly flows towards the Lord, *Bhaktirasāyana* I. 3 ; स्वस्वरूपानुसन्धानं भक्तिरित्यभिधीयते । स्वात्मतत्वानुसन्धानं भक्तिरित्यपरे जगुः—Some say that Bhakti is an unceasing search of ones own true nature ; others hold that it is the enquiry into the truth of one's Self, *Vivekacūdāmaṇi*, 32 ; दर्शनं परभक्तिः स्यात् परज्ञानं तु सङ्गमः । पुनर्विश्लेषभीरुत्वं परमा भक्तिरुच्यते—Vision is Parabhakti, union is Parajñāna, anxiety to maintain that union is Paramabhakti, Yāmunācārya. मद्गुणश्रुतिमात्रेण मयि सर्वगुणाश्रये । मनोगतिरविच्छिन्ना यथा गंगांभसोंबुधौ ॥ लक्षणं भक्तियोगस्य निर्गुणस्य ह्युदाहृतम् । अहैतुक्यव्यवहिता या भक्तिः पुरुषोत्तमे ।—By merely hearing about the qualities of Mine the mind flows constantly towards Me, Who am the repository of all good ; this unbroken flow of mind, just like the current of Ganges emptying into the Bay without a stop, is the mark of Bhaktiyoga beyond the Guṇas ; it is unconditioned and unthwarted love for the Supreme Person, *Bhāg.* III. 29. 11, 12 ; माहात्म्यज्ञानपूर्वस्तु सुदृढः सर्वतोऽधिकः । स्नेहो भक्तिरितिप्रोक्तस्तया मुक्तिर्नचान्यथा ॥ ज्ञानपूर्वः परः स्नेहो नित्यो भक्तिरितीर्यते ॥ Firm love for God more than for anything else, with full consciousness of His glory and magnitude, is Bhakti—and from this Bhakti alone results Release. Supreme love following the wake of previous knowledge and lasting for ever is designated as Bhakti, Madhvācārya in *Mbh. Tātparyanirṇaya*, I. 86, 107. Bhakti should not also be confused with mere emotional excitement or eroticism, as is often done ; nor with fanaticism which sometimes passes for religiosity and leads to all kinds of sectarian quarrels and bloodshed. Again, it is not mere credulousness or blind faith in whatever some priests may claim, or books only labelled as S'āstra may be interpreted to say. It is not also mere scriptural knowledge, logic-chopping, or metaphysical speculations. The word सा (that) in this *Sū.* refers to the Bhakti referred to in the *Sū.* I. The pronoun तत् is often used to denote 'prasiddhi' or common knowledge. The word may therefore be taken to indicate that Bhakti is already well-known to all ; only its real nature and implications are not clearly grasped by everyone. Hence the necessity for a clear definition. There is also a subtle suggestion that the experience of Bhakti is not a rare hallucination eluding all scientific treatment; but that it is a common experience of all devotees, and as such it deserves careful consideration at the hands of all lovers of truth, and is fit to be made the subject of rational enquiry. The phrase परमप्रेमरूपा in the text conveys the sense that real Bhakti, being a transcendental experience of bliss, is different from ordinary love, and that it can never be expressed adequately in words. Supreme Love is an अनुभूति or direct realization that is Mokṣa or liberation itself. This Love is not different from the Bliss of the Divine 'from Which all speech with the mind, turn away not having reached It. He who realizes the Bliss of that Brahman fears not from anything' *Tait.* II. 9. But Nārada, as an exponent of the doctrine of Bhakti, has in some way or other to convey his meaning through words and analogies; hence the method of explaining the unknown in terms of the known, viz. the attempt to convey the idea of the transcendental experience in terms of common love. The word रूप in the expression परमप्रेमरूप is used only to convey this implication. Again the adjective पर or परम (supreme) is employed to distinguish Bhakti from ordinary human love between the sexes. Supremacy of Divine Love is due to three circumstances: (1) It is not based upon selfishness or egoism, and is consequently untainted by any sordid motive—even fear of the Almighty or desire to propitiate Him for personal gains; (2) It prevents any other worldly love in the mind of the devotee; (3) There is complete self-forgetfulness on the part of the lover. Love that is bereft of these qualifications is not Divine Love. प्रेम

or love ordinarily suggests the lover, the beloved, and the bond of love between them. It is a bone of contention among the different schools of thought as to whether any sense of distinction between the three can be felt in the highest spiritual experience. The Non-dualists deny any such distinction, but others hold the view that Love or enjoyment of Bliss cannot be where there is no such distinction. It is, however, commonly admitted by both that the intensity of the experience may be such as to make the lover forget himself as long as he is absorbed in the enjoyment. The difference between the two schools of thought is therefore confined to the question whether the individuality of the experiencing soul is actually lost or not. This is, however, only a metaphysical question, with which the Bhakti Scripture is not primarily concerned.

It would seem, however, that from the point of view of Bhakti also, the union between the lover and the beloved can be said to be complete only where there is absolute merging of the lover in the Beloved; that is, when the experiencing ego is completely dissolved. Comparative study of mysticism convinces us that this is the highest experience of all saints. This complete absorption in the Divine as a result of entrancing love is referred to in Bhakti literature often. Cf. *Bhāg.* X. 29. 15; X. 30. 19, 44; XI. 2. 45-47; XI. 12. 12; etc. Those who love Hari, indeed, lose themselves in Hari—यान्ति तन्मयतां हरेः। 'A Gopī whose mind is given to Kṛṣṇa places her arm on another Gopī and says, "See, I am Kṛṣṇa."'—कस्यां चित् स्वभुजं न्यस्य चलन्त्याहापरा ननु। कृष्णोऽहं पश्यत-

गतिं ललितामिति तन्मना: । Through deep longing for Me the thoughts of the Gopis were firmly fixed on Me and hence they were not conscious of their body, or what was far or near, just as sages absorbed in contemplation, or like rivers that have entered the sea are *not distinguished* by name and form'—ता नाविदन् मय्यनुषङ्गबद्धधियः स्वमात्मानमदस्तथेदम् । यथा समाधौ मुनयोऽब्धितोये नद्यः प्रविष्टा इव नामरूपे । 'Their hearts given to Him, they talked of Him alone; they imitated his sportful activities; they could not think of themselves as different from Him; they sang only of His excellent attributes; they did not think of their homes'—तन्मनस्काः तदालापाः तद्विचेष्टाः तदात्मिकाः । तद्गुणानेव गायन्त्यो नात्मागाराणि सस्मरुः ॥ This very idea is beautifully illustrated by the Sufi poet who describes how in spite of repeated knockings of a lover at his Beloved's door, the latter did not deign to open it until he so far forgot himself as to answer, in reply to a query from within, 'I am thyself.' Jalaludin Rumi says: 'Then shall we rise from the angels and merge in the Nameless.' Another Sufi says: 'When a man becomes annihilated from his attributes, he attains perfect subsistence. He is neither far nor near, neither stranger nor intimate, neither sober nor intoxicated, neither separated nor united; he has no name, or sign, or brand, or mark'—Amir Ali: *Spirit of Islam*, Pp. 172, 213. The Sufi martyr Al Hallaj says: 'I am the Truth, I am He whom I love, and He whom I love is I.' According to Jami, *I* and *thou* have here no place, and are but phantasies, vain and unreal—Browne: *Literary History of Persia*. Cf. also Mohammed's words *Inni-an-Allahu la illaha Ana* which is an exact translation of Isaiah: 'Verily, I, even I, am God, and there is none else.' Witness again the saying of Jesus: 'I and my Father are one.' Saint Paul says: '*Optismum esse unire deo*—the best is to be one with God'; also 'Ye are dead and your life is hid with Christ in God.' Ruysbroeck, the Dutch mystic, says: 'We have lost ourselves, and been melted away into the Unknown Darkness.' Speaking of his experience, the philosopher and mystic John Scotus Erigena says: 'In this state of mystical ignorance, we plunge into the Divine Darkness and lose ourselves in Its life.' According to the Neo-Platonists, the highest stage of union with God cannot be realized by thought, and is possible only in a state of ecstasy in which the soul transcends its own thought, loses itself in the soul of God, becomes one with God. Says Dionysius: 'When the soul considers the greatness of God's might besides its littleness, she casts herself out of herself and out of every creature and is thus reduced to naked nothingness;' also 'It is the nature of love to change a man into that which he loves.' Averroes, the Moorish philosopher of Spain, says that 'it (the individual soul) becomes one with the Universal Spirit or is absorbed in It.' According to Bonaventura, 'The soul transcends itself, enters upon a stage of holy ignorance, and becomes one with the Divine will through love.' The German mystic Eckhart says: 'The soul in her hot pursuit of God becomes absorbed in Him and she herself is reduced to naught just as the sun will swallow up and put out dawn'. 'The soul does not stop till it has passed beyond all differences and has entered the silent desert, into which no difference has even penetrated, which is immovable and supreme over all oppositions and divisions.' 'Whoever would see God must be dead to himself and buried in God.' According to Schelling, the goal is a return to God, to be realized in a mystical intuition in which the soul strips off its selfhood, and becomes absorbed in the Absolute. Cf. also Goethe's lines :

> By nothing godlike could the heart be won
> Were not the heart itself Divine.

The word अस्मिन् (in this) is used in this *Sū.* to denote the object of Love. Nārada is very careful in avoiding the use of any metaphysical or theological designation such as Brahman, Īs'vara, Bhagavān, and Ātman, and personal names like Rāma, Kṛṣṇa, Viṣṇu, and S'iva, so that his teaching may be completely non-sectarian. The indefinite neuter pronoun is very suggestive not only of the transcendence but also of the immanence of God, as *this* in contrast with *that* shows something very near. The object of Bhakti is the Soul of our own souls, the Antaryāmin of the Upaniṣads. The first personal or second personal pronoun would have been mistaken for the subject or object of relative knowledge, and would have given rise to the false notion of God being merely personal. Throughout his work, Nārada avoids a definition of God as in the *Bsū.*, for he feels that to describe God is to bring Him down to the level of the finite objects of relative knowledge. In fact, all descriptions of God can be only relative to the aspirant's spiritual development, and must be coloured by the predilections, capacities, and needs of the person describing, or the persons to whom the description is addressed.

The controversy regarding the nature of God and His relation with the universe and soul are relevant only to the relative plane of worship. Each view of God is only a partial view of the whole truth. Accepting the doctrine of the Chosen Ideal, each aspirant may conceive of God in his own way as the most perfect ideal of his thinking and suitable to his own capacities and needs. He may then love and worship that Ideal with his whole heart. But he should be liberal enough to give the same freedom of thought and worship to others. The aspirant must also not forget that his God is only his own view of the Divine Truth from his level of spiritual development, and that the God of another is but a different view of the same Truth from another view point. S'āṇdilya notes the difference of opinion between Vyāsa and Kas'yapa about the nature of the Deity to be realized, and reconciles both the views thus: 'Kas'yapa declares that realization refers to the Lord, because He is immeasurably superior to the worshipper. Vyāsa says that it refers to the Ātman. S'āṇdilya says that it refers to both, for ultimately both are the same, because of Scriptural authority and reasoning. *S'sū.* 29, 30, 31. The *Chānd.* III. 14. 1-4 shows that Brahman to be worshipped and to be realized is the same as the Ātman in the heart. The major Upaniṣadic texts, *Bg.*, and *Bsū.* echo the same truth. Thus love of God is nothing but love of the Reality or the higher Self of man which he has forgotten; it is the same Indwelling

Divine Spirit that is conceived of in the initial stages of spiritual practice as something different from the soul of man and infinitely superior to him. God thus worshipped is man's ideal of his own future greatness, the ideal into which he has to develop himself by effort. Spiritual endeavour thus begins with separating, in imagination, the God within from the empirical self and investing Him with all the noble qualities which one would like to develop in oneself, but which he does not possess when he begins his religious journey. The individual gradually acquires all the fundamental characteristics of his Ideal, and in course of time feels himself as part of God and finally realizes Him as his own Self. This is echoed in the famous lines: 'When I think of myself as an embodied being, I am your servant: when I think of myself as an individual soul, I am a part of you; but when I realize "I am Ātman," I am one with you. This is my firm conviction'—देहबुध्या तु दासोऽहं जीवबुध्या त्वदंशकः। आत्मबुध्या त्वमेवाहमिति मे निश्चिता मतिः। The various Objects which devotees worship according to their spiritual development may be classified as follows: 1. The Personal God under the aspect and designation of Viṣṇu, Śiva, etc. 2. A concrete representation of the Deity, or a symbol or image (Pratīka or Pratimā) which would remind him of the Personal God. 3. An actual man in flesh and blood, e.g. an Avatāra. 'Such devotion may be directed towards the incarnations of God also. The same results from devotion to well-known incarnations also,' *Ssū.* 46-55. 4. One's own Spiritual Guide or Guru. *Vide Bhāg.* XI. 17. 27. 5. Not any one special individual, but humanity as a whole, *Vide Bhāg*. III. 29. 21-34; VII. 14. 34-38. 6. The whole world conceived as the manifestation of the Supreme Being, *Vide Bhāg*. XI. 2. 41. 7. The Antaryāmin or inner controller of all the objects in the world; *Vide Bṛh*. III. 7. etc. 8. It may be one's own transcendental Ātman, *Vide* Upds. But Parabhakti or the higher Love is possible only when the Chosen Ideal is loved, after the realization of the Divine as one's own very Self. That the devotee may continue to keep his identity separate even after this transcendental experience, is attested to by many authorities: 'Sages delighting in their own Self though they are free from all fetters, still continue to be devoted to Hari, the Personal Deity; Such is the glory of Hari—आत्मारामाश्च मुनयो निर्ग्रन्था अप्युरुक्रमे । कुर्वन्त्यहैतुकीं भक्तिमित्थंभूतगुणो हरिः, *Bhāg*. 1. 7. 10. There are many saints and godmen who retain a little of their individuality to enjoy the bliss of the company of God, because they believe 'it is better to taste sugar than to become one with it.' Others again desire to serve the world and for that keep their individuality. A third type of Bhaktas never cares about keeping their individuality or giving it up, but surrenders the will to God and allows Him to make use of it in any way He likes. But the individuality of these souls who have realized the Divine does not remain the same afterwards as before. Their humanity is only a mask; the Divine expresses Itself through all their deeds and thoughts. Thus according to Nārada one who has realized this Parabhakti is the same as the Jīvanmukta described in *Laghu-yogavāsiṣṭha-rāmāyaṇa*, canto 5, the Brāhmaṇa described in *Mbh.* XIII. 251, the Guṇātīta described in *Bg.* XIV. 22-26, the Sthitaprajña described in *Bg.* II. 55-72, the Bhakta mentioned in *Bg.* XII. 13-19, and the Ativarṇāśramin described in *Sūta-saṁhitā*, Mukti-khaṇḍa, Ch. 5. On the authority of the following passage in the *Jīvanmuktiviveka* and the several scriptural citations assembled there, we may conclude that the same state of realization is referred to by the terms Liberated-in-life, Established-in-wisdom, Lover-of-the-Lord, Gone-beyond-Nature, the truly twice-born, and the one beyond castes and stations—तदेवं विमुक्तश्च विमुच्यते इत्यादिश्रुतय: जीवन्मुक्त-स्थितप्रज्ञ-भगवद्भक्त-गुणातीत-ब्राह्मणा-तिवर्णाश्रमि-प्रतिपादक-स्मृतिवाक्यानि च जीवन्मुक्तिसद्भावे प्रमाणानीति स्थितम्। Thus we can see that the Supreme Divine Love noted by Nārada is not the same as what is generally understood by the term Bhakti or devotion for God. It is, in fact, the culmination of all Yogas, or methods of realization, ending in a complete egoless love of God for the sake of love alone and a realization of God in all creatures, indistinct from one's own Self and expressing itself in the form of unselfish service to God and his creatures in the spirit of Worship. जीवराशिभिराकीर्ण आण्डकोशाङ्घ्रिपो महान्। तन्मूलत्वादच्युतेज्या सर्वजीवात्मतर्पणम्। The Universe is a tree instinct with life; the Lord is its foundation; so service to all creatures is worship of God. *Bhāg.* VII. 14. 36.

Sutra 3. The adjective स्व preceding the word रूप conveys the sense of *own* intrinsic nature. Note the absence of this adjective in the previous *Sū.* While that *Sū.* was meant to be a description of Bhakti from the standpoint of its manifestation in life, this *Sū.* purports to give a description of the same as it is in itself. The word अमृत (immortal) has various shades of meaning, all of which are important in the context, and it is to suggest them all that Nārada has used this word in preference to other words, such as Mukti, Kaivalya, or Apavarga. Accordingly, the present translation of the expression is not merely literal, but is meant to bring out all these suggested meanings. (a) अमृत conveys the sense of freedom from death or change; but the permanence alluded to in the text cannot be interpreted to mean the permanence vouchsafed to us by the physical laws of conservation of energy, or by the biological law of the continuity of the germ plasm as the carrier of life from generation to generation. It cannot also be thought of as mere continuation of life in another birth on the principle of transmigration, believed in by all religions, primitive or civilized, except the organized form of Christianity and Islam. Neither can it refer to the survival of the individual in an astral or ethereal body, as advocated by the spiritualists. It does not also mean the comparatively permanent experience of joy for æons in Heaven, Paradise, Brahmaloka, Vaikuṇṭha, and the like. The ordinary Heaven or Svarga, which all popular religions offer as a reward for good conduct and orthodox performance of rites and ceremonies, is really not permanent, nor is it a place of unalloyed happiness. The Hindu scriptures always emphasize the impermanence of Svarga and celestial pleasures. In fact our sages paint a glowing picture of heaven only to attract to spiritual life those slovenly minds who refuse to move unless some recompense is promised to them in the shape of sensual happiness. We are definitely informed so in *Bhāg*. XI. 21. 23. The Upaniṣads also assure us that everything which is an effect produced by an action must pass away and cannot be permanent. On the other hand, real अमृत or immortality, once it is achieved, can be never lost. Eternal happiness accrues to the Bhaktas, *Ssū.* 8. The eternity of the fruit of self-realization, is emphasized in all important scriptures, see *Chānd*. VIII. 8. 15; *Bṛh*. I. 2. 17; *Bsū*. IV. 4. 22; *Bg*. VIII. 15; etc. (b) अमृत is also a synonym of ambrosia or nectar of bliss. Bhakti is a supremely blissful experience—an unadulterated and unalloyed state of absolute felicity and beatitude. Worldly pleasure and celestial joy pale into insignificance in comparison with the Ānanda, designated as Brahman itself in the Upaniṣads. All other pleasures are partial reflections or manifestations of Divine Bliss through a temporary predominance of the sāttvika mode of the mind, and all craving for earthly or heavenly joys is only an unconscious groping in the dark to gain Spiritual Bliss which is the birthright of each soul. Every desire is a veiled prayer, and every satisfaction a concealed and confused taste of Ānanda. The extremely sweet nature of the spiritual experience is recognised by the Vedic Ṛṣi when he prays 'May I attain to that beloved mansion of His, where those men that are devoted to God are happy, where flows the perennial fountain of nectar, just by the mighty striding feet of

Viṣṇu, in His Supreme Abode,' *Ṛg.* I. 154. 5. The Ātman that is realized is characterized as honey, which is itself Amṛta. *Bṛh.* II. 15. 4. Yājñavalkya tells Maitreyī that every one and everything in this world is loved only for the sake of Ātman or Bliss in the form of Brahman. *Ib.* II. 4. See also *Bṛh.* IV. 3. 32; *Tait.* II. 7; *Chānd.* VII. 23; *Kaṭh.* IV. 5; *S've.* III. 11. *Bg.* V. 21, VI. 21, 27, 28; *Bhāg.* XII. 12. 51; etc. for the blissful nature of God-realization.' One of the beautiful names by which Nammālvār addressed God is 'Ārāvamuda' which means 'Nectar endless'. The word 'Ālvār', which the S'rīvaiṣṇavites use to denote godmen enjoying the highest realization, means those who are immersed in bliss. *Tiruvāymozhi.* II. 8. 4. speaks of Vaikuṇṭha as the region where joy is endless. Pillai Lokācārya's *Mumukṣuppadi* III says, 'Love pursued even after bliss is gained, adds zest to the bliss.' Parās'ara Bhatta speaks of 'love and bliss as one truth.' Kulas'ekhara in the *Mukundamālā* (verse 10) says that he is not aware of any other bliss equal to the nectar of constantly remembering the blessed feet of Hari; and he invites us (Verse 17) to drink the nectar called Kṛṣṇa: for that is the Supreme panacea for all worldly ills and what gives eternal bliss. The *Bhakti-rasayana* opens with a verse which states: 'Bhakti is the supreme goal of man's endeavour; it is incomparable and unalloyed bliss'. The *Nārāyaṇīya* of Nārāyaṇabhaṭṭa says that 'devotion to God, which is sweet in the beginning, in the middle, and in the end, gives the highest bliss'. Tāyumānavar in his famous *Ananda Kalippu* describes the joy of spiritual experience. A similar meaning is conveyed by the saying of Jesus: 'My joy I give unto you and your joy no man taketh from you.' Jesus also speaks of the Kingdom of Heaven and says: 'Enter thou into the joy of thy Lord', *Mat*. XXV. 22, 23. Similar statements are also found in *Quoran*, Pt. XVIII, Ch. XXI, 101, 102 which the commentator explains as referring to the bliss of communion with God; also Pt. XXIII, Ch. XXXVI, where the happiness of heaven is described in one word, 'Peace', corresponding to the S'ānti of the Upaniṣads. Plotinus calls the spiritual state as a 'divinely ineffable harbour of repose'. Fawcett calls it 'joy eternal, the *Energeia Akinesias* whose delight is perfect.' The beauty of this spiritual bliss is never adulterated with even the least trace of misery. 'Every sweet has its sour,' says Emerson, but the bliss of realization is above it. It must also be realized that there is no loss of individuality in this highest experience. Once S'rī Rāmakṛṣṇa said to Narendra (Swāmi Vivekānanda): 'God is like a liquid sweet, would you not dive into the sea? Just think of a vessel with a wide mouth containing syrup of sugar, and suppose you are a fly anxious to drink of the sweet liquid. Where would you sit and drink?' Narendra replied that he would prefer to sit at the edge of the vessel, for if he came to a point beyond his depth he was sure to be drowned. Thereupon S'rī Rāmakṛṣṇa said, 'You forget, my son, that by diving deep into the Divine Sea you need not be afraid of death. Remember, the sea called Saccidāranda is the Sea of Immortality. The water of this Sea never causes death: it is the water of everlasting life. Think not like some foolish persons that you may run to excess in your love of God.' Bhakti is thus no loss of individuality, but only a supreme transcendence of the limitations of individuality and regaining of the true status of the Self. 'Perfect personality is in God only. To all finite minds there is allotted but a pale copy thereof. The finiteness of the finite is not a producing condition of personality, but a limit and a hindrance to its development,' Lotze. (c) अमृत also means Mokṣa or liberation from the cycle of transmigration. It is conceived of both positively and negatively by various schools of thought. The Apavarga of the Nyāya-vais'eṣika school is only a negative conception in as much as it means nothing but release from pain; it is not the positive enjoyment of bliss. It is a complete cessation of effort, activity, and consciousness, and an absolute detachment of the soul from body and mind—an abstract existence without knowledge and happiness. Vātsyāyana is emphatic that Apavarga cannot be a positive manifestation of soul's happiness, and Udyotakara supports him. The Sāṁkhya and Yoga schools speak of Kaivalya as an eternal isolation of the seer from the modifications of Prakṛti or Citta. To them even Release is only phenomenal, since bondage does not belong to the Puruṣa. It is an escape from suffering, and not a manifestation of bliss, because Puruṣa is free from all attributes. Among the Mīmāṁsakas, Jaimini and S'abara never concern themselves with Mukti. Prabhākara conceives of it negatively as a total disappearance of

Dharma and Adharma, and consequent escape from rebirth. It is to him a cessation not only of pain but also of pleasure, and not a state of positive bliss. Kumārila Bhaṭṭa also asserts that libration cannot be eternal unless it is negative in character. So also Pārthasārathi. The Buddhistic schools conceive of the final end or Nirvāṇa as a complete extinction or blowing out even of the self itself, and to the Jains, Nirvāṇa is a disintegration of the Kārmic body. Alone, among the religious and philosophical systems that flourished on the fair soil of India, Vedānta, in all its schools, has emphasized the positive character of the state of Release along with its negative aspect. To the Vedāntin, whether he is a Jñānin or a Bhakta, the summum bonum of existence is the regaining of the natural blissful state of the Ātman, as well as freedom from the miseries of the transmigratory cycle. Nārada emphasizes this double aspect of Vedāntic Release. The emphasis of the Bhakti schools is always on the positive aspect.

Some minor differences among the various schools of Vedānta may be noted here. A point of difference, more important in connection with the present *Sū.* is that the Bhakti schools as well as some teachers among the Advaitins like Maṇḍana do not accept liberation in this very life. They accept final Release only at the fall of the body. This is the view of Christianity and Mohammedanism too. Though the Bhakti teachers thus deny to the most perfect state attainable in this life the right to call itself Mukti, there is not much difference between the Parabhakti (Supreme Love) accepted by them and the Jivanmukti of S'aṅkara. If the sense of freedom from all misery and a sense of eternal Bliss are not possible before death, then it is meaningless to say that Bhakti is Amṛta or immortality. It will be a contradiction in terms to say that immortality can be attained after death. If Mukti is freedom and immortality, it can justify itself only by the soul's experience of its being above death and limitations, in this very life. Hence both Nārada and S'aṅkara accept the realization of immortality in this very embodied life. The following Upaniṣadic passages support it: 'Then the mortal becomes immortal, and attains Brahman *here*'; 'Realizing Him thus, one becomes immortal *here*'; he realizes Brahman; If we have realized the truth here, we know it; while living on this earth we realize That— अथ मर्त्योऽमृतो भवति अत्र ब्रह्म समश्नुते, *Kaṭh*. VI. 14: तमेवं विद्वानमृत इह भवति, *Puruṣasūkta*, *Tait*; अत्र ब्रह्म समश्नुते, *Bṛh*. IV. 4. 12; इह चेदवेदीत् अथ सत्यमस्ति *Ken*. II. 5; इहैव सन्तः अथ विद्मस्तद् वयम् Bṛh. IV. 4. 14. *Vide Jīvanmuktiviveka* (T.P.H., Adyar). (d) अमृत also means unsolicited alms. (द्वे याचितायाचितयोर्यथासंख्यमृतामृते—*Amarakos'a*). The Bhakta never craves for Mukti; he is quite satisfied to enjoy the love of God for love's sake, and to serve Him for the sake of service. Still Mukti comes to him by the grace of God. 'Unlike the Wish-fulfilling tree which has to be approached and solicited if it should satisfy anybody's wish, Thou art always in front of the Bhaktas wherever they are, eager to bless them, even without their asking for any favour, and finally givest them eternal bliss'—

नम्राणां सन्निधत्ते सततमपि पुरस्तैरनभ्यर्थितानप्यर्थान् ; कामानजस्रं वितरति परमानन्दसान्द्रां गतिं च। इत्थं निश्शेषलभ्यो निरवधिकफलः पारिजातो हरे त्वं ; क्षुद्रं तं शक्रवाटीद्रुममभिलषति व्यर्थमर्थिव्रजोऽयम् ॥ *Nārāyaṇīya* 1. 8. Without His grace Release is not possible. यमेवैष वृणुते तेन लभ्यः—It is attained by him alone whom God chooses', *Kaṭh.* II. 22; also जुष्टः तेनामृतत्वमेति—Liked by Him, he attains immortality, *S've.* 1. 6. In the *Mbh.* also we get statements to this purport: 'Only he can realize Nārāyaṇa to whom He is gracious'; 'he who has the grace of Nārāyaṇa realizes Him. He cannot be realized by mere self-effort.' S'ri S'aṅkarācārya who stresses self-effort so often, also recognizes the supreme need of divine grace in several of his writings. *Vide Bhāṣya, Bsū.* II. 3. 41; III. 2. 5; etc.

(1) अमृत also means यज्ञशेष or the holy food left after sacrificial offerings. By the apt selection of the word 'amṛta' to describe the nature of devotion, Nārada means by implication that just as 'amṛta', in the sacrificial sense, is associated with self-effort—for sacrifice which gives rise to 'amṛta' is the result of self-effort—so also Bhakti is associated with self-effort. Supreme love is of the nature described before; it no doubt comes only by the grace of God. But does it come even if a man keeps idle and does not deserve such grace by his self-effort? Divine grace never comes until the mind is purified by continued acts of self-sacrifice. God's grace descends on man always like a breeze, but if he wants to take advantage of it, he must do spiritual practices, as the boatman must unfurl the sails before he can catch the breeze. Thus complete freedom of the will and

self-effort are assured without any prejudice to the doctrine of the grace of God. That God's grace depends upon man's actions is also the view of *Bsū*. II. 3. 42, II. 1. 34; *Yvā*. III. 6. 14, II. 6. 27; and *Bg*. VI. 5. From the above explanation we find that Nārada makes a very happy choice in using the word 'amṛta' to describe the intrinsic nature of Supreme Divine Love, for in that word is contained in a nut-shell the whole doctrine in all its implications. Immortality, bliss, and freedom are the end, and the grace of God and self-effort form the means. All these various ideas—by explicit statement or indirect implication—are sought to be conveyed through the description of the intrinsic nature of Supreme Love, which in short is nothing less than Release itself.

Sutra 4. This aphorism refers directly to the intrinsic nature of Bhakti described in the previous one as Mukti or Release itself. It purports to say that this अमृतत्व, which constitutes the essential nature of Bhakti, is something which the devotee does not directly seek and accomplish; that it is an attainment added to him by the God of Love quite unsolicited; that it is the birthright of every man, irrespective of caste, colour, or creed; and that it makes one upon whom it is bestowed perfect, divine, and contented. लब्ध्वा (having gained) is used in reference to Bhakti as Amṛta or Mokṣa in order to indicate that the devotee does not strive consciously for Mokṣa, but it is conferred on him, unsolicited, by the beloved Lord. As far as the devotee is concerned, his interest lies in loving God and in serving Him and His creation. He simply immerses himself in that Love, and has no thought except that of his Lord. For who can refuse to be absorbed in that ocean of Divine bliss and infinite auspicious Divine attributes and qualities, if he has but the opportunity of knowing them. When Yudhiṣṭhira, was asked why he was so much enamoured of his Lord, he could only retort by asking the question why he should love the Himālayas! Nevertheless God who loves his devotees more than He loves Himself, and who feels pride in considering Himself the servant of His devotees, and is always anxious to do some good turn to them, takes care to bless them with Mukti also. S'rī Rāmakṛṣṇa used to compare God to a loving master who, feeling happy in honouring a devoted servant, makes him sit on the same seat with himself, in spite of the protests of the humble servant. When Mukti, which is a state of union with the Supreme Being, thus comes to the devotee in spite of his desire to escape from the sacrilege of raising himself to the position of his Lord, he simply bows down to the Lord's will as inevitable, for fear of displeasing his Lord, and like an obedient servant accepts His gift as a token of His love, but even then without any consideration of selfish satisfaction. Heaven or hell, liberation or bondage, are all the same to him, and they have the same value as they are equally gifts from his beloved. S'rī S'aṅkara in his *S'ivānandalaharī* expresses the deep longing thus: 'Let me be born as a man or God, an animal or a tree, a gnat, a worm, or a bird. If my heart is immersed in the love of Thy blessed lotus feet, what do I care for any kind of body?'—नरत्वं देवत्वं नगवनमृगत्वं मशकता

पशुत्वं कीटत्वं भवतु विहगत्वादिजननम् सदा त्वत्पादाब्जस्मरणपरमानन्द-लहरीविहारासक्तं चेद् हृदयमिह किं तेन वपुषा ॥ Śrī Kulaśekhara in his *Mukundamālā*, expresses the same idea in many verses, *Vide* verses 3-9. 'Those who have surrendered,' says the Lord, 'their souls to Me do not care for anything except Myself, not even the status of Brahmā, or Indra, or an Emperor, or the lordship of the nether world, or psychic powers, nay, not even freedom from rebirth.' Again, 'Those heroes and saints who are devoted to me as their only goal and refuge, do not care even for Release from birth which I may grant.' *Bhāg.* XI. 14. 14. etc. यत् in the *Sū.* refers to अमृतः, described in the previous *Sū.* as the intrinsic nature of Bhakti. The word पुमान् is specially significant; it implies that the practice of the discipline of Bhakti and the attainment of the state of Mukti it confers, are not restricted by any considerations of caste, colour, or sex. Every human being possessing an earnest desire can cultivate Bhakti and attain Mukti through it. The possession of sub-human bodies is perhaps the only condition that makes the culture of Bhakti impossible. It is not however meant that these sub-human creations have no souls, but only that they have not yet reached a stage of evolution in body and mind which fulfils the minimum requirements of a life of devotion. However, in several devotional books, especially the Purāṇas, we come across instances of birds and animals having gained Bhakti and Mukti; Madhusūdana Sarasvati, the great devotee and philosopher, also maintains in his *Bhakti-rasāyana* that all living beings are entitled to

Bhakti. In this scientific age, we can understand it only as an exaggeration to impress on men how devotion to God can achieve even the seemingly impossible. This is the only conclusion we can arrive at on the subject, seeing that *Bsū.* I. III. 25 maintains that man alone is entitled to spiritual practices and realization. The question of the qualification of superhuman beings (*i.e.*, Gods and demons—Deva and Asura) may also arise here. Most probably Nārada does not take them into consideration in this *Sū.* According to *Bsū.* gods and demons are entitled to spiritual realization.

Nārada, as we have just seen, holds considerations of sex or caste no bar to the practice of devotion and attainment of Release at the perfection of devotional life. Since this is the general view of all teachers of the Bhakti school, and since the number of devotees of the highest type, coming from amongst women and the castes considered lowest are so many, we need not dwell longer on the point. We may just point out here that the opinion of some, who hold that S'ri S'aṅkara believed it impossible for anyone except those born in the Brahmin caste to achieve Release from the transmigratory cycle, is a mistaken one. What S'aṅkara has actually done is only to support, by way of concession to the prejudices of his age, the ineligibility of the अनुपनीत, *i.e.* those that are not invested with the sacred thread, to the study of the Vedas and to follow the disciplines and observances requiring a knowledge of the Vedic text. But for Mukti, which according to him is identical with Jñāna or Self-realization, no one is disqualified by any question of caste, creed, or sex. He admits the possibility of Vidura and Dharmavyādha attaining realization *Bsū.* I. 38. In commenting on *Bsū.* III. 4. 38 he maintains that spiritual realization is possible for all, irrespective of caste, colour, or creed, through Japa, fasting, worship of God, etc. And in concluding the discussion on the *Apas'ūdrādhikaraṇa* he quotes with approval the Purāṇic view that the Purāṇas and the Itihāsas should be taught to all. Now these contain elaborate expositions of all the mystic wisdom of the Vedas, and the *Gītā*—one of the triple foundations of the Vedānta containing the quintessence of the Upanisads—occurs in the *Mahābhārata*, a book classed as Itihāsa, and therefore open to all. This concession therefore only means that S'aṅkara was willing to give the spirit of Vedic wisdom to all; he only denied the letter out of consideration for the prejudices of the age. Nowhere does he deny Mukti, or the chances of gaining it, to anyone. Hence he and Nārada are in complete agreement on this point of the eligibility of all for Mukti.

A Siddha or a perfect man is one who has attained the goal of all spiritual endeavour. The goal of all human aspiration is perfection. Till perfection is attained, practice has to be continued, in spite of the minor attainments and psychic powers that one may come to be endowed with. Perfection is already inherent in man. It is only clouded by Ignorance. When *Māyā* or Ignorance is transcended through spiritual practices the natural perfection of the Ātman manifests itself, as the sun shines when the clouds clear away. The function of Sādhana or practice is only to remove this cloud of Māyā. That devotion to God is one of the methods of attaining this perfection, and one of the easiest and the most direct of them all, is clearly stated in Patañjali's *Ysū.* I. 23. In ordinary parlance the word Siddha denotes a man possessing various superhuman powers. *Ysū.* III. 37 makes it clear that these superhuman powers or siddhis are obstacles to the highest realization. It is not in any such sense the word is used here; and it is clearly emphasized by the immediately following word 'amṛta', translated as 'divinity'. In other words the sign of a 'perfect man' or Siddha is not the possession of miraculous powers, but the attainment of unity with the Supreme Being. Perfection being possible only in God, the man of highest realization is said to become one with God; for, as we have seen, the individuality of man merges in the Supreme Divinity when the highest realization is gained.

The contentment or तृप्ति of the perfect man mentioned in the *Sū.* is to be distinguished from the self-satisfaction of lesser men. While an aspirant is on the road to perfection, he must be filled with a divine discontent. Unless one is dissatisfied with anything less than the Highest, one is not likely to progress in the spiritual path. Only when one reaches the highest perfection, can one safely be contented with oneself. The contentment here referred to is not the kind of satisfaction that comes when some desire is fulfilled; it is an absolute satisfaction arising from the absence of all desires.

There is no reason to think that such a perfect soul will lapse into inactivity; for though he has achieved the highest, the great love that has taken him to God prompts him also to be active in promoting the spiritual welfare of others less fortunate than himself, in a spirit of service. Again mere satisfaction should not be taken to be the test of realization; for then, whenever we are satisfied with some minor achievement, we may not aspire further. The satisfaction of the perfect man is only an accompaniment of realization, and not one that should be consciously aspired after by the aspirant. For such hankering for satisfaction, being itself a kind of desire, will be an obstacle in the way of its achievement. St. John of the Cross says: 'To seek satisfaction in God is spiritual gluttony.' The aspirant must be ready to accept God even if His coming means trouble and tribulation. Madame Guyon says in her *Acquiescence of Pure Love*:

> To me it is equal whether love ordain
> My life or death, appoint me pain or ease.
> My soul perceives no real ill in pain;
> In ease or health no real good she sees;
> One good she covets, and that good alone,—
> To choose Thy will, from selfish bias free,
> And to prefer a cottage to a throne,
> And grief to comfort, if it pleases Thee.

'If God were to will to send the souls of the just to hell—so Crysostom and Clement suggest—souls in the third state would not love Him the less. . . It is only pure love that loves to suffer ', Fenelon. Cf. The words of Job: 'Though He slay me, yet will I trust in Him.' Kunti, mother of the virtuous Pāṇḍavas, prays: विपदः सन्तु नः शश्वत्तत्र तत्र जगद्गुरो । भवतो दर्शनं यत्स्यादपुनर्भवदर्शनम् —O Guide of the universe, let hardships and sorrows come always if during their course we are blessed with Thy vision that puts an end to birth and death, *Bhāg* I. 8. 24. Such should be the attitude of the real Bhakta before he can aspire to the highest. To know the Truth, to realize God, one must, therefore, enter upon a vigorous and persistent endeavour with an absolute indifference to pleasure, pain, or personal satisfaction that may accompany or follow such persuit; otherwise it is impossible to attain to the Truth, *i.e.* to realize God. But when Truth is actually realized, *i.e.*, when the highest Bhakti, which is of the nature of Mukti, is attained, it always brings to the aspirant, an unperturbed sense of satisfaction, which 'having obtained man considers no other gain superior,' *Bg.*, VI. 22.

Sutra 5. The description given here is reminiscent of what we get in *Bg.* II. 55—76; XIV. 22—26; XII. 13—19; *Bhāg.* XI. 2. 48—55; *Laghuyogavāsiṣṭha*, V. 90—97; *Sūtasaṁhitā*, Mukti-khaṇda V, and *Mbh.* XIII. 251. The description in all these places shows that the Bhakta or Jivanmukta is beyond the ego, beyond the three modes of Nature, beyond the duties of castes and stations of life. He is yet full of love and a spirit of service which is always accompanied by an entranced enjoyment of the bliss of Brahman. That all these descriptions refer to the same ideal is plain from the words of Vidyāraṇya and Svapnes'vara, *Vide Supra* p. 50.

Although the participles लब्ध्वा in the previous *Sū*. and प्राप्य in the present one are apparently similar in meaning, on scrutiny we can make out a subtle distinction: the first suggests gaining, while the second connotes attainment. Attainment involves personal effort; and hence the choice of the second word prevents a wrong emphasis being placed on the aspect of grace to the prejudice of self-effort. Nārada never lets slip an opportunity to emphasize both these aspects of spiritual life, as if to correct the misconceptions and dangers arising from partiality to any one of these conditions of God-realization. The *Sū*. states that the perfect man has no more selfish desires. Desires arise from a sense of imperfection or limitation, which is characteristic of the man who identifies himself with the ego. Once the ego is transcended, and perfection is attained, this characteristic disappears. The feeling of imperfection is possible only when a man finds something outside himself, other than himself, an object of seeking. But the perfect man is not aware of anything other than God, his own higher Self. Hence also desires have no place in him. The question may arise here why desirelessness is mentioned as the special mark of the perfect man when it is the accepted creed of all spiritual disciplines that non-attachment for objects of the world is an invariable pre-requisite of all seekers of spiritual good. The author of the Sūtras must have meant to bring into prominence the difference in the quality of the vairāgya or dislike of sense pleasures characteristic of the spiritual aspirant and the perfected one who has attained the goal. As the *Jīvanmuktiviveka* notes, 'at the stage prior to the realization of the goal, the seeker of God is free from cravings, as a result of his vigilant practice of self-control and other virtues; the desires still persist, and are held in control only with some effort, whereas, after realization, there being nothing like the transformations of the mind, desires cease altogether. Though the perfect man seems to respond to such feelings as love and hatred, on account of previous habit, he is pure within as the sky which, though filled with smoke and dust, remains pure'. The difference is noticed in *Naiṣkarmyasiddhi* IV. 69: उत्पन्नात्मावबोधस्य ह्यद्वेष्टृत्वादयोगुणाः । अयत्नतो भवन्त्येते न तु साधकरूपिणः ।—One who has realized the Self is free from hatred, hypocrisy, and violence, and possesses to the highest degree forbearance, straightforwardness, and the rest without any conscious effort; he has no more to practice them as discipline. The *Sreyomārga* also says, 'All that precede the acquisition of realization are means which are brought about by effort, but they are inherent in the case of a perfect man.' The aspirant will always be yearning for liberation which is again a form of desire however exalted it may be, but in a man who has already attained to the goal, no residue of desire, however noble, is left. It is also relevant to note here the distinction made by Patañjali between higher and lower types of Vairāgya. The latter he describes as indifference to the Guṇās arising out of the knowledge of Puruṣa, *Vide Ysū.* I. 15 & 16.

किञ्चित् in the *Sū.* emphasizes this absolute freedom from desires. It is a well-known fact recognized by all books on devotion, and illustrated by the lives of devotees, that true devotees of God would not pray for any worldly gift. Not only that, they would not pray even for Mukti or liberation. 'Those devotees,' says Rūpagosvāmin in *Bhakti-rasāmṛta-sindhu*, I. 2-13, 'who are delighted with the service of the lotus feet of Kṛṣṇa, do not desire even Mokṣa.' But as implied herein, and as openly declared in many devotional works, though these great souls do not desire such things like one who has not reached realization may desire, still they evince another kind of higher craving for worshipping the Lord, singing and hearing His glories and serving the world as the manifestation of the Lord. Even perfected souls who retain their higher ego cannot get over this craving, which is quite different from worldly desires depending upon the lower ego for its existence. For further elucidation of the point consult *Bhāg.* I. 4. 12; I. 7. 10; II. 1. 7; III. 25. 34; III. 29. 13; VII. 9. 41; and IX. 21. 12. It is evident from these citations that the prayer of Rantideva that he may be present in all beings and undergo all the sufferings for their sake, so that they may be relieved of all their misery, and that of Prahlāda to lift up foolish people from Saṁsāra, cannot be considered as mere egoistic desires. When we examine the lives of the greatest spiritual men like Buddha, Christ, and Rāmakṛṣṇa, we find the same phenomenon. Buddha gave up the bliss of Nirvāṇa that he might be born again and again to serve the world. When Swāmi

Vivekānanda once told Śrī Rāmakṛṣṇa that he loved to remain rapt in divine contemplation, the latter retorted that that was all right for many, but that he expected something better from him, meaning thereby that the Swāmī should not hanker after his individual salvation, but desire for the salvation of the world. Again when Śrī Rāmakṛṣṇa tested him by asking him to pray to the Mother for worldly prosperity, the Swāmī attempted several times to obey his command, and when he was asked why he could not, he said that the moment the thought of the Divine Mother came into his mind, he lost all desire for worldly prosperity, and hence could pray only for Bhakti. We see also how he was actuated by the intense desire to spread the Gospel of Śrī Rāmakṛṣṇa. We read of Christ's desire to save the souls of sinners and bring down the Kingdom of Heaven on earth, and of Mohammed's desire to teach the Arabs the principles of religion and spirituality. Nārada could possibly have nothing to object to such cravings arising in the hearts of the highest devotees.

Freedom from grief implied in the phrase न शोचति has this implication: Ordinarily sorrow is considered to be a characteristic of Tamas. Vide *Bg.* XVIII. 28 & 35. But here it includes all kinds of worldly pleasures also, whether Sāttvika, Rājasika, or Tāmasika; the reason being that all worldly pleasures must be preceded, accompanied, or followed by grief. Thus *Bg.* XVIII. 36 & 38, makes it clear that the so-called Sāttvika pleasure must always be earned by hard practice; that Rājasika pleasure turn out to be poison in the end; and that

Tāmasika pleasure is a delusion. Patañjali also says in *Ysū.* II. 15 that to the thinking man everything is painful because they bring pain either as consequence, or as anticipation of loss of happiness, or as fresh cravings arising from impressions of happiness, or as counter-action of qualities. According to Patañjali all these are based on ignorance and ego, and must be included under the common name of Kleśa or misery. A man can expect to be free from such misery only after the realization of Truth. Such a man is beyond both pleasure and pain arising from merit and demerit, and is beyond all grief. Hence 'sorrow' includes all worldly joy, which has always got misery either as its root or fruit. As absence of desire, the absence of grief in a perfect man does not signify that he is devoid of sympathy for the miseries of others. To one who feels his neighbour as oneself, it is impossible not to sympathize with him in his miseries. To be a Bhakta is not to develop a stony heart and be careless about the woes of mankind. Sympathy is divine, and if God himself is moved to be born for the relief of such misery, there is nothing to prevent a perfect man, who has become divine, from feeling sorrow for the sufferings of his oppressed neighbour. In fact this sympathy is only another expression of his divinity. But we must take care not to take all cases of sympathy to be a sign of God-realization, though no doubt a man of divine sympathy may be said to have transcended his humanity. For we must remember that some sympathy is possible to a selfish man also. A mother sympathizing

with her child, a huntsman with his dog, and a cultivator with his bullock, are indeed cases of sympathy, but the ego is at the bottom of their feeling. They sympathize because the child or dog or bullock belongs to them. Real sympathy is possible only for the Bhakta who has transcended the bourne of ignorance and who feels the whole world as himself. The presence of this sympathy, which is also a kind of grief caused by the grief of others, is not intended to be denied in a Bhakta by this *Sū*. For example, see Prahlāda's sympathy for the miseries of those who are immersed in Saṁsāra, as described in *Bhāg*. VII. 9. 43 & 44:
नैवोद्विजे परदुरत्ययवैतरण्यास्त्वद्वीर्यगायन महामृतमग्नचित्तः । शोचे ततो विमुखचेतस इन्द्रियार्थमायासुखाय भरमुद्वहतो विमूढान् ॥ प्रायेण देव मुनयः स्वविमुक्तिकामा मौनं चरन्ति विजने न परार्थनिष्ठाः । नैतान् विहाया कृपणान् विमुमुक्ष एको नान्यं त्वदस्य शरणं भ्रमतोऽनुपश्ये ॥
'With my mind deeply immersed in the rare ambrosia of singing Thy glories, I do not care for the Vaitaraṇi (the river of Hell) so difficult to cross. But I sympathize with those who, immersed in deep ignorance, bear this burden of Saṁsāra for the sake of sense pleasures, and consequently have no inclination to seek after that ambrosia. Most sages intent upon their own release contemplate Thee in perfect silence, but they do not think of the welfare of others. I do not seek such release for myself, leaving these helpless creatures to themselves. I do not find any other than Thyself to be able to protect those who are going astray.' The same idea is illustrated by the self-sacrifice of Śibi, Jīmūtavāhana, and Dadhīci in our Purāṇas, and by the lives of Buddha and Christ.

Freedom from hatred is the next sign of a perfect man (न द्वेष्टि). As noted by Patañjali in *Ysū.* II. 8, hatred is always directed towards some object or person that causes pain or injury to oneself; and Vyāsa, commenting upon the *Sū.*, says that it is the nature of anger to get rid of such offending object or person. S'aṅkara also, in commenting on *Bg.* III. 37, remarks that it is obstructed desire that reappears in the guise of hatred and anger. Thus if Kāma is desire to obtain pleasurable objects, Dveṣa or hatred is desire to get rid of unpleasant or painful objects. So when a man is in a stage when there is no possibility of any desire or pain, he cannot be subject to hatred. 'The body is the cause of pleasure or pain; the Ātman has nothing to do with it; for it all concerns the gross and the subtle bodies, which are material in their nature. If one chances to bite one's tongue, with one's teeth, with whom should one be angry for causing that pain? If one limb of a person is struck by another limb, with whom should one be angry?' *Bhāg.* XI. 23. 51 to 56. This is the attitude of the perfect man who has become one with all creation. Moreover, to the Bhakta everything happens only by the will of the Lord, and if, therefore, he hates anyone, it will be equal to hating God Himself. Hence to him everything that comes from his Beloved is only a token of His love, and as such is always welcome. Here also this anger must be distinguished from that righteous indignation against the evils of Society or against the oppressors of humanity, as for example S'rī Kṛṣṇa's against Kaṁsa, Narakāsura, etc. or Rāma's against Rāvaṇa, Virādha, etc., or Jesus Christ's against the money-changers inside the temple whom he whipped out, or Mohammed's against the oppressors of the devotees of the one God. Such indignation is not a manifestation of Dveṣa (anger), and is not included under this *Sū*. The same is the case with the real renunciation of a Paramahaṁsa who is repelled by all that tends to cloud his vision of God.

न रमते ; that is, does not rejoice over anything. Ordinarily one rejoices when some desire is satisfied or some likelihood of pain is removed. This is the relative joy arising from merit, which is perishable in nature and is based on the ego born of Avidyā or ignorance. The true devotee overcomes joy and sorrow of this type. As *Kaṭh.* II. 12 says, 'The wise man relinquishes both joy and sorrow, having realized that ancient Effulgent One.' But this does not mean that the devotee has no joy at all resulting from the transcendental experience of the Divine. As the *Vivekacūdāmaṇi*, 522 points out: 'What wise man would discard that enjoyment of Supreme Bliss and revel in things unsubstantial? When the exceedingly charming moon is shining, who would wish to look at a painted moon?' The Bhakta is always immersed in this higher joy, in which the ego is completely absent. As Plotinus says, 'They are no more two, but one; the soul is no more conscious of the body or mind, but knows that she has what she desired, and that she is where no deception can come, and she would not exchange that bliss for all the heaven of heavens.'

नोऽत्साही भवति in the text means, 'Nor does he exert himself.' Generally a man exerts himself for gaining some desirable object or for getting rid of something undesirable. The Bhakta has no special desires of his own, nor does he wish to get rid of anything, because everything to him is a manifestation of the Lord. So why should he exert himself ? But this does not mean that he is an idler or is insensitive. The idea is the same as the 'Sarvārambha-parityāgī' of the *Bg*. XII. 16 and XIV. 25. S'rī S'aṅkara takes this latter word to denote one who gives up all activities prompted by selfish desires. S'rī Kṛṣṇa makes it clear that even the Siddha must work so long as he inhabits a body *Bg*. III. 5 & XVIII. 11. The body and mind form part of universal Nature and obey the laws of Nature; no amount of external force can divert the body and mind from obeying the laws of their being. The only difference between the activities of a perfect man and those of an ordinary man is that the one is not prompted by the ego, and hence is not affected by the consequences of attachment like the other. Vide *Bg*. III. 25, 28, & 33. It is a common error to consider S'aṅkara an advocate of total inactivity. He only advocates complete freedom from the duties of a householder during the stage of spiritual practice so as to prevent distractions to Samādhi, and confines his objections against a perfect man's activity to those rites and ceremonies which are based on an ignorance of the true nature of the Self. His main objection is against the view of a certain school of Vedāntins who consider that the perfect man is still subject to ritualistic injunction. The main aim of his attack also seems to be to defend the order of Sannyāsa from the attacks of ritualists who consider all renunciation of rituals sinful. S'aṅkara is not against unselfish action on the part of a perfect man ; nay he puts it in so many words that such action is not at all action (*vide* his comment on *Bg*. II. 11 ; III. 25; IV. 20; V. 7 ; XVIII. 66). In such a sense only the Siddha may be considered to be not acting. The *Bhāg*. XI. 7. 11 also says that what is absent in the perfect man is egoistic action : Beyond the reach of both merit and demerit, a perfect man will, like a child, desist from prohibited actions, but not through a sense of evil ; he may also perform enjoined actions, but not through an idea that it will conduce to merit. Thus we see all authorities are unanimous in considering that there is nothing contradictory in a perfect man's still living a dynamic life in the world. What Nārada too means here is that such a man cannot feel that he is doing any work, and that he cannot be expected to do work with selfish motives. To sum up our discussion, the perfect man, having transcended the ego, comes to have a type of non-attachment that is spontaneous, and not the result of any effort. He has no desire, except the desire to love the Lord and serve the world as His manifestation ; he has no hatred except indignation against evil and unrighteousness. His happiness consists not in the relative joys of the world, which are always concomitants of pain, but in the bliss of the Divine. And he does not exert to promote his own self-interest, but works for the good of all, without any sense of ego or of any feeling of external compulsion, in a spirit of service to God.

Sutra 6. The description of the perfect man is continued. It is pointed out that no particular standard or uniformity of behaviour and conduct can possibly be expected of a perfect man. Having surrendered his whole being completely to the Lord, and having merged his individuality in Him, the true Bhakta is not conscious of doing anything of his own accord or for his own sake. He feels like a dry leaf at the mercy of the wind ; he is made use of by the Lord Himself as His instrument to carry out His inscrutable purpose in this world. So far as the Bhakta himself is concerned, he is always immersed in the bliss of Self-realization and service of the Lord To all external appearance, however, he may sometimes behave just like any ordinary man, scrupulously discharging all the duties pertaining to his station in life, and thus set an example to men of lower spiritual evolution than himself. Often he may be seen to override accepted codes of social customs and conventional rules of propriety, so as to break the chain that clogs the wheels of progress, and thus become liable to be scorned and criticized by the conservatives. At other times he may appear to be inactive, being immersed in the bliss of Samādhi, and appear dead to his surroundings like a stock or stone. Thus Nārada wants us to understand how difficult it is to judge from a man's external behaviour whether he is a perfect man or not, as some of our modern behaviourists would advocate. Even when he is active externally, he is internally calm and quiet, so that he may be said to be an extraordinary combination of calmness and activity at the same time.

The word ज्ञात्वा (having known) denotes the transition from the idea of attainment in the previous *Sū.* to the idea of knowing. It suggests that spiritual realization is not really an attainment of something external to the aspirant, a status or power or a different world like heaven or Brahmaloka. It is not something produced as a result of action, whether in the nature of external rites and ceremonials or internal meditation, severally or in combination. It is only a recognition or realization of man's real status, his own inherent nature, the truth behind the phenomena, which is always self-existent and self-effulgent, but was obstructed by ignorance and egotism. Both spiritual practice and grace of God, referred to in the two previous aphorisms, are required only for the removal of obstructions. Were spiritual realization otherwise, it would never be permanent, as it is the law of Nature that everything that comes into existence in time must also inevitably pass away. There is again a subtle suggestion that there is no real distinction between Bhakti and Jñāna in their higher reaches, just as the radii of a circle, however divergent they may be towards the circumference, must inevitably meet at the centre. The differences in nomenclature are based only on differences in the methods of approach and consequent differences in expression in life. In the highest stage of realization they are the same. Thus S'ri Kṛṣṇa describes the Jñānin as Ekabhakti or one whose devotion is centred in a single entity, *Bg.* VII. 17. That Bhakti and Jñāna are inseperable is stressed diversely in *Bg.* VII. 14, 19, 29 ;

IX. 13; X. 10, 11; XI. 54; XIV. 26; XV. 19; and XVIII. 54. The description of Bhakti given in *Bg.* XII. and of Jñāna given in *Bg.* XIII differ very little practically. All this shows that S'rī Kṛṣṇa held that both cannot be made compartmental. 'In the stage of highest devotion, he knows Me, knows what in truth I am and who I am,' *Bg.* XVIII. 55. It may, however, be objected that S'aṅkara speaks of Bhakti as only a stepping-stone to Jñāna. But in understanding the meaning of this statement, we should not forget that what he refers to is the lower Bhakti, which is only a discipline and as such only a means to Jñāna or the highest realization. On the other hand, when Rāmānuja and other teachers speak of Jñāna as a stepping-stone to Bhakti, Jñāna to them means only the lower intellectual knowledge, which is a discipline, and Bhakti the higher realization. It is in the very nature of things impossible to conceive of a higher stage than the highest realization. In his *Bhaktirasāyana*, Madhusūdanasarasvati also raises the question whether Bhakti and Brahmavidyā (the science of Brahman) are the same, and if so what necessity is there for a treatise on the doctrine of Bhakti. In reply he points out that there is a necessity for a separate treatise as the two are different in respect of four things, *viz.*, Svarūpa (form), Sādhana (means), Phala (result), and Adhikāra (qualification). He points out: 1. in Bhakti the mind melts out of Love and takes the form of the Beloved, 2. in Brahmavidyā there is no such melting of heart; the mind is only concentrated on the undifferentiated Brahman; 3. In the former the mind is Savikalpa (with modification), in the latter it is Nirvikalpa (without modification). With respect to the means, he points out that whereas Brahmavidyā is dependent on the study of the major texts of the Upaniṣads such as 'Thou art That', Bhakti arises by a study of such treatises as describe the glories of the Lord. With respect to result, love of God is what is aimed at through Bhakti, and destruction of ignorance by Brahmavidyā. So far as qualification is concerned, every living being is entitled to Bhakti, but not so to Brahmavidyā, which is only for specially qualified aspirants. It will be seen that the whole discussion has reference only to the disciplinary stage and not to the stage of realization. But unlike other teachers, Madhusūdana gives an equal and independent status to both as methods of realization. यत् in the *Sū.* refers to प्रेम and अमृत in the previous aphorisms.

The word मत्त means either intoxicated or mad. Taking it to mean intoxicated, the Bhakta may be compared to the 'mattabhṛṅga' or the bee which gets intoxicated by drinking honey. It is quite common in Upaniṣadic literature to compare the Ātman to Madhu or honey. The Sufis often compare it to wine. The use of wine in Christian liturgy, of the Soma juice in Vedic Yajña, or of liquor in the S'ākta worship is meant to symbolize this enjoyment of the sweetness of Divine Bliss. The perfectly illumined soul is in uninterrupted enjoyment of this honey or wine, which is so sweet and health-giving. Just as people under the influence of wine are sometimes seen to develop strength and express their latent talents, so the realization of God and constant enjoyment of Divine Bliss make man spiritually and morally pure and healthy, and fit to undertake any kind of hard work in the service of God and man. It makes the dumb eloquent, and the lame cross mountains, as the poet says. The fool becomes a poet, and the weak and cowardly become heroes under its influence. Witness how Jesus, the carpenter's child, became the wisest man of his age, and brave enough to defy the might of the Roman Empire, or how Prahlāda dared to disobey his father whom all the world dreaded and obeyed. The idea of intoxication also suggests that the conduct and behaviour of the perfected soul are sometimes as inscrutable as the ways of the Lord Himself. No man can foresee or predict what he may or may not do under particular circumstances. He has no will of his own, as he has already surrendered it completely to the Lord. He is not the slave of so-called commonsense or reason, which often makes a man cold and calculating and selfish, nor is he in the grip of conventional laws of society or scriptures. He is under the benign influence of a higher Power than human, and his behaviour and conduct depend upon how this higher Power makes use of him for Its own inscrutable purposes. He is simply an instrument in the hands of God, and is happy to be made use of as He thinks best. His conduct, being sometimes strange, and at other times unintelligible from the standpoint of ordinary human reason and experience, may often appear similar to those of lunatics though his behaviour can never go against Dharma. A St. Francis of Assisi preaching to birds, his little sisters as he calls them, or his persuading a wolf, whom he calls his brother, to a better life ; a Buddha sacrificing his life to save that of a goat ; a Christ atoning for the sins of mankind and forgiving the enemies who brought about his death ; a Rāmakṛṣṇa daring to slap his patroness and refusing to accept a gift of ten thousand Rupees ; a Vivekānanda giving up his prospects of worldly prosperity—are these not supreme examples of madness from the point of view of commonsense realists ? Nārada is not alone in characterizing a Bhakta as intoxicated. Nammālvār says, 'If men were drunk with the love of God, they ought to dance like madmen in the streets. If they cannot do that, they are not love-smitten.' S'rī Rāmakṛṣṇa says that a true devotee who has drunk deep of the wine of Divine love is like a drunkard, and as such cannot always observe the conventional rules of propriety. The god-intoxicated man is unconscious of himself. To the external world he is like a drunkard. S'rī Rāmakṛṣṇa once said that when he saw the feet of the Mother, he felt as intoxicated as if he had drunk five bottles of wine. According to the same Master, the Bhakta may be found sometimes laughing, sometimes weeping, and at other times dancing and singing, being moved by different emotions, and may even be found moving about like an unclean spirit or a madman. See also *Bhāg.* V. 10. 13 ; XI. 2. 40 ; XI. 3. 32 ; etc. European mystics also often compare the state of realization to a state of intoxication or madness. Thus Plato in his *Phaedrus* calls it 'saving madness'.

Again, when the Christian mystic says, '*Sangina Christi, inebria me*', he is asking for such a gift of supernal vitality, a draught of that wine of Absolute Life which runs in the arteries of the world. In the *Fioretti*, it is told of John of Parma how he was drunk of the chalice of the spirit of Life delivered by Christ to St. Francis. Again Mechthild of Magdeburg says, 'I would drink, for a space, of the unmingled wine.' Emerson in his essay on the Oversoul points out that a tendency to insanity has always attended the opening of the religious sense in man, as if he was blasted with excesssive light. The trances of Socrates, the union of Plotinus, the Vision of Porphyry, the conversion of Paul, the Aurora of Boehme, the convulsions of George Fox and the Illumination of Swedenborg are all of this kind. We thus see how Nārada is justified in characterizing figuratively the Siddha as intoxicated or mad. S'rī Rāmakṛṣṇa used to say that all people are mad, the only difference being that while some are mad after lust and gold, others are mad after God. We should take care, however, to remember that we cannot make queerness or unreasonableness a test of realization. For while some God-intoxicated souls may appear mad at times, all of them need not necessarily be queer always.

The word स्तब्ध in the *Sū.* is used metaphorically to denote absence of activity. When the devotee is in the presence of his Beloved in a state of rapture he becomes fascinated and loses all power of action as a man dead drunk loses all capacity for independent motion, or as a bee which has drunk too much honey is not able to fly. Moreover, when he has reached the stage of perfection, there is no further possibility of any activity even by way of spiritual practice, as he has nothing more to achieve. This does not, however, mean that he is idle. But even while he appears to be active externally when he is not in Samādhi, it is no more the devotee that is acting, but it is God who acts through him. This is the whole burden of S'ri Kṛṣṇa's teaching on work. Among mystics, Ruysbroeck describes the life of one who has achieved this state as 'ministering to the world without, in love and mercy, whilst inwardly abiding in stillness and utter peace.' The term आत्मारामः (immersed in the Higher Self) gives the reason for the apparent inconsistencies of conduct mentioned above. Ātman being the same in all, absorption and delight in Self only implies loving service of the world. That such rapt contemplation of God and service are not inconsistent is clear from *Bg.* IV. 18, 19 : V. 24, 25 etc.

Sutra 7. A distinction between Love of God and love of worldly objects, especially, sex attraction is stressed in this aphorism. In Bhakti, the mind naturally renounces sense pleasures : in Kāma it gets engrossed in them. Being therefore of a contradictory nature, Bhakti cannot be equated with Kāma. From the point of view of ancient psychology, this reason for drawing a distinction between Bhakti and Kāma may be sufficient. But modern psychologists would not be satisfied by this apparent difference in the object of interest in the two forms of love. They demand better reasons for giving spiritual experience a higher basis than man's instinctive energies which manifest as desires. A consistent attempt is made in modern times to find a sexual origin for the so-called higher experiences of saints and mystics. According to modern psychology, an expression of desire need not always imply the flow of the mind towards an external object. When a person fails to obtain satisfaction for his instinctive cravings in the real world outside, owing to social taboos, keenness of competition, and the rest, his desires take a subterranean course. Unknown to the person, they remain submerged in the unconscious levels of the mind, and with added force derived from their suppression by mental censorship, they seek satisfaction in the world of phantasy, accompanied by various abnormal and unhealthy mental symptoms. Many a psychologist is inclined to classify the subjective experiences or spiritual intuitions of the saints and mystics along with these abnormal mental manifestations, and attribute them to the same cause, namely, the suppression of fundamental instincts, especially, the sexual. This theory of the sexual genesis of spiritual experience is based upon the following facts: (1) Very often there is seen a correspondence between the setting in of puberty in man, and the experience of conversion which is generally taken as the dawn of the spiritual sense. (2) In all religions and schools of thought emphasizing mystic experience, there are very strong sex taboos, and abstinence from sexual indulgences is held to be an unavoidable condition for the efflorescence of this mystical faculty. (3) The so-called higher experiences of saints, it is held, can be interpreted in terms of suppressed sex, as in the case of many forms of mental abnormalities. (4) In the writings of almost all the important mystics, sex symbolisms have been used to give expression to their aspirations and realizations. On the basis of these and other facts, spiritual love and experience are explained by psychologists as a suppressed expression of sexuality, which is by common consent Kāma *par excellence.*

The following remarks may be made by way of criticism of this theory: (1) The doctrine of correspondence between puberty and the experience of conversion is too simple a generalization, as it ignores all data that is inconvenient to it. Thus there are many cases of famous figures in religious history like Prahlāda, Dhruva, Naciketas, Kaṇṇappar, Jesus, Rāmakṛṣṇa, and Dayānanda, who showed signs of spiritual enlightenment even from boyhood. Such instances become perplexing in spite of the Freudian theory of infantile sexuality. In the generality of men it may be otherwise: but all that can be argued from this is that the spiritual faculty in man, like other faculties, generally gains its full expression only with the maturity of the body. (2) No doubt various forms of sex taboos are enforced in societies by the influence of religious sanction. But this can be accounted for by the fact that religion and morality have always gone hand in hand. The connection between spiritual awakening and perfect continence is, however, more significant.

It must be noted that the continence of the true aspirant and the repression, of which psychologists are so well aware, are poles asunder in their method and results. As far as result is concerned, what happens in repression is a degeneration of mind, and in a spiritual experience a higher development of it. As for method, repression is accomplished through fear, unnatural application of force, dissimulation, and ignorant evasion of the problem. The result of it is that sex tendencies and impressions remain submerged, and manifest as phantasies accompanied by mental disorders. In the case of a genuine spiritual aspirant practising continence, sex is fearlessly and intelligently faced and analysed, and thus, instead of being allowed to remain submerged as a crude animal propensity, its energies are transformed into a higher power for the enrichment of man's psychic being. But even this is not to be identified or equated with spiritual illumination; for what perfect continence does is only to provide the right subjective environment, a pure mind and body, in which alone spiritual experience can gain full expression.

And as for what this spiritual experience is, it will be nearer truth to recognize its distinctiveness instead of equating it with any of the other tendencies that psychologists generally classify under instincts. In fact there are writers on the psychology of religion who speak of a special religious instinct. Thus Rutgers Marshall writes in his *Instinct and Reason*: 'Religious activities, like the expression of all true instincts, seem often to be spontaneously developed in man. The masses of mankind do not have to be argued into the expression of religious feeling. Rather it is true that rationalistic and other barriers must be raised to prevent the expression of religious force that is found in various degrees'. As to what the primary nature of that spiritual instinct is, Prof. Rudolph Otto, more than any one in modern times, has attempted to describe in his *Idea of the Holy*. He defends its *a priori* character, and gives it the new name of the *Numinous*. Starbuck, too, in his paper on the *Instinctive Basis of Religion* maintains what he calls the Cosmo-æsthetic and teleo-æsthetic senses to constitute the ultimate religious instinct in human nature. Prof. Jastrow writes in his *Study of Religion* as if the existence of a religious instinct is axiomatic. Prof. Hocking in his *Human Nature and its Remaking* speaks of the instinctive motive of religion to be a specific craving for restoration of creative power. Even those who do not agree to a special religious instinct must admit that 'human lives begin not only with biological instincts common to all members of the race but with certain other tendencies to action and feeling which are not shared by all, but are found only in particular individuals', just as in the case of a genius for music or the like. In his *Psychology of Primitive Cultures*, Bartlett admits such tendencies and calls them 'individual difference tendencies'. The saints must have possessed such a tendency, which differentiates them from others. This tendency may be described as the 'tendency to fix their attention beyond and above the reality of the senses, accompanied by a striving for profounder realities leading to a spirit of renunciation of immediate material enjoyment in order to obtain a felicity of a more lasting and universal character', De Sanctis' *Religious Conversion.* Mc Dougall, too, admits as follows in the Symposium on *Instinct and Reason* in the British Journal of Psychology: 'There are many facts which compel us to go further in the recognition of innate mental structure, such facts as the special facilities shown by individuals in music, in mathematics, in language, and other aesthetic and moral endowments. The question of the extent and nature of the innate endowments or innate mental structure remains one of the largest fields of work for psychology.'* The Hindus would attribute such special tendencies and aptitudes to tendencies acquired in previous births. *Vide Bg.* VII. 19 & VI. 44. Even Leuba admits in his article in *Religion in Transition* that 'there is one fact of enormous significance, a fact incontestable and verifiable by everyone: an urge works in every man, it is present already in the animal world, to create the perfect in every aspect of life.' It is this urge for perfection that the religious man feels in his heart as the attraction exerted by God Who is the embodiment of all human values such as Truth, Goodness, and Beauty. This is true love and this is the real spritual faculty or instinct as interpreted by Bhaktiśāstra. Thus, whether it is due to a special instinct common to all men, or to a tendency peculiar to special individuals, or to a general urge for perfection which is in evidence in all life but which becomes conscious in man, the religious experience is something unique in itself and not attributable to any of the other instincts like the sex. It would be far safer to admit with Hegel that religion, philosophy, and art are the final values towards which the world is striving.

(3) As for the third point, namely, the possibility of interpreting spiritual experiences by the same laws applicable to the phantasies of mental defectives, it has to be remarked that from a psychologist who is committed to a naturalistic interpretation of all spiritual phenomena, nothing more can be expected. But to one who does not share his prejudice, the vast difference brought on the personality of a saint and of a mental defective by their respective experiences, is a positive proof for tracing it to different origins. 4. Lastly, with regard to the use of erotic symbolisms by mystics in their writings and utterances, it will be very hasty and superficial to attribute their experiences to sex instinct from this fact alone. There is nothing to prove that they were prompted to use such language by any sexual craving. The true explanation of this fact can be had if we take the following facts into consideration : (*a*) Sex being the most powerful emotion known to the natural man, the language employed for its expression offers the most suitable medium to the mystics for conveying a glimpse at least of a transcendental experience that enraptures their soul. (*b*) As the highest Bhakti involves the union of the individual soul with the universal soul, the mystics find for it a handy illustration in the union of two persons in love. (*c*)

Again many philosophical systems conceive God as the only Puruṣa or male, and look upon all individual souls as females, related as his wives. Thus if we find sex symbolism in the writings of mystics, it is to be attributed to various influences, poetical, philological and philosophical, and not to anything sexual in their spiritual experiences. In addition to these facts, it must also be remembered that mystics employ symbolisms drawn from many aspects of life other than sex. Thus in the forms of Bhakti known as Dāsyabhāva (servant's attitude), Sakhya (attitude of a friend), Vātsalya (parental attitude), and S'ānta (philosophical attitude), various imageries and expressions of love other than sexual are used. If the spiritual experiences attained in these cases are to be explained in terms of non-sexual instincts corresponding to these images, what we arrive at is not an explanation of facts but a mere confused understanding of them. Far simpler would it be to accept the presence of a specific aspect in the human mind responding to stimuli that are distinctively spiritual. But it may be admitted that, like all instincts, it too does not express itself in isolation in our life. Ordinarily, when it takes the form of a sentiment, it gets intertwined with other instincts, and thus in the life of the common man, the spiritual sense may be found mixed with many worldly tendencies. But in the highest spiritual realization, the mind is thoroughly purged of its fleshly affections. For, in the words of S'rī Rāmakṛṣṇa, a mind that is attached to sex and possessions can help us only to understand worldly objects. It is only when the instincts have been purged of their natural taints by what Nārada calls 'nirodha', (restraint or renunciation), that the mind becomes capable of grasping the higher truths. Regarding a mind that has thus been refined and filled with love of the Highest, it is absurd to talk of 'compartmental' instincts. All its energies have been unified into one form, and there is only one instinct in it, namely, the passion for God. It is this withdrawal of the mind from its instinctive expressions, both in the objective and subjective fields—whether as flight towards its natural objects or as indulgence in wish-fulfilment through repressions and phantasies—that Nārada indicates by the term 'nirodha'. Because this 'nirodha' is involved in Bhakti, and the illumination it gives, Bhakti cannot be described as of the nature of desire.

Sutra 8. This *Sū.* explains the special characteristic of 'nirodha' noticed in Bhakti. The particle तु (but) is intended to draw attention to this speciality. According to the *Sū.* Nirodha is not of the nature of repression condemned by Psychologists as harmful to human personality but of the nature of sublimation. The expression Lokavedavyāpāra covers all activities which a human being is capable of. Such activities are twofold: worldly activities and scriptural duties. The former includes all physical, chemical, vital, and psychological actions and reactions noticed in a human organizm in the natural environment to which it is related as part to the whole. The latter consists in man's peculiar urge to realize his highest destiny. This distinguishes man from the rest of the animal kingdom. All activities that have for their motive Dharma and Mokṣa, the highest ends which man alone is capable of pursuing, may be broadly considered as Vedavyāpāra. Education, culture, philosophy, religion, art, morality, social service, and the rest when pursued for Dharmic ends come under scriptural duty thus conceived. The word Nyāsa used in the *Sū.* means both renunciation and dedication, the positive and negative aspects of a single impulse. The renunciation of worldly activities and scriptural duties does not here mean the forsaking of such activities themselves, but the effacement of the ego and its associates such as craving, selfishness, and attachment, resulting from the activities (Cf. *Bg.* III. 5—8, XVIII. 5—9). The activities cannot be stopped ; they can only be dedicated for the purpose of God-realization and divine service (*Bg.* III. 30, XVIII. 57) by an entire surrender of the individual soul to the Divine (*Bg.* XVIII. 66). This implies complete consecration of body, mind, and their powers to God.[1] Such consecration is a discipline

[1] What has been emphasized in the *Sū.* as the dedication of the individual soul to the Divine Reality by complete self-surrender and absolute union in identity is not only the final word of all spiritual and religious discipline, but also the inescapable conclusion to which science and philosophy tend. A glance at psychology and biology, physics and philosophy only reinforce the ancient conclusions of Vedānta. Experimental psychology has to-day proved that human mind is dynamic and that human behaviour is but a play of an active principle whether called a purposive or hormic energy ramified into a number of instincts, or a primary urge for power, or a fundamental psychic energy, or a primary sex instinct called libido, or the progressively organized reflexes producing synthetic novelties. Just as the different schools of psychology are positing one fundamental and primary psychic energy at the bottom of all psychic activity, we find also that the biologists are stressing on a

of the seeker and a spontaneous sign of the man of realization; for the latter then sees the whole world as

fundamental and primary evolutionary activity at the bottom of all biological phenomena whether considered merely as mechanical, or as vital, or even as mental. Darwin has recognized it as a blind, mechanical struggle for existence giving rise to a progressive evolution of the species. Among recent scientists it is considered as a special force or energy comparable to the other recognised forms called Biotic Energy (Benjamin Moore); or as a developing principle or tendency in and behind all organized matter (John Burrows); or as some originative impulse within the organism which expresses itself as variation and mutation and in all kinds of creative effort and endeavour (Geddes and Thompson); or as the inherent growth force (Goethe); or as life-force (Bernard Shaw); or as an internal factor tending towards perfection (Nägelli); or as the struggle of the spirit within to be superior to matter, to escape from the trammels of matter, to secure a fuller individual life and a larger freedom (Albert P. Mathews). E. W. Mac. Bride, Professor of Zoology in the Imperial College of Sciences, London, says that all living matter is endowed with something which strives to meet adverse circumstances and control its own growth. On the basis of experimental evidence Hans Driesch, the German Biologist, has declared that life is due to the presence of a non-material factor—a perfecting principle which is mental in nature. To Henri Bergson the *élan vital* or 'Mind Energy' is the primordial world principle, the basic reality of all being, the source and ground of all evolution, a vital impulse or push or creative ground pervading Matter, insinuating itself in it, overcoming its inertia and resistance, and determining the direction of evolution. 'There is but one creative process', says Prof. Patten, 'common to all phases of evolution, inorganic, organic, mental, and social. That process is best described by the term co-operation or mutual service'. In the view of General Smuts there is one operative factor in the universe which organizes, integrates, and synthesizes; and the world tends towards wholes—atoms, molecules, cells, plants, animals, and man in regular succession. 'Biology is a study of the larger organisms, whereas physics of smaller organisms', Whitehead. Professor Wheeler of the Harward University explains this tendency to form wholes by attributing it to their social nature, their irresistible tendency to cohere and organize themselves into more and more complex emergent wholes. In his *Mind in Evolution* Hobhouse is led to think that mind in the infinitely varied form of its activity, from the groping of unconscious effort to the full clearness of conscious purpose, may be the essential driving force in all evolutionary change. He considers the world to be a process of rational development of the nature of Effort in which the principle of development is the principle of rational harmony or love. 'Life emerges from his Beloved. The following statements of scriptures stress this beautifully : यत् करोषि यदश्नासि यज्जुहोषि ददासि यत् ।

matter, and mind from life, in a series of stages in the course of evolution, as a result of higher and higher levels of organization,' says Lloyd Morgan ; and in explaining the agency that lifts the world to higher and higher levels, he says : 'For better or for worse, I acknowledge god as the nisus through which activity emergents emerge and the whole course of Emergent evolution is directed'. Physics had already reduced all matter to electrons and protons and the latter to functional units of Energy. Recent writers on physics, astronomy, and even mathematics have felt the necessity for God to explain the facts confronting in their respective fields. Thus science has climbed reluctantly and against much determined opposition from Realists and Naturalists, higher and higher, from Matter to Energy, from Energy to Life, from Life to Mind, and from Mind to God in its search for an explanation of Cosmic phenomena. Philosophical enquiry also has arrived at a single principle called Cosmic Intelligence or Life designated as Hiraṇyagarbha or Prāṇa in the Upds, *Primum Mobile* by Aristotle, Demiurges by Plato, Nous by Anaximander, *Natura Naturans* by Bruno and Spinoza, the Will to Power by Neitzche, the Unconscious Will by von Hartman and Wundt, the Absolute Will by Schopenhauer, the Pure Creative Energy by Schelling, 'Spiritual Life' by Euken, and the Powe. that makes for Righteousness by Matthew Arnold. The Unknowable of Spencer, the Thing-in-itself of Kant, the Absolute Ego of Fichte, the Absolute Idea of Hegel, the Absolute Self of Idealists, the Absolute Experience of Bradley and Royce, and the Oversoul of Emerson are still higher philosophical concepts of the same Reality. These descriptions, however, represent the results of a purely intellectual rational search for the source and substratum and goal of the world phenomena. Religion speaks of the same Being, although in a slightly more emotional, and sometimes in an anthropomorphic, setting from the standpoint of intuitive experience. What the scientist has found necessary to concede reluctantly as a result of his observation and experiments in respect of the phenomenal universe, and what the philosopher found as the inevitable conclusion when he tried to rationalize and interpret the totality of experience by mere discursive reason and reflective thought, the religious man felt and loved and served, the mystic experienced and enjoyed, the theologian tried to prove by cosmological, theological, ontological, moral, and æsthetic arguments. It is the same Reality that we are to recognize in the God of the theists, the Bare Pure One of Plotinus, the Perfect Beauty of St. Augustine, the Divine Wilderness of Eckhart, the Father of Spirits of Berkeley, the Love that gives all things, described by Jacopone Da Todi, the Wayless

यत्तपस्यसि कौन्तेय तत्कुरुष्व मदर्पणम्, *Bg.* IX. 27 ; त्वत्पादपद्मार्पित-चित्तवृत्तिः त्वन्नामसंगीतकथासु वाणी । त्वद्भृत्यसेवानिरतौ करौ मे त्वदङ्गसङ्गं

Abyss of Fathomless Beatitude of Ruysbroeck, the Heart of the Universe of Jacob Boehme, the Heavenly Bridegroom of Mechthild, the Matchless Chalice and Sovereign Wine of the Sufis, the Jehova of the Jews, the Zeus of the Greeks, the Providence of the Stoics, the Jupiter of the Romans, the Inferable One of the Neoplatonists, the Father in Heaven of the Christians, the Dharmakāya or the S'ūnya of the Buddhists, the Allah of the Moslems, the Ahur Mazda of the Parsees, and the Brahman, Paramātman, Īs'vara, Puruṣottama, Bhagavān, and Ekam Sat of the Hindus. We read in Cleanthus' Hymn to Zeus: 'O God, most gracious, called by many a name, Nature's Great King, through endless years the same; Omnipotent, who by Thy just decree controllest all; Hail, Zeus, for unto Thee behoves Thy creatures in all lands to call.' Plutarch too says: 'One Sun and one Sky over all nations, and one Deity under many names' (Vide also, Bhāg. I. 2. 11. III. 32. 26-36; Yogavāsiṣṭha III. 1. 12; III. 5. 6-7; V. 87. 19-20). It is this one Truth that the devotee realizes, loves, and serves. Thus according to all science, philosophy, and religion one single substance, one God, is realized as the source, substratum, and goal of all cosmic phenomena organic as well as inorganic, human and subhuman—the Tajjālan of the *Chānd*. and the Janmādyasya yataḥ of *Bsū*. 'Whatever else may be certain', wrote William James, 'this at least is certain—that the world of our present natural knowledge is enveloped in a larger world of some sort of whose residual properties we at present can form no positive idea'. Herbert Spencer observes in his *Principles of Sociology*: 'But one truth must grow ever clear—the truth that there is an Inscrutable Existence, everywhere manifested, to which the man of science can neither find nor conceive either beginning or end. Amid the mysteries which become more mysterious the more they are thought about, there will remain the one absolute certainty that he is ever in the presence of an Infinite and Eternal Energy from which all things proceed.' Let us remember the words of Francis Bacon that it is only a little Philosophy that leads to Atheism. All physical, chemical, vital, psychical, moral, social, and spiritual processes found anywhere in the universe are but a progressive manifestation of the one Divine urge expressed as the individual's pilgrimage to Perfection. This inner urge in every being proclaims the eternal presence of the Divine in the heart of man and the universe. He is the Antaryāmin who works out the salvation and perfection of every individual not only by an initial push but by a steady and persistent pull from the front, as He is not only the cause but also the goal of all evolution. It is this steady pull exerted by Him, this attraction of His Infinitude,

लभतां मदङ्गम् ॥ त्वन्मूर्तिभक्तान् स्वगुरुं च चक्षुः पश्यत्वजस्रं स शृणोतु कर्णः । त्वज्जन्मकर्माणि च पादयुग्मं व्रजत्वजस्रं तव मन्दिराणि ॥ अङ्गानि ते पादरजोविमिश्रतीर्थानि बिभ्रत्वहिशत्रुकेतो । शिरस्त्वदीयं भवपद्मजाद्यैर्जुष्टं पदं राम नमत्वजस्रम्, *Adhrā.* IV. 1. 91-93 ; वाणी गुणानुकथने श्रवणौ कथायां हस्तौ च कर्मसु मनस्तव पादयोर्नः । स्मृत्यां शिरस्तव निवासजगत्प्रणामे दृष्टिः सतां दर्शनेऽस्तु भवत्तनूनाम् *Bhāg.* X. 10. 38 ; जिह्वे कीर्तय केशवं मुररिपुं चेतो भज श्रीधरं पाणिद्वन्द्व समर्चयाच्युतकथाः श्रोत्रद्वय त्वं शृणु । कृष्णं लोकय लोचनद्वय हरेर्गच्छाङ्घ्रियुग्मालयं जिघ्र घ्राण मुकुन्दपादतुलसीं मूर्धन् नमाधोक्षजम् *Mukundamālā* 10 ; also *Sivānandalaharī* 7 and *Stotraratna* 54 and 57. All

Bliss, Intellegince, Holiness, and other attributes that theology calls God's love for man, or Grace ; and it is the natural response of the individual to this benign influence that appears as the evolutionary urge to perfection or the spiritual urge for God-realization or Bhakti and in the lower forms as the passion of the unregenerate for sense pleasures. 'The Greek naturalists saw,' says Santayana, 'that the Infinite Substance of things was instinct with a perpetual motion and rhythmic order which were its life and that the spirit of man was a spark from that universal Fire'. It is thus the love of human spirit for the cosmic Spirit that is at the root of all evolutionary activity. The most natural direction of all our activity should therefore be towards God-realization or union of the part to the whole. Nyāsa or dedication of all activity is therefore scientific and natural. All the various powers of body and mind of man are evolved only for this purpose, and they attain their fruition only when they are utilized for that reunion to their source, or God-realization. Any other use of these powers is only misuse of it, and all worldly miseries result from such misuse. In self-surrender through love all the powers of mind and body and spirit co-operate to bring about this desired goal. Hence Nyāsa is the most essential of all spiritual practices. It is also easy, natural, and pleasant, because to give up a lower attraction for a higher one does not involve serious strain when it is recognized to be so. The whole of Varṇās'ramadharma was meant to be an effective institution touching every aspect and function of life for schooling the aspirant in the practice of this grand principle of Nyāsa. (Vide *Mnu.* V. 56. *Bhag.* I. 2. 13, 5. 22 ; XI. 5. 11. etc.). For one who is perfect in Nyāsa the whole life is a Yajña or worship at the altar of the Master of Sacrifices enthroned in the heart of all beings, and it is the attainment of Perfection.

the activities of a true devotee of God are thus sublimated into worship. The difference between such a person and an unenlightened man is that while the former is absolutely selfless and unattached the latter is selfish and attached to the results of his action. What is renounced by the Bhakta is not external activities but the ego. Even the distinction of sacred and secular activity disappears for an illumined soul; because every work is sacred to him in as much as it is an expression of his love for God. यद्यत्कर्म करोमि तत्तदखिलं शंभो तवाराधनम्, whatsoever I do, O God, all that is Thy worship—S'aṅkara, *S'ivamānasapūja*. On the other hand, in spite of all care on the part of an unenlightened man to mark off sacred duties, he cannot make them *really* sacred as long as the basis of his action is *ego* which disappears completely only when Self is realized fully.

Sutra 9. तस्मिन् refers to Nyāsa in *Sū.* 8. अनन्यता or unification implies this: In the perfected man the primary instincts common to all members of the human race are all organized into the sentiment of love of God. They are not destroyed completely but they give up their distinctive characteristics and modes of reaction, and merge themselves in the Divine love and are completely unified into one. They are merely sublimated, and remain as suppliers of energy necessary for service and worship in which the love of God expresses itself. There is unification in another sense also. The man of realization has no interest of his own. He feels the woes of the world as his own, and moved by sympathy for the suffering of creatures, completely forgets himself in active service. There is also unification in a still higher sense, in so far as the ego of such a person becomes identified with God and his will with God's will.

उदासीनता or indifference noticed in such a great soul has this meaning: Though the sublimated instincts remain, they do not react even in the presence of their natural stimuli, as such reaction cannot co-exist with the predominant sentiment of Love, to which they are opposed. But they do react when such reaction is helpful for the expression of Divine Love. The two terms are further explained by Nārada himself in the next two Sūtras.

Sutra 10 emphasizes how in a perfected man sublimation is effected by the withdrawal of the instincts from their natural field of action and by the redirection of their energies towards the Paramātman, Who is the support of all. Before God realization the ego supplies the support of all instinctive reactions, and such reactions require also the presence of particular stimuli. But in the state of realization, both these supports are absent. Hence the very conditions necessary for their natural expression do not exist. But even though these do not exist, they have got a better support in the Self of all selves, namely, God.

Sutra 11 maintains that love of God never ends in sloth or idleness. A true devotee will dislike only such works as are hostile to divine love; but with the energy thus saved by the abandonment of undesirable works, he would vigorously perform others that are favourable to and consistent with devotion. This latter kind of works may range from pious duties like worship and prayer to actions of world-wide significance performed in the spirit of dedication inculcated by S'rī Kṛṣṇa.

Sutra 12. What is शास्त्ररक्षण or protection of scriptures? Scriptures of mankind are nothing but the records of the spiritual realizations of Ṛṣis; we see many of the scriptures woefully neglected not only by the masses, but even by the educated and so-called religious people. They have practically become dead. The reason for this is that the experiences recorded therein have become meaningless to the later generations. The truths preached by the ancient sages must be felt to be useful to us at the present time also. This can be achieved only if persons living even at present, whom we venerate, embody these truths and follow the scriptures in their actual life. As S'rī Kṛṣṇa says in *Bg.* III. 21, the masses are always led to follow in the footsteps of those whom they look up to as leaders. The truths of the scriptures must be re-lived before our own eyes, and their usefulness demonstrated publicly, before the ordinary man adopts them for guidance in his life. If, therefore, perfected men do not follow the scriptures, then woe unto the scriptures! Thus scriptures need the protection of the persons who have realized Truth, as otherwise they are liable to be neglected or misinterpreted. Again, every old text is not a S'āstra. What may have been useful in the past may cease to be so in course of time under other circumstances and surroundings.

Progress in culture and civilization also necessitates many readjustments in the scriptures. Every age must, therefore, have its own men of realization who can test the scriptures in the light of their own spiritual experiences. Only such rules and texts deserve to live as can stand those repeated tests. Only the perfected men can find out what is of real value in the scriptures and sift the grain from the chaff. Perfected men are to protect the S'āstras also in the sense of making them understandable to people and applicable in their lives by the example of their own life and teachings.

Sutra 13. The case that is being considered here is that of a man whose realization has become well established. Therefore there can be no risk for him. He can never have a fall. Realization once gained and fully established can never be lost. Nor need he be afraid of becoming wicked in life, for all his propensities for vice have ceased with the disappearance of his ego before the onset of self-realization. In fact, it is the conduct of a perfected man that sets the standard of Dharma. He is however more anxious about the risk of a fall for others who are likely to imitate him and follow in his foot-steps. He will therefore be very scrupulous in setting an example to others lest they should have a fall. His one consideration will be the welfare of others.

Sutra 14. Social customs are meant by लोक in the text. Ways of life that are not specifically enjoined by the scripture, such as specific dress, rules of etiquette, and the rest denoted thereby are merely conventional. The perfect man is not always bound by them;

he may behave in such matters with much freedom. But even though his ways may not be sanctioned by the letter of the law or custom, they rest on his realization and are more in accordance with the spirit of Dharma. It is these latter actions which generally bring about innovation in the scriptural injunctions in course of time. Again new situations may necessitate a fresh application of the truths of the scriptures. Only the man of realization can show how departures from the current practice can be made, and yet without any disrespect for the scripture. तावत् specifies the extent to which such a person may take liberties with existing rules; *viz.*, as far as necessary for saving the world from pitfalls, for escaping from undue notice of the public, or for not wounding the feelings of society. भोजनादिव्यापार includes such natural activities as sleep and physical exercise, unavoidable for life. शरीरधारण means not mere existence but preservation of health. One cannot serve God and his creation without a healthy mind in a healthy body. A man of realization considers his own body and mind as not belonging to himself but to God and to the society which brought it into being and nourished it till he attained perfection; and as such he takes care of it as a trustee for them, though he does not care for it for his own sake. He can never be negligent and careless about them, as he has no ego of his own which may lead him to such carelessness.

Sutra 15. In this and the succeeding nine aphorisms Nārada gives us a few descriptions of Bhakti as given by some writers who have preceded him, and shows how his own view is more complete than that of any of his predecessors. In *Sū.* 15 he explains the impossibility of describing this ineffable experience, as well as the inevitability of differences in view, the moment one tries to bring it down to the level of thought. The nature of realization is, as we have seen, indescribable. Still some sort of description cannot be avoided at least for the benefit of the future generations. All such descriptions must inevitably fall short of the actual truth ; they can at best be only approximations to the reality. What can actually be observed and described are only the external marks which constitute the expression of the subjective experience. Description is an intellectual process, and therefore the quality and perfection of the description must depend upon capacity for correct observation, clear analysis, and adequate expression ; the theological and temperamental prejudices of the observer, the needs and capacities of the audience, and the requirements of time and locality always lend colour to such descriptions. No two minds are constituted exactly alike, and as such there is plenty of room for मतभेद or differences and variety in the descriptions of the same experience. Thus, those who are predominantly intellectual in outlook must necessarily give an intellectual colouring ; those with an emotional bent are bound to describe it in terms of emotion, and those of a dynamic temperament must view it from an ethical standpoint. In fact it is only such characteristics of the perfect man as are appealing to one's mind that can find a place in one's description. Differences in description need not therefore be interpreted as pointing to differences in the experience itself.

Thus in *Bhāg.* III. 25. 32 & 33, Maitreya says that Bhakti consists in the mind naturally settling upon the Highest Truth, the root of all existence as well as of the senses; and in III. 29. 11 & 12 Kapila describes it as uninterrupted thought flowing towards God seated in the hearts of all creatures, like the flow of waters of the Ganges towards the sea. In *Vp.* we find Prahlāda praying that the love which the undiscriminating have for the objects of the senses be turned into Bhakti by being directed towards God. In the *Devībhāg.* we read: 'As oil poured from one vessel to another falls in an unbroken stream, so when the mind in an unbroken stream thinks about the Lord, we have what is called supreme Love.' The *Nāradapāñcarātra* describes it in one place as service of the Lord of Indriyas through the Indriyas without being clouded by Upādhis and purified by being directed towards Him; and in another place of the same work the author describes it as an unintermittent stream of thought based on the love of God without attachment for anything else. S'rī Sañkara describes it in the *Vivekacūdāmaṇi* (verse 17) as constant thought on the real nature of one's own Self, and says in the *S'ivānandalaharī*—(verse 61) that we have Bhakti when the thoughts approach the feet of the Lord and stick to them permanently, as the seed approaches the Ankola tree, an iron needle the magnet, a virtuous wife her husband, or a creeper a tree. S'rī Rāmānuja in *S'rībhāṣya* I. 1. 1 identifies Bhakti with loving meditation. Jayatīrtha in *Nyāyasudhā* says : तत्र भक्तिर्नाम निरवधिकानन्तानवद्यकल्याणगुणत्वज्ञानपूर्वकः स्वस्वात्मात्मीयसमस्तवस्तुभ्योऽनेकगुणाधिकोऽन्तरायसहस्रेणाप्यप्रतिबद्धो निरन्तरप्रेमप्रवाहः—Bhakti is an incessant flow of love preceded by the knowledge that God is possessed of unequalled, unsurpassed, infinite auspicious qualities, which exceeds one's love to oneself, one's relations and belongings, which is not retarded or shaken by a thousand troubles and difficulties. Sāṇḍilya in his *Bhaktimīmāṁsā* describes Bhakti as Supreme Love of God, and Svapnes'vara in commenting on the *Sū.* says that this love results from the realization of the greatness of the Lord. *Bhaktirasāyana* (I. 3 & II. 1) describes it as an unintermittent flow of thought towards God whose form is indelibly impressed upon the heart which has melted in love. In the *Bhaktirasāmṛtasindhu* I. 11, Rūpagosvāmin describes it as constant enjoyment of God unobstructed by desires for anything else, and unclouded by Jñāna or Karma. Yāmunācārya, speaks of the vision of God as Parabhakti ; union with Him as Parajñāna and fear of separation from Him as Paramabhakti. Manavāḷa-mahāmuni in his *Dramidopaniṣat-sāra-saṅgati* speaks of Bhakti as the direction towards God of that love which the undiscriminating have for the objects of the senses (*Vide* supra pp. 39-42.)

Sutra 16. In this and the next two aphorisms Nārada states the views of three teachers on the characteristics of Bhakti. On a careful perusal, it can be seen that these three views are selected because they represent three expressions of love in deed, word, and mind. The three views are not mutually contradictory and exclusive, but may be taken as supplementing each other. First comes the view of Vyāsa.

In the various Purāṇas and the *Mbh.* Vyāsa gives a complete description of the various aspects of Bhakti. The one particular mode of Bhakti specially attributed to him here is only one among them. Probably the reason for this specification is that before he met Nārada and was initiated by him into Bhakti, he used to emphasize the dynamic aspect of spiritual life, as in the *Mbh.* Even in the *Bhāg.*, the scripture of Bhakti *par excellence*, the Bhaktas are delineated by him as living an intensely active life of worship and social usefulness. The word 'anurāga' ordinarily means only mere love, but in Bhakti-s'āstra it means the love that arises out of the recognition of the divinity and glory of God after realization. Cf. Svapnes'vara's comment on *S'sū.* 2. Technically पूजा or worship means all those activities, mental as well as physical, undertaken for satisfying a superior being on whom one is dependant, and for whom one feels a kind of reverence. It is a phenomenon characteristic of all religions. It includes all kinds of rituals and ceremonies, which are symbolic expressions of religious emotion. There is a general belief that formal worship is characteristic of only the first stages of Bhakti. But Nārada here quotes the authority of Vyāsa to show that worship may be continued even after realization. Witness for example how S'aṅkara, Rāmānuja, Madhva, Gaurāṅga, and

Rāmakṛṣṇa engaged themselves in worship even after realization. In fact it is only the worship of a man of self-realization that really deserves the name, as it is he, who has a full vision of the glory of the Lord whom he worships, alone that worships Him truly with his whole heart and soul untainted by the ego. आदि (and the like) in the *Sū.* refers to sacred dance, celebration of festivals, building and renovation of temples, social service, acts of charity, devotional works of art such as painting and sculpture, and the rest.

Sutra 17. The whole world likes to speak of the beloved. आदि here implies all expressions of love in word, prayer, Japa, study, and exposition of scriptures, discourse on spiritual topics Harikathā, Saṅkirtana, composition of hymns and songs, and theological literature. While external activities of the Bhakta are helpful to others by way of example, the verbal expressions provide help by way of precepts also. Thus *Bg*. X. 9 says, 'With their hearts fixed on Me and their life absorbed in Me, constantly discussing and conversing with one another about me, they are contented and rejoice'. *Bhāg*. X. 1. 4 says, 'Who else but a butcher would feel reluctant to listen again and again to the recital of the excellent attributes of the most glorious Lord, constantly sung by persons free from desires?' Witness the example of Nārada who always goes about singing the glories of the Lord in ecstacy. Vyāsa, Vālmiki, and Tulasidās composed the epics under the inspiration of Bhakti. The Aḷvārs, Mirābāi, Kabir, Tukārām and a host of other Bhaktas like Jayadeva did the same.

Parīkṣit delighted himself in listening to the glories of the Lord recited by S′uka. S′rī Rāmakṛṣṇa and Gaurāṅga immersed themselves in Saṅkirtana. S′rī S′uka says in the *Bhāg.* X. 1. 16, 'Enquiry about the Lord Vāsudeva's stories purifies three people—him that describes, him that enquires, and him that listens.' Bhīṣma thinks that the singing of hymns is the best of all Dharmas. (Vide Visṇu-S′ahasranāma). Even in the *Ṛgv.* we read, 'O glorious, all-pervading Lord, we worship thee by mere repetition of thy name.' The Mantra occurs also in the *Yajurveda.* The Lord Himself says that He is the Japa-yaña among all Yajñas.

Sutra 18. S′āṇdilya seems to think of the danger of mere physical and verbal expressions which are possible even without the proper spiritual background of delight in the Self. He, therefore, warns us not to take every such expression as in itself being a characteristic of Bhakti. Bhakti is more spiritual than physical or verbal, and only in so far as the physical or verbal expression is prompted by the fullness of heart, it deserves to be considered a characteristic of Bhakti.

Sutra 19. Narada here gives his own view: it is more comprehensive and points out the very essence of Bhakti. तु in the text draws our attention to the difference in view. अखिलाचार: (all activities) implies that Nārada does not narrow down the life of the Bhakta to rituals, chanting of sacred 'Namas', and similar activities that are strictly called devotional. Complete self-surrender is the prime characteristic of Bhakti; and every action done with this attitude has a due place in devotional life. For self-surrender is only another name for the effacement of the ego, and any work that is selfless has a place in spiritual life. परमव्याकुलता Extreme anguish is another sign. Extremes always meet, and the Bhaktas feel a great delight when they reach the stage of realization when the slightest forgetfulness brings the pangs of separation, and consider that as the highest culmination of Bhakti. It is not possible for a man of God-realization to forget Him at any time. This is therefore meant to show that there is no possibility of forgetting Him, as the mind is automatically prevented from such forgetfulness by the anguish which he would have to feel if he were to forget Him.

Sutra 20. Among such examples in historical times the names of Nammāḷvār, S'rī Caitanya, and S'rī Rāmakṛṣṇa may be mentioned. Nārada gives the pre-eminent example in the next *Sū.*

Sutra 21. All the devotees of the Lord consider these illiterate cowherd-women of Vṛndāvana as the paragons of Bhakti. The Lord S'rī Kṛṣṇa says in *Bhāg.* X. 32. 22, 'I cannot sufficiently reward your devoted service even through the grant of long life in heaven,—the service of you who have resorted to and worshipped Me, conceiving a pure and faultless relation to Me, and having cut asunder the very hard ties of domestic life. May your righteousness be its fullest reward'. 'They have given their heart and soul to Me. They consider Me their very life, and for My sake they have abandoned their nearest relatives. I always support those who, for

My sake, give up all worldly advantages and pleasures. When I, the most beloved of lovable objects, am at a distance, the women of Gokula ever think of Me and remain lost to all worldly interests owing to extreme anxiety caused by separation. Somehow with great difficulty the Gopīs who have set their heart and soul on Me are supporting their lives on messages of my return to them'; *Ib.* X. 46. 4-6. 'With their minds fixed on Me through love, they knew neither their kinsmen, nor their bodies, nor things far and near, as sages in the superconscious state know not name and form—like unto rivers merging in the waters of the ocean. Not knowing My real nature, the Gopīs, who were ignorant women, desired Me as their sweetheart (in the beginning), yet they attained Me, the Supreme Brahman by hundreds and thousands through the power of holy association,' *Ib.* XI. 12. 12-13. Again Uddhava says: 'How blessed should it be to live in Vṛndāvana as one of the shrubs or creepers or plants or herbs that come in contact with the dust of the feet of these Gopīs, who abandoned their kinsmen and the path of the Āryas, hard to give up, and resorted to the feet of Mukunda, sought after by the Vedas—these Gopīs who embraced the lotus feet of the Glorious Krishna, set on their bosom in the Rāsa dance, and were rid of all worldly ills. *Ib.* X. 47. 61, 62. Again in *Bhāg.* X. 44. 15 the women of Mathura speak of the Gopīs thus: 'Blessed are the women of Vraja, who, while milking, pounding, churning, washing, rocking cradles, lulling their crying babes, sprinkling, cleansing and the like, sing the praise of Hari with a devoted and loving heart; their throats are choked with tears, and mind devoted to Him; their path is that of constant remembrance of the Lord. Indeed they deserve to be congratulated in every way.' Within historical times also the love of the Gopīs for Kṛṣṇa has been the theme of music, poetry, and painting. The Vaiṣṇavite saints got their inspiration from this love of the Gopīs. Nimbārka, Jayadeva, Gaurāṅga and Vallabha, founded their theology on this Vṛndāvana Līla. Even in modern days we find Śrī Rāmakṛṣṇa and Swāmi Vivekānanda waxing eloquent and poetic on this topic. Śri Rāmakṛṣṇa often used to fall into Samādhi whenever he heard or thought of the Gopīs. Once he remarked, 'The devotion of the Gopīs is the devotion of love, constant, unmixed, and unflinching.' Swāmi Vivekānanda remarks: Gopīlilā is the acme of the religion of love, in which individuality vanishes and there is communion. It is in this līlā that Śrī Kṛṣṇa shows what He teaches in *Bg.*, 'Give up everything for Me'. Go and take shelter under Vṛndāvanalīlā to understand 'Bhakti'. But there are not wanting people who cannot see anything in this except a sex passion. Even the worthy Parīkṣit could not understand it and in *Bhāg.* X. 29-12, he raises the doubt, 'They knew Him only as their sweetheart, not as Parabrahman. How was it then that those whose thoughts were swayed by Guṇas could escape the current of Guṇas?' Śuka tries to clear the doubt by pointing out that what matters is concentration of mind on Hari, whether through feeling of hatred or love or fear. The Lord Himself supports the view in

Bhāg. XI. 9. 22. Parīkṣit does not seem to be satisfied, for he raises the question again. This time he asks how Bhagavān could descend so low as to cater to the sex cravings of the Gopīs. S'rī S'uka takes shelter this time under the excuse that divine beings should not be judged by human standards. Vide *Bhāg.* X. 33. 30-38. The real answer for clearing the doubt raised by Parīkṣit is given by S'rī Kṛṣṇa Himself first in His talk to the Gopīs in *Bhāg.* X. 22. 26, where He points out that even the lower desires of those who approach Him for their satisfaction are like the grain which is fried and boiled, and cannot therefore grow into a plant. Such is the wonderful effect of association with an extraordinarily holy personality like S'rī Kṛṣṇa; for the dynamic influence of such a being sublimates even the vulgar desires into the holy passion of Bhakti. That this fact of the Gopīs' realizing Brahman, even though they first approached Kṛṣṇa as their sweetheart, is solely due to the power of holy association, is again emphasized by Kṛṣṇa in *Bhāg.* XI. 12. 13. Swāmi Vivekānanda says in his lecture on The Sages of India ? : 'There are not wanting fools, even in the midst of us, who cannot understand the marvellous significance of that most marvellous of all episodes. There are, let me repeat, impure fools, even born of our blood who try to shrink from that as if from something impure. To them I have only one thing to say, 'First make yourselves pure'; and you must remember that he who tells the history of the love of the Gopīs is one who was born pure, the eternally pure S'uka, the son of Vyāsa. So long as there is selfishness in the heart, so long is love of God impossible. Aye, forget first the love for gold, and name and fame, and for this little trumpery world of ours. Then, only then, you will understand the love of the Gopīs, too holy to be attempted without giving up everything, too sacred to be understood until the soul has become perfectly pure. People with ideas of sex, and of money, and of fame, bubbling up every minute in the heart, daring to criticize and understand the love of the Gopis! This is the very essence of the Kṛṣṇa Incarnation.' Thus it is clear on the evidence of these pure souls, who can be expected to have the right to pronounce an opinion on the subject, that the love of the Gopīs, even though it might have begun in the lower plane, rose up to the highest plane of selfless love of God, and as such, in the final stages it deserves to be considered the acme of perfection in Bhakti.

Sutra 22. The phrase तत्रापि implies that in spite of the fact that the Gopīs' love for S'rī Kṛṣṇa is artistically portrayed in the language of human love and so liable to be misunderstood by the vulgar, the true nature of it is quite different. People, who are carried away by the human picture, fail to see that the thought was never absent from the minds of the Gopis that Kṛṣṇa was not a man but the Supreme Being. The words जार and अस्वरूपविदः used in *Bhāg.* XI. 12. 12 depicting the attitude of the Gopis are only an अर्थवाद to eulogize the supreme value of सङ्ग or company. These two words, moreover, apply only to the preliminary stage of their relation with S'rī Kṛṣṇa and not to the final stage referred to in the last *Sū*. *Bhāg*. X. 29. 31.33, 37; X. 31. 4, 5; and several other verses clearly state that the Gopīs were not after a human lover, but the Paramātman Himself. The Gopīs who were witnessing the several super-human deeds of S'rī Kṛṣṇa in succession would not have forgotten his divinity at any time. As *Bsū*. IV. 1. 5 suggests, without the knowledge of उत्कर्ष or माहात्म्य no worship or Bhakti is possible. But as one progresses in the path of Love and the relation with the Beloved grows intimate, His glories less and less attract the attention of the lover, until at last he realizes his Beloved as his very Self.

Sutra 23 definitely marks off the difference between the earthly and the divine love. All love other than that for God is in one sense unlawful; to love any creature as a creature and not as the Divinity embodied in it is unlawful. 'Nothing so defileth and entangleth the heart of man', says Thomas a Kempis, 'as the impure love to creatures'.. The same saintly author continues in the words of the Lord: 'Thy regard for thy friend ought to be grounded in Me; and for My sake is he to be beloved, whosoever he be . . . Without Me friendship hath no strength, no continuance; neither is that love true and pure, which is not knit by Me.' Cf. also *Bhāg*. IV. 3. 22.

Sutra 24. The mistress is utterly selfish; her love is mercenary. She does not care for the happiness of her paramour. In pure love and Bhakti there cannot be any trace of selfishness. The lover does not at all care for his own happiness. He is willing to court suffering to make his beloved happy. Exactly so is the case of the Gopīs who did not love Kṛṣṇa through any selfish motive. They were ready to give up all for making Him happy. Their happiness depended only on His happiness. This *Sū.* therefore brings out the second great difference between Bhakti and earthly love, *viz.*, utter unselfishness.

Sutra 25. We have seen that in Nārada's description of the highest Bhakti as exemplified in the lives of the Gopīs of Brindāvan, all the functions of the mind, *viz.*, intellect, emotion, and will, are fully represented. The intellect is found to be active in cognizing the glory and majesty of God, the emotion in experiencing the delight of divine bliss, and the will in consecrating all activities by complete surrender to Him. Now the question arises whether the highest realization consists merely in the enhancement and purification of these various powers of the mind. In this and the succeeding eight aphorisms, Nārada discusses this question and comes to the conclusion that Parabhakti or the highest spiritual realization is something more than all these, although all these too incidentally result from such realization, and that it really does not constitute the *result* of any spiritual practice, but is a mere *manifestation* of some inexplicable, ineffable experience of the natural perfection of the soul. Incidentally the relative importance of the various powers of the mind in producing the conditions necessary for such manifestation of the already existing perfection of the soul, is also considered. Superiority is claimed for

Bhakti not as a particular method of attainment over others, but as the highest spiritual realization or Para-bhakti. As paths the various kinds of spiritual practices involving the exercise of various powers of the mind, are all equal. Karma stands for Karmayoga, the exercise of the will; Jñāna stands for Jñānayoga, the excercise of the intellect and reason; and Yoga stands for the Bhaktiyoga or the exercise of the emotions. The question may arise as to why Rājayoga is not represented in this scheme. The answer is given by Madhusūdana-sarasvati in his *Bhaktirasāyana* by stating that Rāja-yoga is only a department of Jñānayoga. Or it may also be taken that Rājayoga, being only the Yoga of meditation, is a part of all the three Yogas, as noted in *S'sū*. 19: 'Yoga is for the benefit of both, because of its indispensability in both.' The Bhagavān himself classifies the Yogas as only three in number, from the psychological standpoint, in *Bhāg*. XI. 20. 6: 'With a view to effect the liberation of men, I have inculcated three Yogas or methods, *viz*., those of knowledge, work, and devotion. There is no other means anywhere.' Even the highest spiritual experience itself is liable to be evaluated from the standpoint of one or other of these several powers of the mind. Thus S'aṅkara considers it a kind of vision of Truth. S'rī Rāmānuja, Caitanyadeva, and others view it as an experience of the highest love. Thr Smṛti writers like Yājñavalkya consider it as the highest Dharma. अयं तु परमो धर्मो यद् योगेनात्मदर्शनम् —The realization of the Ātman through the Yogas is the highest Dharma—*Yāj. Smṛti* I. 8. Among modern writers on

Religion in the West, we find the same difference in the emphasis. For example, (*a*) the intellectual school is represented by Max Muller, Herbert Spencer, Von Hartman and others. Max Muller says in his *Origin of Religion* that religion is an apprehension of the Infinite In his *First Principles*, Herbert Spencer characterizes it as a complete recognition of the ultimate mystery. In his *Religion of the Future*, Von Hartman speaks of it as a consciousness of our practical relation to an invisible spiritual order. Romanes in *Thoughts on Religion* conceives of it as a department of thought, having for its object a self-conscious and intelligent being. In his *Philosophy of Religion* Hegel describes it as a know ledge possessed by the finite mind of its nature as absolute mind. Jevons in his *History of Religion* calls it a perception of invisible things, of Him, through the things that are made. Munsterburg in his *Eternal Values* speaks of it as a form of apprehension through supra-personal consciousness. (*b*) The emotional school is represented by Schleirmacher, Rudolf Otto, Tiele, Mac Taggart, etc. Schleirmacher tells us that religion consists in certain feelings of absolute dependence upon God. Tiele says: It is a pure and reverential disposition which we call piety, its essence consisting in adoration, which is a compound of holy awe, humble reverence, grateful acknowledgment of every token of love, hopeful confidence, lowly self-abasement, a deep sense of one's own unworthiness and shortcomings, total self-abnegation, an unconditional conservation of one's whole life and one's whole faculties, and a desire to

9

possess the adored object and to call it entirely one's own. To Mac Taggart, it is an emotion resting on the conviction of a harmony between ourselves and the universe at large. Pfleiderer says that in the religious consciousness, knowing and willing are not ends in themselves as in science and morality, but rather subordinated to feeling as the real centre of religious experience. Stratton says that it is an appreciation of an unknown world, usually an unseen company. Greenleaf Thompson says that it is an aggregate of those sentiments of the human mind arising in connection with relations assumed to exist between the order of nature and a postulated supernatural. Commenius says that it is an inner veneration by which the mind of man attaches and binds itself to the Supreme Godhead. Professor Rudolf Otto calls it the *mysteruim tremendum et fascinans.* (c) The Practical or Voluntaristic School has its representatives in Prof. James and others. To James it is a harmonious adjustment to an unseen order on which our supreme good depends. Reville sees in it a harmonious synthesis between one's destiny and the opposing influences he meets in this world. Stanley calls it a biological mode of reaction to high superiorities of environment. Frazer takes it as a propitiation or conciliation of powers superior to man which are believed to control and direct the course of Nature and of human life. Marshall calls it the restraint of individualistic impulses to racial ones. Comte considers it the regulation of individual nat ıre. Davidson views it as placing oneself in harmony with time's environment.

Sabatier views it as a commerce, a conscious and willed relation, into which a soul in distress enters with the mysterious power on which it feels that it and its destiny depend. The most notable protagonist of this view is Kant, who calls it a recognition of all our duties as divine commands. A careful consideration of these views would make it clear that all of them are only partial views of the real truth, and that they really represent only the external opinion of third persons about the spiritual consciousness as it manifests itself in others, and to which they themselves are strangers. Their views cannot be therefore held to be correct. The spiritual experience in itself has nothing to do with the powers of the mind, which have to be transcended in the final stages of Sādhana. It is something unique and refuses to be described in terms of the mental powers, although all the faculties have to be purified and intensified and united before such realization takes place.

Sutra 26 gives one of the reasons of the superiority of spiritual experience to the various Yogas. The Yogas are only methods of practice and are needed only so long as one has not realized the highest. They only help the aspirant on his way to the goal. The Parabhakti described above is, on the other hand, the goal itself, and as such is superior, in that the Yogas are useless when it is once attained. The Yogas represent a lower stage in spiritual development and Parabhakti represents the highest stage. Instead of saying that it is the fruit, Nārada says it is of 'the nature of' fruit. This is only to indicate that, although in the ordinary way it may be spoken of as a result of spiritual practice, really it is not the effect of any Sādhana done by the aspirant. If it is an effect, then it cannot be everlasting, as everything that has come into existence must also pass out of existence in the natural course of things. In fact the eternality of this experience is the one thing that distinguishes it from such things as the experience of heaven. S'āṇdilya also speaks of it in the same strain, Vide, *S'sū* 8 ; 9. That Parabhakti is not the effect of any action or effort on man's part, is again adverted to in *Sū* 30.

Sutra 27 gives another reason why Sādhanas or Yogas are inferior to Parabakti. Sādhana or spiritual practice is self-effort, and so one must be conscious of oneself as a separate individual. The man of realization is one who has transcended this ego-consciousness. In fact it is the ego that prevents the manifestation of Parabhakti. The *Sū.* should not, however, be taken to indicate that even God is partial and has His own likes and dislikes. Even a spiritual aspirant should be free from such partiality ; then what to say of God ! To attribute this partiality to God would be to go against Bhagavān's own words in the *Bg.* IX. 29 : 'Alike am I to all beings. To Me there is none hateful or dear.' The grace of God is always there, only the ego prevents man from taking advantage of it. If man utlilizes his ego in such a way as to annihilate the ego itself, he is able to benefit by it. It is not the fault of the fire if it warms a man who approaches it, but not one who is away from it. Vide also *Bsū.* II. 1. 34 : 'Partiality and cruelty cannot be attributed to God because that depends upon other things, *i.e.*, He dispenses according to the merit and demerit of the individual soul." *Of* also *Bhāg*. X. 80. 6 ; VII. 9. 27.

Sutra 28. S'aṅkarācārya emphasizes the function of the intellect in attaining the highest realization and subordinates other functions to it. In fact all the Dars'anas, except perhaps the Pūrvamīmāṁsā, promise Mukti only to those who have clear vision of Truth. Of. also Christ's saying · 'Thou shalt know the truth and the truth shall make you free.' The Buddha makes Right Understanding the first of his eightfold Noble Path and the Jainas include Right Knowledge in their Ratnatraya or Triple Panacea for the cure of Samsāra. There is no doubt that spiritual practice must begin naturally with thinking about what we have to attain and knowing the means to attain it. That is the reason why every system of religion insists upon some sort of scriptural study under some teacher. Even to love God, or to practice virtue, some kind of previous thought and knowledge is essential. Thus Walter Hilton, the Christian mystic, says, 'When thou goest about to pray, first make and frame betwixt thee and God a full purpose and intention ; then begin and do as well as thou canst.' *The cloud of unknowing*, a Christian treatise on mysticism, says Prayer may not goodly be gotten in beginners or proficients, without thinking coming before.' All medieval Christian theologians and mystics emphasize that steady and methodic thought must precede any spiritual practice. St. Teresa harps on the supreme need for 're-collecting the mind', i.e., collecting the scattered thoughts and concentrating the intellect on the business in hand. This emphasis on the reasoning faculty is surely not out of place, for there are some who disparage reason on the strength of *Kaṭh.* II. 9 and *Bsū.* II. 1. 11. But these authorities only tell us that mere reasoning, independent of the other functions of the mind, and of help got from the experience of others, may not lead to the highest. But surely there is no sense in believing that one should leave one's brains behind, immediately one turns towards God! It is indeed true that all mental powers must be transcended before one realizes the highest. The soul must indeed outstrip its instruments in its flight towards God; especially during the last stages of the quest where it is a 'flight of the Alone to the Alone'. But those who are still far from this stage will only be injuring themselves by trying to anticipate this moment. This stage can never be attained by mere annihilation of intelligence and reason. A particular seeker's view of the truth as experienced by him must be coloured by the contents of the mind acquired previously—the apperceptive mass, as the psychologist would call it. Therefore it is always advantageous to have a reasonable idea of God to begin with. The worthier and purer our ideas of God, arrived at by a proper use of the intellect, the purer, worthier, and truer our interpretation of our experiences will be. But we should take care not to mistake this for mere dry intellectualism. As Nārada points out later on in *Sū*, 74, the aspirant should not take delight in vain argumentations and scholastic disputations for their own sake. The proper place for reason is provided for in spiritual practice by the insistence on reflection or Manana. Manu says that he only knows Dharma who understands the teachings of the scriptures with the help of reason and none else. The *Yogavāsiṣṭha* says that one should discard even the words of Brahma if it is against reason. Bhagavān, after teaching Arjuna the whole of Brahmavidyā, tells him at the end that he should understand it critically and then adopt such of the teachings as seem reasonable. Bṛhaspati says that in all consideration of Dharma, if reason is not given its proper place, there may be loss of virtue. Jaimni says in *Jsū*. I. 3. 3 and I. 3. 11 & 12 that wherever there is conflict in Śāstra, one should remove the conflict by use of reason. Thus we see how all our great teachers have given the highest place for reason in spiritual practice. But it is one thing to give it its legitimate place in the scheme, and another thing to say that reason alone is the means of attainment. Therefore some others reject this one-sided view as shown in the next *Sū*.

Sutra 29. The mind is a homogeneous entity and cannot be cut up into water-tight compartments. In exercising one function prominently, the others are also unconsciously exercised. One would do well to give exercise to all the functions, because they will be mutually strengthening and the goal will be attained sooner. Reason by itself is like a man and love is like a woman, says S'rī Rāmakṛṣṇa. The one can go only as far as the drawing room, while the other can enter the inner apartments. Ruysbroeck says, 'Where intellect must stay without, love and will may enter in.' In the words of the *Cloud of Unknowing*, 'It is the blind intent stretching towards Him, the true lovely will of the heart which gains the goal.' St. Augustine also thinks that man is nothing but his will. William Law says: 'The will makes the beginning, the middle, and end of everything. It is the only workman in nature and everything is its work.' The Bible says: 'The Kingdom of Heaven is taken by violence.' The *Cloud of Unknowing* says in another place: 'By the least longing man is led to be the servant of God, not by faultless deductions of dialectics, but by the mysterious logic of the heart.' Thus if intellect refuses the aid of feeling and will, it remains dry intellectual dogma. If love is unassisted by intellect and will, it may be blind sentimentalism; and if will is not helped by knowledge and love, it remains merely meaningless, aimless activity. In fact it would also seem impossible for each of the functions to work separately in isolation. How can a man know the highest without putting forth effort to know, and without being prompted by the love of Truth! So also is it possible for anybody to love truly without knowing the object of his love, and without exerting himself to serve his Beloved? It is not also possible to exert one-self for somebody without knowing and loving him. Thus all the powers of the mind always co-operate with one another.

Sutra 30. To say that Bhakti, as spiritual realization, is its own fruit means that it has no cause or that it is not the effect of anything else. The explanation of this is as follows: We have seen that all self-effort in the form of spiritual practices holds good only in the realm of Avidyā or Māyā. The results of these practices are also within the province of this Māyā, *i.e.*, realm of causality. These practices cause the destruction of ego, or purify the heart. But spiritual experience is not mere destruction of the ego, or purity of the heart. It is the eternally perfect nature of the Self revealing itself spontaneously when the obstructing causes are removed. Efforts do not cause this experience, because where the experience takes place, one has transcended the law of causation; it is impossible to relate that absolute state to spiritual practices on the links of cause and effect. Moreover, we have also seen how such practices by themselves are powerless to produce even the conditions necessary for this Self-manifestation, unless assisted by the grace of God. As the Self pushes on towards reality, God rushes in on it. If the aspirant takes one step towards God, God takes two steps towards his devotee. Grace is only the theological expression to indicate this inflow of Divine energy, which is considered to be the response made by God to human effort. Really, however, grace presses in upon us eternally, and merely awaits our voluntary appropriation of it. As Walter Hilton puts it: 'Though it be so that prayer is not the cause of grace, nevertheless it is a way or means by which grace freely given comes to the soul.

Sutra 31. The allusion in the word राजा is to the well-known story of the prince who was lost by his father in his childhood and was taken care of by some hermit in the forest. When the boy, who was ignorant of his parentage, and who considered himself a mere hermit, heard of his parentage accidentally, nothing new is produced but he is only reminded of an existing fact. So one is reminded of one's true status when one realizes the highest Self. The reference in the word गृह is to the experience of the wayfarer who returns home after a long absence. The home continues to be his home even in his absence, but the distance which obstructed his enjoyment is removed when he comes back. The pleasant experiences of his home were clouded by his long absence, but they are again revived as soon as he comes back. Nothing new is produced by his coming back. The reference in भोजन is to the experience of the hungry man when he has his dinner. The dinner does not produce any new satisfaction but only removes the disturbance caused by hunger. When the uneasiness is removed, the natural satisfaction remains undisturbed. These illustrations show how spiritual practices really work. They result only in removing the obstructions to the natural experience of the Self, which is eternal and never produced by any effort on the part of man.

Sutra 32. Not as a result of the hearing of the news does the hermit become a prince. He was a prince already and no status was added to him by his mere hearing. The wayfarer's satisfaction is also there already, nothing new was added to him by his return. So also the satisfaction of having a healthy body is already there; taking of food does not create anything new, but only removes the disturbance caused by hunger. With this *Sū.* the discussion on Parabhakti comes to an end.

Sutra 33. The Part dealing with Parabhakti ends here. Parabhakti is the highest Realization which is of the nature of Mokṣa. A religious aspirant should therefore accept it as the summit of all values; it is not an auxiliary value or a means to a higher human end. The Bhakti school considers Mokṣa in any other form than Paramaprema, or Supreme Love as stated above, trivial. Cf. the following statements: नारायणपराः शान्ताः न कुतश्चन बिभ्यति । स्वर्गापवर्गनरकेष्वपि तुल्यार्थदर्शिनः—*Bhāg.* VI. 17.28; धर्मार्थकाममोक्षेषु नेच्छा मम कदाचन । त्वत्पादपङ्कजास्वादजीवितं दीयतां मम—*Npāñc*; भुक्तिमुक्तिस्पृहा यावत् पिशाची हृदि वर्तते । तावद्भक्तिसुखस्यात्र कथमभ्युदयो भवेत्—Jivagosvāmin.

Sutra 34. The rest of the book—that is, the 41 Sūtras beginning with the present one,—may be considered as the Second Part. It is devoted to a consideration of the means to the highest spiritual realization. The natural perfection of the human soul is manifested only when the various faculties of the mind are purified and co-ordinated harmoniously; and spiritual practices are meant to effect this through the cultivation of the various faculties of the mind. Bhaktiyoga is mainly concerned with the culture and purification of the emotions; and Nārada confines himself to the discipline of Bhakti alone in the present work. In Bhaktiśāstra the culture of the intellect has a place only in so far as it is necessary and helpful to the proper development of emotions; and the development of emotions is effected through zealous love of God, designated as devotion or Aparabhakti. Devotion is only a means; it is to be distinguished from Supreme Love or Parabhakti, Vide *Sū.* 3. According to the scriptures of Bhakti all religious endeavour is for the attainment of Aparabhakti, which is the direct means to obtain Parabhakti or Supreme Love which is Realization itself. Nārada now describes the various disciplines that help one to achieve this devotion. These disciplines fall into two groups, one positive and the other negative. They help the aspirant to avail himself of the divine grace, which always seeks to bless the aspirant with devotion to the Lord. The aphorism with which we are now dealing forms an introduction to the whole of the ensuing discussion. Nārada does not want to base his teachings solely on his own experiences; for however much he might have been personally helped by particular practices, these need not be equally helpful to all owing to differences in circumstances and environments, social and psychological. He therefore proposes to deal only with the universal elements of spiritual practice which have been accepted as necessary by all teachers of Bhakti, Vide, *Sū.* 43 etc. It is, as it were, the experiments and experiences of one great teacher tested in the light of those of others, and thus the grain separated from the chaff. The following teachings must therefore be taken as the essence of Bhakti discipline. Since the doctrines taught by Nārada are entirely bereft of all sectarian bias, they may safely be adopted by all religious seekers irrespective of birth, persuasion, and sect. If any of the teachings of a particular teacher or sect goes against the universal and essential principles set forth below, one should be extremely cautious in accepting them; for they are likely to affect injuriously the attainment of the end in view. Difference in opinion is admissible regarding the highest Realization which is indescribable, Vide, *Sū.* 15. But in the sphere of Aparabhakti the means described are all capable of being scrutinized by the discriminating intellect, and the essentials may easily be found out. There is, therefore, no room for difference of opinion here; and only such methods are presented here which are accepted by all as important and unexceptionable. The teachers (आचार्याः) mentioned in the *Sū.* are those who have had firsthand experience of the upward struggle and the consequent Realization; and who, being deeply moved by the miseries of the world, stretch out a helping hand to those who have not yet dared to begin the ascent. These apostles of divine love must be distinguished from mere writers of religious books who have not tread the spiritual path or experienced the religious goal, but have only a knowledge of these from reports. Writers of this kind are not safe guides; this is the force of the word आचार्यः, derived from the root चर् with the prefix आ implying the sense of 'practice'. The verb गायन्ति in the text literally means 'sing'; it is chosen to suggest the idea of joy which accompanies the spiritual ministration to others. The true teacher's instructions come spontaneously because he feels a celestial joy in helping others.

Here we are to remember that all spiritual practice, as pointed out by Śaṅkarācārya in his commentary on *Bg.* II. 55, consists in putting forth the necessary effort to develop in an aspirant the qualities and characteristics which are always present in a man of the highest Realization. These characteristics, mostly mentioned in Ch. I, may be classified into two groups: 1. Absence of the evils of Bondage; 2. Presence of the divine bliss characteristic of Liberation. A spiritual aspirant must necessarily therefore exert himself every moment to cultivate virtues falling within either of these groups in all aspects of his life. He should reject everything that subjects him to the bondage of transmigration and its attendant evils and adopt everything that expresses the bliss of divine life. The negative and positive aspects of spiritual practice are really the obverse and reverse of the same coin. The seed decays and disappears before it develops into a tree; similary in spiritual life unless the lower stages are given up the higher ones cannot be attained. Unless you cease to be what you are, you cannot be what you ought to be. But according to the outlook of the seeker, sometimes the negative aspect is stressed and at other times the positive one. Those who emphasize the negative aspect argue that the goal is attained when the obstruction is removed: those who stress the positive discipline argue that even the obstructions can be removed only with the help of some positive effort. It is like striking a match to get rid of darkness. It is foolish to attempt, they say, to remove darkness by merely pushing it aside. Both the arguments are right from two distinct viewpoints; but it is dangerous to emphasize one at the expense of the other. Thus excessive asceticism in the name of conquering the flesh and subduing the mind should not banish all noble feelings helpful for the attainment of the goal. Again in the name of positive practices one should not cling on to worldly enjoyments relegating renunciation to the group of impractical ideals. A happy combination of the positive and the negative practices is not impossible; and spiritual teachers have emphasized this synthesis. A careful consideration of the miseries and evils of the world is enough to prompt a wise man to reject the world *in toto*. But it is only when this dispassion for the world is coupled with a knowledge of and faith in the possibility of attaining higher divine bliss that spiritual endeavour becomes firm and productive of the best result. Renunciation and service, detachment from worldly objects and practice—this twin discipline form the corner-stone of all spiritual discipline, *Bhāg.* IV. 22. 21.

Sutra 35. The essence of the negative aspect of spiritual practice is presented here. That consists in the renunciation of the ego. It is immaterial whether an aspirant begins with negative or positive practices first. That is left to the capacity, opportunity, and convenience of the individual. But real success comes only when the positive and negative practices are pursued simultaneously, as their mutual cooperation is essential for success. The advantage in putting this negative practice first may be that even the most sluggish seekers who do not care to practice any of the positive virtues will stear clear of all danger; for negative practice prevents an aspirant from retrograding even though no progress is made. To maintain one's human nature is the first step towards achieving divinity. Before getting an athletic body one should see that one is free from disease. The particle तु standing towards the beginning of the *Sū.* suggests that the aphorism is an answer to the following possible objection: Suppose the highest realization is only a kind of love. Why not then begin practice by loving all pleasurable and attractive things of the world? If the highest end of the aspirant is happiness or bliss, why not begin by trying to enjoy as much sense pleasures as possible? The answer is that such a procedure is risky, as it is based on false premises; for the Bliss that is sought as the goal of spiritual practices is eternal and natural, whereas the joys that the senses give in the world are fleeting, surpassable, impure, and intermittent. Their reality is of quite a different order from that of Divine Bliss, and unless the lower is transcended the higher cannot be got. Hence Visayatyāga is emphasized. Here we have taken Viṣaya in the sense of objective reality—exactly the sense in which S'rī S'aṅkara employs the word in the very first passage of his famous *Sārīrakabhāṣya*. So long as one is alive, awake, and observing, one cannot refuse to see the objective world; nor is it possible for one to escape it however much one may try to run away from it. But one can refuse to consider it as *real*, if one has the wisdom and courage. Advaitic authorities recognize three orders of reality, absolutely real, empirical, and apparitional. The Divine Reality alone is Pāramārthika or absolutely real; the world of everyday experience is Vyāvahārikasat or has reality only for purposes of experience and usage. The vision conjured up by a magician has only the semblance of reality; it is Prātibhāsikasat. The absolutely real is unchangeable and indestructible under all circumstances. This test cannot be applied to the other two orders of reality as they vanish in sleep and just after the magical show, respectively. So they cannot be *really* real; they are apparently real, or real for the time being only. Only God who forms the substratum of all objective and subjective phenomena, exists eternally without in the least foregoing His real nature under any circumstance, and in all states of consciousness. To know this ephemeral nature of all subjective as well as objective phenomena is what is meant by Viṣayatyāga. त्यागः प्रपञ्चरूपस्य चिदात्मत्वावलोकनम्—Renunciation means looking upon the universe as essentially Pure Consciousness, *Aparokṣānubhūti*, 106. In the earlier stages of spiritual striving, this can be practised only by actually abandoning as worthless all objects that excite and tempt the lower mind. S'rī Rāmakṛṣṇa includes all these in his pithy phrase 'woman and gold'. This avoidance of the object itself is necessary only in the early stages, and need be practised only with reference to objects which are capable of causing attachment and bondage. The Sannyāsa order of life represents the highest stage of this kind of Sādhana, in which man has to retire from society. All practices that are laid down by the S'āstras as duties of the other Ās'ramas or stations of life represent this renunciation in its preliminary stages, and are graded in such a way that they may enable the aspirant to slide into Sannyāsa without any unnecessary strain. Practice of renunciation of sense objects must, however, be voluntary and not forced. Thus the poor man does not benefit by his giving up food on a fast day, because he does so under compulsion, neither does the patient who is prevented by the doctor from taking ordinary food, nor he who is segregated from his family for considerations of health. The renunciation in these cases is not voluntary. First of all there must be the capacity and possibility of enjoying the object; only voluntary surrender of such an available chance of enjoyment constitutes true renunciation. This renunciation of objects should not also be carried to absurd lengths, as is done by many ascetics who practice self-torture for its own sake. Such extreme asceticism is a disease which has its root in some aberration of the mind; and one who is addicted to it is a fit subject for psycho-analytic treatment. What constitues such extreme cases is to be judged from the circumstances of each case. On the other hand, examples of Janaka, Rāmānanda Roy, Puṇdarīka-Vidyānidhi, Vidyāraṇya, and the like, are often cited by worldly-minded people as authority for convincing themselves that there is no real necessity at all to practise this kind of renunciation. These examples however, are rather exceptions that prove the rule, and are in fact not fit to be taken as models to be followed by the beginner, who runs the risk of getting entangled in the meshes of Māyā. These instances only prove the fact that when one has attained Parabhakti, one need not practise this form of Sādhana. From that time, worldly objects will not have the power to tempt him from the path of virtue and love of God. Only they who have reached this stage can safely dare to beard the lion in his own den! *Kumārasambhava*, 1. 59. says: They alone are heroes whose hearts will not yield even in the presence of temptation;—विकारहेतौ सति विक्रियन्ते येषां न चेतांसि त एव धीराः । The devil's tempting Jesus and Māra's attempt to seduce Buddha point to the same truth. For the novice, therefore, it is safer to keep out of temptation. Bhiṣma's words in *Mbh.* XII. 180. 30, 33 are worth reproducing here: न खल्वप्यरसज्ञस्य कामः क्व च न जायते । संस्पर्शात् दर्शनाद्वापि श्रवणाद्वापि जायते ॥ अप्राशनमसंस्पर्शमसंदर्शनमेव च । पुरुषस्यैष नियमो मन्ये श्रेयो न संशयः ॥—There is no possibility of desire arising in a man who does not know the pleasureableness of an object. And this pleasureableness is known only by actual contact with it by sight, touch, hearing, and the rest. Safer it is therefore for a man not to enjoy or see or touch such objects. Again, it is often advocated, by people who cannot give up worldly enjoyments, that these enjoyments are required as a necessary prelude to renunciation, since only such enjoyment leading to satiation could put down the desire for enjoyment once for all. This also is a dangerous doctrine. For never is it possible to suppress desire by enjoyment. Says the *Mbh.* II. ch. 63, Yayātigāthā as well as *Manu.* 11, 94. न जातु कामः कामानामुपभोगेन शाम्यति । हविषा कृष्णवर्त्मेव भूय एवाभिवर्धते ॥

यत्पृथिव्यां व्रीहियवं हिरण्यं पशवः स्त्रियः । नालमेकस्य तत्सर्वं इतिमत्वा शमं व्रजेत् ॥—' Desires are never quenched by enjoyment. It rather inflames them all the more, as ghee only inflames fire and does not put it out. The entire riches of the earth is not enough to satiate one greedy man; reasoning thus, man should be contented. Therefore, says the *Yogavāsiṣṭha*, VI. 77. 81, 83, 'the slightest desire must be nipped in the bud by abstinence, as it would otherwise lead to perdition, just as one would destroy the sprout of a poisonous tree. Hook the fish of desire by abstinence.'

सङ्गत्याग means renunciation of all attachment. It shows that mere renunciation of an object of enjoyment is not sufficient, unless it is accompanied by a renunciation of all attachment to it mentally. If objects of enjoyments are given up by force, it is repression, and it would lead to all kinds of evil consequences. described in detail by psycho-analysts. Mere renunciation of external objects of enjoyment (says *Bg.* III. 6, 7), all the while pondering over sense pleasures within oneself, is a false way of renunciation. It is far better to renounce all attachment mentally even while enjoying them externally. The statement cited above only asserts that of the two kinds of renunciation the latter is superior to the former if it is possible. There is no condemnation of external renunciation implied in it; nor the hint that one may be going on indulging in external pleasures on the plea that on is mentally detached. Mind being the basis of all sense operations, when the mind turns away, the senses too will follow. It is not possible to enjoy carnal or sensual pleasures when the mind refuses to find any interest therein. So when there is mental renunciation external renunciation naturally follows, for there is no incentive then for enjoyment. Nārada is an advocate of the necessity of both the kinds of renunciation, internal and external. His view may be compared to the one expressed in *Mbh*. XII. 219. 17; 162. 17: त्याग एव हि सर्वेषां युक्तानामपि कर्मणाम् । नित्यं मिथ्याविनीतानां क्लेशो दुःखवहो मतः ॥ त्यागः स्नेहस्य यस्त्यागो विषयाणां तथैव च ॥ External renunciation is absolutely necessary in the early stages; while internal renunciation is essential at all times. Where total renunciation of objects is not possible on account of special circumstances, one should be particularly careful to practice mental renunciation at least, and be free from attachments to objects. The objective and the subjective forms of renunciation form the basis of all spiritual practice. द्रव्यत्यागे तु कर्माणि भोगत्यागे व्रतानि च । सुखत्यागे तपो योगं सर्वत्यागे समापना ॥ तस्य मार्गोऽयमद्वैधः सर्वत्यागस्य दर्शितः । विप्रहाणाय दुःखस्य दुर्गतिस्त्वन्यथा भवेत्—Good work is for renouncing wealth by way of gifts; vows are for giving up sense pleasures; eschewing of luxuries is for austerity and spiritual striving; the finality of everything is total renunciation. The steps shown just above undoubtedly lead to that total renunciation. That total renunciation cures all mysery; without renunciation there is no escape from mysery; *Mbh*. XII. 219. 18, 19; cf. also *Bhāg*. XI. 23. 46. The view of S'rī Kṛṣṇa in regard to Karmatyāga and Phalatyāga is acceptable to Nārada also, see *Sū*. 11, 14, 48, 62. The various kinds of renunciation to be practised are given in aphorisms 43-49. Renunciation is not complete until ego is completely destroyed.

Sutra 36. In the previous *Sū.* the general principle underlying the negative aspect of spiritual practice has been enunciated as external and internal renunciation; that is to say, renunciation of ego and its various expressions in life as well as every object that has a tendency to exercise and strengthen the lower instincts and impulses of man. There one has only to avoid scrupulously things, thoughts, feelings, and actions which are incited by self-interest and worldly outlook, which if unchecked and uncontrolled would perpetuate Samsāra. The present *Sū.* goes one step further. It insists that one should never rest contented by mere avoidance of evil, but must follow it up consciously by an active practice of good for its own sake. One should actively try to express in one's life all the divine perfections, which one inherently possesses. The Divine is eternally present in the human breast as the Antaryāmin, and man's divinity and perfection, though temporarily smothered by the ego, is incessantly struggling for self-expression. In positive Sādhana one takes advantage of this natural urge of the human soul for perfection. All possible circumstances and situations are created favourable for its expression. Thus the natural capacity of man to distinguish the true from the false, the right from the wrong, the beautiful from the ugly, and to love and appreciate truth, goodness, and beauty for their own sake, and to guide his life in the light of these, is to be constantly exercised and strengthened. Only so far as he makes use of this capacity to manifest his divine perfection does he earn the title to be considered a human being at all. Even the natural instincts and impulses are not bad in themselves. They have their own beneficient purpose to serve in the early stages of spiritual ascent. They can be pruned and trimmed and guided into right channels by the process of sublimation. Undesirable thoughts, feelings, and habits will have to be counteracted by the cultivation of their contrary ones through constant and repeated exercises. Such exercises run counter to the demands of the natural man. It is an up-hill task; and tremendous will-power has to be summoned in the beginning to swim against the current of one's own inherent tendencies or past Saṁskāras. All training in scientific and philsophical method and outlook, cultivation of the æsthetic faculties and refining the mind through that process, ceaseless effort to lead a virtuous life with the aid of constant selfless service, and a hankering for truth, beauty, and goodness—all these are needed for the spiritual ascent of man. Philosophy and science, art and morality, all serve as handmaids to religion which is the manifestation of the divinity already in man. The culture of Sattva quality and the acquisition of Daivīsampat spoken of in *Bg*. XIV and XVI are meant for this purpose; and they are to be achieved through Tyāga and Yoga.

अव्यावृत (uninterrupted) implies that spiritual practice must be constant, steady, and punctual. स्वाध्याया-योगमासीत योगात्स्वाध्यायमावसेत् । स्वाध्याययोगसम्पत्त्या परमात्मा

प्रकाशते ॥ Holy study and spiritual practices such as concentration and meditation must alternate without the least gap; as a result of it the Supreme Self will manifest Itself, *Vp*. VI. 6. 2. *Adhyātmopaniṣad* says: निद्राया: लोकवार्तायाः शब्दादेरर्थविस्मृतेः। क्वचिन्नावसरं दत्त्वा चिन्तयात्मानमात्मनि ॥ Never allowing room for drowsiness, gossip, distraction due to external sounds, and forgetfulness, always meditate on Ātman within you. स तु दीर्घकालनैरन्तर्यसत्कारासेवितो दृढभूमिः—It becomes firmly grounded by long, constant efforts with great love for the end to be attained—*Ysū*. I. 14. आवृत्तिः असकृदुपदेशात्—An aspirant has to repeat the practice, for it is taught by many statements in the scripture, *Bsū*. I. 4. 1. The necessity of such effort is emphasized in *Bg*. VIII. 14 also. Breaks in spiritual practice are not advisable if one can possibly avoid them. They not only nullify the good effects of previous practice, but often cause positive, permanent injury. It will be opening the gates of the fortress to the enemy who has been once driven out. There are of course noble exceptions like Vis'vāmitra who, in spite of repeated falls, persisted till the highest was attained. To the wise and courageous every failure is only a stepping-stone to success. But to the craven-minded man, one failure is sufficient to unnerve him and induce him to give up the struggle for good. As Bhartṛhari says, 'The craven-minded do not dare to begin at all for fear of obstacles, the ordinary man retires and gives up the attempt once for all when he meets with obstacles in the course of his struggle, but the hero is he who persists in the face of innumerable obstacles that try to thwart him from attaining his object'. In fact it only adds to his zest if the hero meets obstacles that come in the way. He never yields of his own accord. But circumstances may be such often as to compel him to take rest and gather strength for a fresh endeavour. Break may thus come in spite of one's best efforts; but then one should begin again as soon as the weather clears and circumstances once more become favourable. Thus, if on account of any disease or other causes, practice has to be suspended temporarily, the earnest aspirant should take up the thread again at the first opportunity. Even if obstacles come, the struggle itself is not to be given up and the inner fire must still be kept burning. This spirit of struggle itself against odds gives a continuity to the Sādhana in spite of the temporary lull. In such cases, the principle of *Bg*. II. 40 and VI. 40 holds good and saves him. These passages point out that if one engages oneself in spiritual practices in the right spirit and method, one does not come to grief even if a break appears in the middle due to circumstances beyond one's control. धर्मकार्ये यतन् शक्त्या नो चेत् प्राप्नोति मानवः। प्राप्तो भवति तत्पुण्यं अत्र मे नास्ति संशयः— I have no doubt that a spiritual aspirant shall get great merit even though he may fail to reach his end in one life by earnest holy endeavour, *Mbh*. V. Such breaks are not real breaks at all, as there is continuity of inner aspiration and struggle even in periods of lull. While commenting upon the expression 'yatatām api siddhānām' (*Bg*. VII. 3.) S'aṅkara takes care to note that a man who struggles sincerely for the highest end is already as good as a Siddha, meaning thereby that it is this sincere struggle that really constitutes the real practice. Breaks become injurious only if they are caused by wanton negligence, or carelessness, or temptations of the flesh or senses. Any conscious yielding to such temptation and sin makes a man weaker, and thus causes more or less permanent injury. It will be like the fate of the man who, while trying to climb up a tree, lets loose his hold in the middle of his ascent on account of his carelessness or being tempted to catch at some other attractive object such as a beautiful bird flitting near him. It is this yielding to weakness and temptation that one has to be afraid of.

A doubt may arise here as to the very possibility of such continuity in practice. No doubt, activity cannot go on continuously for any length of time, as it causes fatigue. There must be intervals of rest; and real rest only helps in the furtherance of the object in view. Over-enthusiasm, sometimes on the other hand, leads to over-exercise, and this in its turn leads to untoward consequences, such as diseases and madness. But rest does not necessarily mean abstaining from all activity. As psychologists have pointed out, and educational practice bears out, rest need be only a change of work. Again it is only when work is undertaken without interest that fatigue often intervenes to cause trouble. If one is really interested in the activity or its results, it ceases to be a task and takes on the form of play. It is well known how, even if the exercise of muscles involved in play is more strenuous and taxing than ordinary work, the latter often causes fatigue sooner than the former. That is why Patañjali and other Ācāryas insist upon the element of interest in and reverence for the ideal. One should take interest even in the struggle. 'The prize,' says Robert Browning, 'is in the process'. A good way of keeping up interest is to provide sufficient variety, which also provides the necessary rest. Such variety in the nature of the activity is therefore allowable and should not be mistaken for discontinuity, since the spirit behind the various activities as well as the struggle to express the Divine perfections will have their own continuity in spite of the apparent break in the external activity. Thus meditation and worship, Japa and Saṅkīrtana, study and service of devotees, acts of loving charity and performance of one's own daily duties, pilgrimages and witnessing of drama on noble themes—all may be given their rightful share in the scheme of practice, and may be allowed to alternate with one another, to provide the necessary rest and interest. That it is possible to have these varieties and yet to have continuity in real Sādhana is illustrated by Sri Rāmakṛṣṇa in his own life and teachings. Note the various illustrations he gives, such as that of the village maiden carrying water on her head, the wife awaiting her husband's arrival while at the same time cooking his meals with one hand, and nursing her child with the other. The word 'Bhajana' (loving service) in the text is correlated with Bhakti. Bhajana represents the activity, while Bhakti the emotional accompaniment of it, Primarily any act done out of love for God is, therefore.

Bhajana. Also, such acts as are accompaniments or expressions of love, as witnessed in the life of real Bhaktas and taught by them, may be voluntarily undertaken by the Sadhaka to cultivate this love for God. Thus prayer and worship, chanting and music, social service and meditation, study and service to Guru, all may be undertaken as Bhajana, even if they are not in the first instance the result of love, for these are sure to result in such love in the long run. Psychologists like James and Lange have emphasized this aspect of emotion as accompaniments of certain physical changes. Only these activities must be undertaken sincerely and consciously for the sake of cultivating this love, as otherwise they may degenerate and become harmful. Prahlāda's enumeration of nine kinds of this Bhajana—श्रवणं कीर्तनं विष्णोः स्मरणं पादसेवनम् । अर्चनं वन्दनं दास्यं सख्यमात्मनिवेदनम् ॥ *Bhāg*. VII. 5. 23, 24—provide not only the variety but also the exercise for Bhakti culture. One may also put mentally into various kinds of relationship with God such as that of a parent, a friend, a servant, and the like, (*Vide* Sūtras 66 and 82) to induce this kind of love for the Lord. Thus the different practices that help to cultivate this love is Bhajana or loving service. Vide also *Bg*. IX; *S'sū*. II. 2 and *Adhrām* III. 10. 21-28 for further details.

Sutra 37. We have seen above how steadiness and unbroken continuity is necessary in spiritual practice. Now Nārada gives an answer to a possible objection that may be levelled against this requirement. The objection may be stated thus: However necessary and advisable it might be to spend one's whole time in spiritual practices, one cannot avoid spending some time at least in meeting such innocent demands of the physical body as hunger, sleep, calls of nature, and attention to cleanliness, which even a perfected soul cannot escape. Again, as long as one remains a member of a certain social group, one has to adjust oneself to the requirements of such groups, and one is compelled to observe various customs and etiquette, such as Āśauca. He has also to attend to the discharge of his social obligations. When Bhagavān says in *Bg.* III. 25 that even a man of realization must actively participate in bringing about the welfare of society, how can a novice escape from it? It would thus seem impracticable to spend the whole time in spiritual practices alone, and a break in the continuity is inevitable when one is obliged to attend to such things. Such continuity is still possible and practicable, says Nārada in reply, as the mind can continue to meditate on God and his blessed attributes, even when the body is occupied in the discharge of such obligatory duties, with the help of hearing and singing—भगवद्गुणश्रवणकीर्तनात् । The main purpose of spiritual endeavour is to purify the mind; and according to the Bhakti scriptures the best way to succeed in it is to seek constant, loving association with the Lord in one's own heart. By any method whatsoever one should focus the mind on God—तस्मात् केनाप्युपायेन मनः कृष्णे निवेशयेत्—*Bhāg.* VII. 1. 31. Always one should remember God; never should God slip away from memory; all rules are but ancilliary to these two—स्मर्तव्यः सततं विष्णुः विस्मर्तव्यो न

जातुचित । सर्वे विधिनिषेधाः स्युरेतयोरेव किङ्कराः । The essence of all Yoga consists in withdrawing the mind from the sensual objects and fixing only on God—एतावान् योग आदिष्टो मच्छिष्यैः सनकादिभिः । सर्वतो मन आकृष्य मय्यद्धावेश्यते यथा । *Bhāg.* XI. 13. 14. The mind abhors a vacuum; it must be engaged in something or other. If it meditates on sense objects it becomes worldly; if it remembers God it becomes divine—विषयान् ध्यायतश्चित्तं विषयेषु विषज्जते । मामनुस्मरतश्चित्तं मय्येव प्रविलीयते ॥ *Bhāg.* XI. 14. 27. The evils of pondering over sense objects that excite passion are given in *Bg.* II. 62, 63. Therefore noble souls are always intent on the Divine, *Bg.* IX. 13, 14, 27. Since the mind has the property of getting the colour and odour of the object with which it is in contact, the scriptures repeatedly advise to do all acts carefully remembering the Lord and finding delight in godly work—कुर्यात्सर्वाणि कर्माणि मदर्थं शनकैः स्मरन् । मय्यर्पितमनश्चित्तो मद्धर्मात्ममनोरतिः ॥ *Bhāg.* XI. 29. 9. All impurities of the heart are wiped off and a perfectly auspicious state is soon engendered by dwelling on the Lord continually, *Bhāg.* II. 3. 10, 20-24; III. 33. 6, 7; VI. 2. 11, 12, 16, 17; XII. 3. 43-49; *Vp.* II. 6. 38-43; VI. 8. 21, 57. That is why devotees of the highest type do not like anything else—एवमेकान्तिनां प्रायः कीतनस्मरण प्रभोः । कुर्वतां परमप्रीत्या कृत्यमन्न्यन्न रोचते ॥ *Haribhaktivilāsa.* Hence meditation is the essence of all positive spiritual practice. *Vide Bhāg.* II. 3. 10.

It is a psychological fact that thinking is possible only with the help of visual or auditory symbols; hence words and sentences are indispensible in the remembrance of

God, if the mind is not entirely lost in a visualized form. Thinking is sub-vocal speech mostly; and ideas and words are intimately connected. In continuous meditation an unbroken series of words and passages are, therefore, necessary. The employment of language in support of meditation is what is meant by S'ravana and Kīrtana; these are mutually dependent because speaking without hearing and hearing without speaking are plainly impossible. Both speaking and hearing may be done either by the same person or different persons. Speech employed for sustained meditation may also be loud or silent. Even in silent meditation a kind of internal S'ravaṇa and Kīrtana will be going on; only the same person is the speaker as well as the hearer in this case. When the Kīrtana and S'ravaṇa are conducted in company the group must be of unanimous intent. तच्चिन्तनं तत्कथनमन्योन्यं तत्प्रबोधनम्। एतदेकपरत्वं च ब्रह्माभ्यासं विदुर्बुधाः—Reflection on the Truth, mutual instruction, and absorption in it form the spiritual discipline, *Pañcadas'ī*; cf. also *Bg*. X. 9. These verbal aids designed to draw the mind to the Divine and keep it intent on Him takes various forms. It may be study of scriptures or enquiry into the texts that expound Divine truths. Sometimes it may take the form of composing and singing songs and hymns, or producing other kinds of religious literature purely for devotional purposes and not for profit. Vyāsa's composing of *Bhāg*. under the instruction of Nārada and S'uka's reciting it to Parikṣit may be taken as examples. The efficacy of Saṅkīrtana and S'ravaṇa are thus referred to in *Bhāg*. X. 90, 49 and 50: 'One who seeks to develop devotion to His feet should listen to accounts of the deeds that wear away all enslaving Karma, of the foremost of the Yadus—the deeds which accord with the sportful forms which the Supreme Being assumes for the purpose of protecting the righteous life taught by Him. By virtue of the devotion which grows every hour and minute by listening to, the singing of, and constant contemplation of, Mukunda's glorious stories, mortal man attains his abode which is beyond the range of Yama's inevitable force and for whose sake even kings left inhabited places and retired to the forest.' *Bhāg.* XII. 4, 40 says : 'To a man tossed and distressed in the wild fire of various sorrows and intent on crossing the impassable sea of Saṁsāra there is no raft other than constant listening to, and drinking of, the excellent essence of the sportful activities of the Almighty Lord Puruṣottama.' *Bhāg.* II. 1. 5 says : 'Therefore, O Bhārata, Hari, the Lord and protector and soul of all, must be heard and sung and remembered by those who wish to be free from all fear.' *Vide* also *Ib.* I. 5. 22. III. 3. 31, XII. 12. 47 to 65.

Often Kīrtana may consist only in the thoughtful repetition of various divine names, formulas, or symbolic syllables. It is accepted by spiritual adepts that repetition of the Mantras form the highest help to meditation. The *Yogaśikhopaniṣad* II. 8 says, मननात् त्राणनाच्चैव मद्रूपस्यावबोधनात् । मन्त्रमित्युच्यते ब्रह्मन् मदधिष्ठानतो ऽपि वा ॥ Since reflection and saving power are connected with the 'holy formula' and also because it forms the abode of Brahman and helpful in realizing God it is called Mantra.

Such Mantras may consist of a single syllable, a word or words, a single verse, or even a number of them; the last type is called a **मालामन्त्र.** These Mantras are very important, and their repetition is what is generally known as Japa. To call on God by His hallowed names is as old as religion. Desirous of obtaining realization, says the Ṛgvedic verse, we only take Thy name—अस्य जानन्तो नाम चित् विवक्तन। महस्ते विष्णो सुमतिं भजामहे। *Ṛgv.* VII. 104. 12. The same verse occurs in the *Yajv.* also with the variation बृहत for महस in the second line. The *Sāmv.* I. 2. 9. 2 states: We use no sacrificial stakes, we slay no victims, we worship entirely by repeating Mantras—नकि देवा इनीमसि न कथा योपयामसि मन्त्रश्रुत्यं चरामसि। *Rāmapūrvatāpinī Upd.* I. 4. declares that Rama established the path of Righteousness by His deeds and the path of knowledge by His Name—धर्ममार्गं चरित्रेण ज्ञानमार्गं च नामतः। तथा ध्यानेन वैराग्यमैश्वर्यं स्वस्य पूजनात्॥ The *Yogacūdāmaṇyupaniṣad*, 87, 88, emphasizes the value of constant Japa for self-purification and realization—वचसा तज्जपेन्नित्यं वपुषा तत्समभ्यसेत् मनसा तज्जपेन्नित्यं तत्परं ज्योतिरोमिति। शुचिर्वाप्यशुचिर्वापि यो जपेत् प्रणवं सदा। न स लिप्यति पापेन पद्मपत्रमिवाम्भसा। The *Mbh.* also says that the aspirant reaches the highest by Japa—जपमावर्तयन् नित्यं जपन् वै ब्रह्मचारिकम्। तदर्थबुध्या संयाति मनसा जापकः परम॥ The various religious practices prescribed in the S'rutis which are hemmed in by all kinds of rules and restrictions cannot be done by all. Therefore by giving up such practices and merely repeating the Name of God one attains everything—विहितमखिलकर्म ब्राह्मणानां मुनीन्द्रैर्विधिनियमसमेतं शक्यते नैव कर्तुम्। तदखिलमपि हित्वा यो महादेवशब्दं पठति फलमशेषं प्राप्नुयात्सोऽनवद्यम्। *Brahvaip.* All these passages reveal what a high place the sages of antiquity gave to the divine name. Buddhism, Christianity, and Islam also have the same consideration for the Divine Name. 'Let them also that love thy name be joyful in thee' *The Psalms*, 5. 11. Give unto the Lord the glory due to his name', *Ib.* 29. 2. 'O magnify the Lord with me,

And let us exalt his name together.' *Ib.* 34. 3, 4;
'Make a Joyful noise unto God, all the earth:
Sing forth the glory of his name:
Make his praise glorious.' *Ib.* 66. 1-3.
'I will lift up my hands in thy name.' *Ib.* 63. 5.

The superiority of Japayajña is noticed by the sages who composed the Smṛtis again and again. Says Vasiṣṭha: ये पाकयज्ञाश्चत्वारो विधियज्ञसमन्विताः । सर्वो ते जपयज्ञस्य कलां नार्हन्ति षोडशीम् ॥ *Mnu.* II. 86 says: बिधियज्ञात् जपयज्ञो विशिष्टो दशभिर्गुणैः । उपांशु स्यात् शतगुणः साहस्रो मानसः स्मृतः ॥ These statements make it clear that Japa is superior to all burnt sacrifices and other Vedic rites, and that even in Japa mental repetition is most effective. Yama states that Japa is the most excellent sacrifice—जपयज्ञस्तु यज्ञानां सर्वेषामुत्तमः स्मृतः । *Padmp.* says: यावन्तः कर्मयज्ञाः स्युः प्रदिष्टानि तपांसि च । सर्वे ते जपयज्ञस्य कलां नार्हन्ति षोडशीम् ॥ Us'anas states: दानात् शतगुणो यागो यागात् शतगुणो जपः । The Tantrasāra sums up by stating: जपनिष्ठो द्विजश्रेष्ठः सर्वयज्ञफलं लभेत् । सर्वेषामपि यज्ञानां जायतेऽसौ महाफलः—A spiritual aspirant intent on Japa will get the result of all sacrifices, and hence Japayajña gives the best result. जप्येनैव तु संसिध्येद् ब्राह्मणो नात्र संशयः । कुर्यादन्यन्नवा कुर्यात् मैत्रो ब्राह्मण उच्यते ॥—A spiritual man attains his goal through Japa alone whatever else he may perform or not, *Mnu.* II. 87. जपस्तु सर्वधर्मेभ्यः परमो धर्म उच्यते ।

अहिंसया च भूतानां जपयज्ञः प्रवर्तते—Japa is the most excellent Dharma ; for it involves no injury to any creature, *Mbh.* Bhiṣma emphasizes this while relating to Yudhiṣṭhira the Thousand Names. S'aṅkara, in commenting on the passage, observes—हिंसादिपुरुषान्तरद्रव्यान्तरदेशकालादिनियमानपेक्षत्वमाधिक्ये कारणम्—The superiority of Japa is based on its freedom from dependence on any other particular objects, time or place, or other requirements as well as the fact that no injury is involved in it as in other sacrifices. Moreover while other Yajñas are not permitted for all, Japa can be practised by all irrespective of age, sex, caste, and stages of life, at all times and in all places in one form or other. There is another advantage also in repeating Divine Names ; it does not stand in need of any special instruction from anybody else—हरिसङ्कीर्तनस्यास्य नोपदेशः कथञ्चन । किन्तु ब्रवीमि सौम्य त्वं कथयस्वाशुचिर्न हि ॥ *Brahmāṇḍap.* ; also see *Brahp.* I. 97. 166. There is not any observance of ceremonial purity in repeating Lord's name mentally—चक्रायुधस्य नामानि सर्वदा परिकीर्तयेत् । नाशौचं कीर्तने तस्य पवित्रो भगवान् हरि ॥ *Dakṣasmṛti.* न दोषो मानसे जप्ये सर्वकालेषु सर्वदा ॥—says the *Vais'ampāyanasaṁhitā.* न देशकालनियमः शौचाशौच विनिर्णयः । परं सङ्कीर्तनादेव राम रामेति मुच्यते—*Vais'vānarasmṛti.* Specifications of place and time are given only to help certain individuals ; for instance, the *Prapañcasāra* says : समुद्रतीरेप्यथवाद्रिशृङ्गे समुद्रगानां सरितां च तीरे । जपेद्विविक्ते निज एव वा गृहे विष्णोर्गृहे वा पुरुषो मनस्वी ॥ These restrictions are in no way a bar to the general principle that one may practise where one gets concentration—यत्रैकाग्रता तत्राविशेषात् *Bsū.* IV. 1. 11. In the beginning, says

S'rī Rāmakṛṣṇa, a man should try to concentrate his mind in a lonely place to avoid distraction ; but when he has gained the power of mental concentration by constant practice, his mind will always rise above his environment and rest in God wherever he might stay. एकान्ते गुह्यदेशे च तस्माज्जप्यं समाचरेत्—In a solitary place protected from distraction Japa should be practised, *Kūrmap.* Aṅgiras also says : प्रछन्नानि च दानानि ज्ञानं च निरहङ्कृतम् । जप्यानि च सुगुप्तानि तेषां फलमनन्तकम् ।—Gifts given without making it public, knowledge acquired without vanity, and Japa done in secrecy will be infinitely potent in their result.

Regarding the varieties of Japa and their description we get these statements in Smṛti works : त्रिविधो जपयज्ञः स्यात्तस्य भेदं निबोधत । वाचिकाख्य उपांशुश्च मानसस्त्रिविधः स्मृतः ॥ त्रयाणां जपयज्ञानां श्रेयान् स्यादुत्तरोत्तरम् । यदुच्चनीचस्वरितैः स्पष्टैः स्पष्टपदाक्षरैः । मन्त्रमुच्चारयेद वाचा जपयज्ञः स वाचिकः ॥ शनैरुच्चारयेन्मन्त्रमीषदोष्ठौ प्रचालयन् । किञ्चित् शब्दं स्वयं विद्याद् उपांशुः स जपः स्मृतः ॥ धिया यदक्षरश्रेण्यां वर्णाद वर्ण पादात् पदम् । मन्त्रार्थचिन्तनाभ्यासो मानसो जप उच्यते ॥ यो भवेदचलज्जिह्वो दशनावरणो जपः । स मानसः समाख्यातो जपश्रुतिविभूषणैः ॥ ओष्ठस्पन्दनमात्रेण यत्तूपांशु तदध्वनि । कृत्वा जिह्वां निर्विकल्पां चिन्तयेत्तद्धि मानसम् ॥ जपस्तु त्रिविधः प्रोक्तः स तूच्चोपांशुमानसः ॥ उच्चादुपांशुरुत्कृष्टः उपांशोरपिमानसः ॥ उच्चैस्त्वेकगुणः प्रोक्तो ध्वानो दशगुणः स्मृतः । उपांशुःस्यात् शतगुणः साहस्रो मानसः स्मृतः ॥ The import of these passages is that Japa can be performed in three ways : Loudly, uttering to oneself, and repeating merely in mind without the least movement of vocal organs. If the efficacy of loud utterance is one unit, that of uttering a little loud is ten, of muttering to oneself with the movement of lips a hundred, and of repeating in thought alone without vocal movement a thousand units. Of these, it is better for beginners to begin with loud repetition. It is only after long practice that one can do the Upāṁs'u, and with still greater practice, the Mānasa. The mental Japa is the most efficacious of all. It is this mental Japa that one can practise always even when the hands are employed otherwise. There is, however, a danger in monotonously repeating Mantras mentally for a long time while sitting quiet. The mind becoming stilled, there is a likelihood of one's getting asleep unconsciously. It is therefore advisable for beginners whenever and wherever possible to have recourse to loud chanting, which keeps them quite awake and attentive to the object which they meditate upon. That is why we find S'rī Rāmakṛṣṇa, Caitanyadeva, and other saints laying such great emphasis on loud chanting or Saṅkīrtana. The danger of sleep is much less when the singing is done in congregation. An assembly of devotees creates a special atmosphere favourable to meditation. Devotional music is also helpful in concentrating the mind. Thus mass prayers and congregational music are highly beneficial for beginners. Among the other conditions noticed in the scriptures for ensuring success in Japa, first of all there are some external restrictions which are helpful. The *Prapañcasāra* says that one should have a light stomach, and should have had sound sleep, before one sits for meditation on a proper seat in an equable spot, with closed eyes and turning to the east—सुजीर्णमितभोजनः सुखसमाप्तनिद्रादिकः सुशुद्धतलसद्गृहे विरहिते च शीतादिभिः । पटाजिनकुशोत्तरे सुविशदे च मृद्वासने निमीलितविलोचनः प्रतिविशेत्सुखं प्राङ्मुखः ॥ प्रसा-

रितं वामकरं निजाङ्के निधाय तस्योपरि दक्षिणं च। ऋजुः प्रसन्नोऽवहितेद्रिय: सन्नाधारमत्यन्तसमं स्मरेत् स्वम् ।—Let him sit straight with the palms of the hands placed in the lap, right over the left, well stretched; let him have his mind and senses alert and calm and remember that he is a harmonious and undistracted agent performing the act of Japa and meditation. The aspirant must not be nodding his head and exposing the teeth; he must repeat distinctly and clearly—स्वरवर्णपदैर्वाक्यं शुद्धमावर्तयन् जपेत्। न कम्पयेच्छिरोग्रीवं दन्तान् नैव प्रकाशयेत् ॥ S'aṅkha. Bhāradvāja says that Japa is adversely affected by spitting, yawning, getting angry, feeling sleepy or hungry, as well as by inadvertence, and seeing low and sinful people—निष्ठीवजृम्भणक्रोधनिद्रालस्यक्षुधा-मदा: । पतितश्वान्त्यजालोका: दशैते जपवैरिण: ॥ Restraint of the mind, purity, silence, reflecting on the meaning, freedom from distraction, and absence of indifference are the causes that contribute to success in Japa—मन: संहरणं शौचं मौनं मन्त्रार्थचिन्तनम् । अव्यग्रत्वमनिर्वेदो जपसंसिद्धिहेतवः । Bṛhaspati. Again while doing Japa one should not be pacing about, laughing, looking at someone by the side, leaning on a wall, talking in the middle, having the head covered, placing one foot or hand over the other, leaving the mind to wander about, and uttering aloud so that others may hear—न प्रक्रमन् न च हसन् न पार्श्वमवलोकयन् । नापाश्रितो न जल्पन् च न प्रावृतशिरास्तथा । न पदा पदमाक्रम्य न चैव हि तथा करौ । न चासमाहितमना: न च संश्रावयन् जपेत् ॥ Vyāsa. The *Smṛticandrika* says that Japa and other religious duties done while running, standing, and doing some other work along with it or numbering on the sacred thread are fruitless—धावतस्तिष्ठतश्चैव स्वेच्छया कर्म कुर्वत: संख्यां चैवोपवीतेन जपहोमादि निष्फलम् ॥ Some other helpful practices based on tradition are :—प्रदक्षिणे प्रणामे च पूजायां हवने जपे । न कण्ठावृतवस्त्रः स्यात् दर्शने गुरुदेवयोः । आचार्यमेकभक्तं च भगवन्मन्दिरं जलम् । अश्वत्थमग्निमर्कं च पृष्ठीकृत्वा जपेन्नतु ॥ *S'āṇḍilyasmṛti.* नाभेरधः स्वकायं तु स्पृष्ट्वा प्रक्षालयेत् करम् । Marici. यदि वाग्यमलोपः स्यात् जपादिषु कथञ्चन । व्याहरेद्वैष्णवं सूक्तं स्मरेद् वा विष्णुमव्ययम् ॥ *Yogiyājñavalkya.* Of these some rules are very necessary ; for instance seated posture. If Japa is done while standing or walking attention will be distracted by the strain of the muscles, and if it is done lying down one may easily go to sleep. So *Bsū.* IV. 1. 7 says that concentration can be better had in a seated posture. One has to meditate on his chosen Ideal as his own very Self while doing Japa, *Bsū.* IV. 1. 3. The *Chānd.* II. 22. 2 says : मनसा ध्यायन् अप्रमत्त: स्तुवीत—Contemplating in the mind, one should repeat the Mantra vigilantly. Hence to get perfection in Japa one should know the meaning and Deity ensouled in the Mantra—मन्त्रार्थं मन्त्रचैतन्यं यो न जानाति साधकः । शतलक्षप्रजप्तोऽपि तस्य मन्त्रो न सिध्यति ॥ मन्त्रचैतन्यमेतत्तु तदधिष्ठानदेवता तज्ज्ञानं परमेशानि भक्तानां सिद्धिदायकम् ॥ *Mahānirvāṇatantra* III. 31, 35. This leads us to the necessity of the knowledge of the meaning of the Mantra and the need of its repetition several times.

Although it is often stated that a single utterance of the name is sufficient to save one, it is safer to remember that it is only an exaggeration to create faith in the efficacy of Japa, as Japa itself means repetition. If the above claim were true, then every one would have been saved long ago. It may be true that one proper utterance of the name with the proper spirit and S'raddhā may be sufficient to save the most highly qualified aspirants. But if a person finds out the sweetness of the Divine name, he will not renounce it even after realization. Therefore, if a man gives up repetition after the first utterance, we may take it for granted that he has not done the Japa properly, and that he has not realized the sweetness of it. This claim of the Bhakti school is something like the claim of S'aṅkara that the Mahāvākya need be heard only once in the case of highly qualified aspirants. But S'aṅkara himself qualifies his own claim later on in his *Bhāṣya* on *Bsū.* IV. 1. 1 & 2, where he says that in the case of ordinary aspirants repetition must be continued until perfection is reached. Therefore Japa and Saṅkīrtana must be done repeatedly and zealously, for it is only repetition of words that can support repetition of ideas continuously. This point is made clear in *Ssū.* 75, where it is argued: 'If you say that this will result in the non-performance of severe austerities and penances which are prescribed for heinous sins, we reply, not so, because of its constant performance till death.' This makes it quite clear that Japa and chanting must be repeated till they produce the desired effect. Even those who think that a single utterance of the name is enough to produce the desired effect, admit that such effect is not produced in all cases. They attribute this failure not to the inefficacy of the utterance, but to the presence of obstructions in the shape of Prārabdha and Nāmāparādha. The Nāmāparādhas (the ten faults in Japa) are mentioned in *Padp.* where Sanatkumāra instructs Nārada. It is summarized in the following verse: सन्निन्दासति नामवैभवकथा श्रीशेशयोर्भेदधीः अश्रद्धा·श्रुतिशास्त्रदेशिकगिरां नाम्न्यर्थवादभ्रमः । नामास्तीति निषिद्धवृत्तिविहितत्यागौ च धर्मान्तरैः साम्यं नामनि शंकरस्य च हरेः नामापरधा दश ॥ It is also said that these sins can be got over by continuous Japa alone for a long time—नामापराधयुक्तानां नामान्येव हरन्त्यघान् । अविश्रान्तप्रयुक्तानि तान्येवार्थाकराणि च । This is an admission of the necessity of repetition.

Yet another question of great importance is whether Japa should be done consciously and intelligently with full knowledge of the meaning of the Mantras and faith in their efficacy before it becomes spiritually effective. Some Bhaktas believe that even unintelligent and unconscious utterance of the name of God is sufficient for salvation. Vide *Bhāg.* VI. 2. 18. The story of Ajāmila is also quoted in support of this view. But the story of Ajāmila is given in illustration of another point altogether, mentioned in *Bhāg.* VI. 1. 19. This verse speaks of the efficacy of the remembrance of the Lord, and not of an unintelligent utterance of a mere word. The verse succeeding the one referred to also makes it clear that the story should be taken only as an illustration of this principle. What happened in his case is that he was reminded of God and His grace as a result of a casual utterance of the name of the Lord, and that it was the devotion engendered by this remembrance that saved him. It is also described later on in the same book how he performed intense Tapas and realized God. If a casual utterance could have saved him, there would have been no necessity for his subsequent spiritual practices noted in *Bhāg.* VI. 2. 40—44. The purpose of the story is again given in the concluding verse of the same chapter, where it is stated that it is meant to show what an efficacy Japa with proper faith must have, if mere utterance, like that of Ajāmila, has so much power! It is only a Purāṇic emphasis on the efficacy of the repetition and remembrance of God's name. The story of Ajāmila comes in the *Skp.* also in a slightly varied form. There also it is made clear that it was the Bhakti that resulted from remembrance of the Lord that saved him. इत्युक्त्वा भगवद्भक्तिं आलम्ब्यात्मानमात्मनि । ततः सायुज्यपदवीं लेभे तन्नामकीर्तनात् ।

We shall now consider the question whether knowledge of the texts used for Japa is necessary. Speaking about the efficacy of Praṇavajapa, *Chānd.* I. 1. 10, says: 'Both perform spiritual practices—he who knows and he who does not know. But knowledge and ignorance are different in their effects. That alone, which is performed with knowledge, faith, and meditation, becomes spiritually effective—तेनोभौ कुरुतः यश्चैतदेवं वेद यश्च न वेद । नाना तु विद्या चाविद्या च यदेव विद्यया करोति श्रद्धयोपनिषदा तदेव वीर्यवत्तरं भवति । It is again emphasized by Yāska in his Nirukta: स्थाणुरयं भारहारः किलाभूदधीत्य वेदं न विजानाति योऽर्थम् । योऽर्थज्ञः स सकलं भद्रमश्नुते स नाकमेति ज्ञानविधूतपाप्मा । He who repeats a Vedic Mantra without understanding its meaning is like an ass carrying a load of sandal wood; it knows only the weight of the load but does not enjoy the fragrance. The *Rgv.* verse—उत त्वः

पश्यन् न ददर्श वाचं उत त्वः शृण्वन् न शृणोत्येनाम् । उतो त्वस्मै तन्वं विसस्रे जायेवपत्य उशती सुवासा:—emphasizes the importance of the knowledge of the meaning of the Mantra. This Vedic idea again occurs in *S'vet*. IV. 8 : ऋचोऽक्षरे परमे व्योमन् यस्मिन् देवा अधि विश्वे निषेदु: । यस्तन्न वेद किमृचा करिष्यति य इत्तद्विदुस्त इमे समासते ॥ Of what avail are the Veda to him who does not know the indestructible highest Ethereal Being in whom the Gods and the Vedas reside ? Only those who know that are satisfied. मन्त्रार्थज्ञो जपन् जुह्वन् तथैवाध्यापयन् द्विज: । स्वर्गलोकमवाप्नोति नरकं तु विपर्यये ।—These words of Hārita also stress the necessity of knowing the meaning of the Mantra as it would otherwise lead to harmful results. Patañjali's *Sū.* तज्जपस्तदर्थभावनम् makes it clear that Japa must be accompanied by meditation on the meaning of the Mantra. This however should not be understood to mean that one should be aware of the grammatical or etymological meaning of all the words constituting a Mantra before one can be benefited. It is enough if the word enables him, by virtue of the psychological principle of association of ideas, to meditate on God and His blessed attributes. To any one the real meaning of a word is only what he understands by it. Thus even if one does not know the meaning of the Praṇava or the Gāyatrī as a scholar understands it, it is enough if one has the notion that these Mantras mean God and consequently one is reminded of Him when one repeats the Mantra. For it is the meditation that really matters and not the word that helps it. We may even go to the extent of saying that even if some Sanskrit or Arabic words really mean something obscene or indecent to a scholar, the devotee who sincerely uses them as a Mantra to remind himself of God is benefited by such use. It is on this basis that we can explain how people who repeat Sanskrit Mantras without understanding their grammatical or etymological significance are still benefited.

This leads us to another question, namely, whether certain special words have got any unusual efficacy as advocated by some teachers. There is, however, a school of thought which believes that the special sounds of certain Mantras create special kind of vibrations in the body and the atmosphere, which are of special help for spiritual practice. We are not sure of any such special efficacy. Any word which enables a man to keep the idea of God in his mind is a Mantra to him, although it may be only gibberish to another. It need not therefore be in any special language, like Sanskrit, Arabic, or Hebrew, but it may be in one's own mother tongue. Special Mantras which have been tested and found to be effective in actual use in the past and coming down to us charged with spiritual significance have also an appeal to the mind of the novice, who is thereby predisposed to have some faith in its efficacy. These are no mean advantages; but that supplies no data to conclude that particular words or particular languages have superior efficacy in themselves.

So long as one has not transcend the limitations of one's mind, one cannot meditate on the attributeless Absolute or Nirguṇabrahman. The mind can grasp only attributes, and God is the repository of all perfection to a Bhakta. The aspirant has therefore to meditate upon the blessed attributes of God. Nārada is very particular that only such of the qualities of God as we ourselves wish to acquire should be meditated upon. Really everything belongs to Him. If good belongs to Nature, evil also belongs to it, and to none else. But it is foolish to meditate upon evil. That is the reason why devotees like Rāmānuja emphasize that the Lord is the repository of all auspicious qualities, conveniently omitting as useless, the darker side of Nature. The S'āktas on the other hand delight in meditating on the darker side also. Nārada thinks this dangerous and therefore advocates only meditation on the blessed qualities. We have concrete examples of the danger of meditating on the darker side, in the degeneration of many Vaiṣṇava and S'ākta devotees who do not observe this sane rule. Again, it is made particularly clear that mere physical descriptions of the beauty of God's personal form does not aid one in the acquisition of the necessary virtues. It requires therefore to be emphasized that one should prefer singing and hearing about the moral and spiritual perfections of the Lord than of His physical beauty.

It is the mental S'ravaṇa and Kīrtana and Japa that can be continued even while one is engaged in ordinary activities of life; for it is these that will enable one to keep up the continuity of spiritual practices in spite of apparent breaks. This continuity is also provided for in our Smṛtis by making it incumbent on the twice-born to repeat various Mantras when he is attending to various daily duties of life such as eating and bathing, as well as social functions like marriage. By this device our scriptures convert every human activity into spiritual practice.

The word भगवान् is very great and significant. Bhaga in early Vedic literature meant 'dispenser', patron, or gracious lord as applied to the Gods, especially Savitṛ. As a qualifying word it was used to denote dignity, beauty, majesty, or excellence. In *Ṛgv*. I. 164. 40; VII. 41. 4; X. 60. 12; and *Athar*. II. 10. 2; V. 31. 11, the word Bhagavat is used in the sense 'blissful'. अथो वयं भगवन्तः स्यामः means 'may we be the repositories of good qualities'. In the Purāṇas the word came to denote the Supreme Divine Reality and as such a synonym of Brahman and Paramātman—वदन्ति तत् तत्त्वविदः तत्वं यद् ज्ञान मव्ययं। ब्रह्मेति परमात्मेति भगवानिति शब्यते—*Bhāg*. I. 2. 11. That the word Bhagavān is the term by which Brahman or Paramātman is referred to by devotees for the sake of worship is clear from *Vp*. VI. 5. 66-79: यत्तदव्यक्तमजरमचिन्त्यमजमव्ययम्। अनिर्देश्यमरूपं च पाणिपादाद्यसंयुतम्। विभु सर्वगतं नित्यं भूतयोनिरकारणम्। तद् ब्रह्म तत्परं धाम तद् ध्येयं मोक्षकांक्षिभिः। श्रुतिवाक्योदितं सूक्ष्मं तद्विष्णोः परमं पदम्। तदेव भगवद्वाच्यं स्वरूपं परमात्मनः। वाचको भगवच्छब्दस्तस्याद्यस्याक्षयात्मनः। एवं निगदितार्थस्य तत्तत्त्वं तस्य तत्वतः। ज्ञायते येन तज्ज्ञानं परमन्यत्त्रयीमयम्। अशब्दगोचरस्यापि तस्य वै ब्रह्मणो द्विज। पूजायां भगवच्छब्दः क्रियते ह्युपचारतः। शुद्धे महाविभूत्याख्ये परे ब्रह्मणि शब्यते। मैत्रेय भगवच्छब्दः सर्वकारणकारणे। सम्भर्तेति तथा भर्ता भकारोऽर्थद्वयान्वितः। नेता गमयिता स्रष्टा गकारार्थस्तथा मुने। ऐश्वर्यस्य समग्रस्य धर्मस्य यशसः श्रियः। ज्ञानवैराग्ययोश्चैव षण्णां भग इतीरणा। वसन्ति तत्र भूतानि भूतात्मन्यखिलात्मनि। स च भूतेष्वशेषेषु वकारार्थस्ततोऽव्ययः। एवमेष महान् शब्दो मत्रेय भगवानिति। परमब्रह्मभूतस्य वासु-

देवस्य नान्न्यगः। तत्र पूज्यपदार्थोक्तिपरिभाषासमन्वितः। शब्दोऽय नोपचारेण त्वन्यत्र ह्युपचारतः। उत्पत्तिं प्रलयं चैव भूतानमगतिं गतिम्। वेत्ति विद्यामविद्यां च स वाच्यो भगवानिति। ज्ञानशक्तिबलैश्वर्यवीर्यतेजांस्यशेषतः भगवच्छब्दवाच्यानि विना हेयैर्गुणादिभिः। "That which is imperceptible, undecaying, inconceivable, unborn, inexhaustible, indestructible; which has neither form, nor hands, nor feet, which is almighty, omnipresent, eternal; the cause of all things and without cause, permeating all, itself unpenetrated, and from which all things proceed, that is the object which the wise behold, that is Brahman, that is the Supreme State, that is the thing spoken of by the Vedas, the infinitely subtle, supreme condition of Viṣṇu. That Essence of the Supreme is defined by the term Bhagavat; the word Bhagavat is the denotation of that primeval and eternal God; and he who fully understands the meaning of that expression is possessed of holy wisdom, the sum and substance of the three Vedas. The word Bhagavat is a convenient form to be used in the adoration of that Supreme Being, to whom no term is applicable; and therefore Bhagavat expresses that Supreme Spirit which is individual, almighty, and the cause of causes of all things. The syllable 'bha' implies the cherisher and supporter of the universe. By 'ga' is understood the leader, impeller, or creator. The dissyllabic 'bhaga' indicates the six properties—dominion, might, glory, splendour, wisdom and dispassion. The purport of the syllable 'va' is that elemental Spirit in which all beings exist, and which exists in all beings. And thus this great word Bhagāvan is the name of Vāsudeva, who is one with the Supreme Brahman, and of no one else. This word therefore, which is the general denomination of an adorable object, is not used in reference to the supreme in a general signification, but a special one. When applied to any other thing or person it is used in its customary or general import. In the latter case it may purport one who knows the origin and end and revolutions of beings and what is wisdom and what is ignorance. In the former it denotes wisdom, energy, power, domination, might, glory, without end and without defect." It is evident from this citation that primarily the word stands for the One Supreme Divinity whom S'rī Rāmānuja characterizes not only as the repository of the six divine perfections enumerated above, but also as endowed with the eight attributes mentioned in *Chānd.* III. 14. 2 and many others—अखिलहेयप्रत्यनीककल्याणैकतानस्वेतरसमस्तवस्तुविलक्षणानन्दज्ञानानन्दैकस्वरूप स्वाभाविकानवधिकातिशयज्ञानबलैश्वर्यवीर्यशक्तितेजःसौशील्यवात्सल्यमार्दवार्जवसौहार्दसाम्यकारुण्यमाधुर्यगाम्भीर्यौदार्यचातुर्यस्थैर्यधैर्यशौर्यपराक्रमसत्यकामसत्यसङ्कल्पकृतित्वकृतज्ञताद्यसङ्ख्येयकल्याणगुणौघमहार्णव etc., शरणागतिगद्य. God according to this conception is संयद्वाम—the repository of all Good qualities. The last verse from *Vp.* quoted above stresses this idea. Rāmānuja therefore styles Him as possessing Ubhayaliṅga (twofold marks)—freedom from imperfections and abundance of perfections. Such a description of God is extremely useful for the worshipper, for he approaches the Divine as an object of worship. So S'aṅkara also characterizes the Saguṇabrahma as endowed with these six perfections. Since the word भगवान् is most aptly used for the Supreme

Reality as the goal of worship, by secondary or figurative usage whoever is glorious and venerable, divine and adorable, is also addressed by this term. Hence the incarnations are also referred to as Bhagavān (*Vide Ssū.* 50) and we are asked to worship them. Rāmānuja extends the use of the word to the five manifestations of God called Para, Vyūha, Vibhava, Hārda, and Arcā and advises us to worship them. As for worship *Ysū.* I. 37 advocates meditation even on the heart of a man of realization. So human Gurus are also considered fit to be worshipped in the *Svet.* VI. 23 and especially in the Purāṇas and Āgamas. We may consider that the word 'Bhagvān' used in the *Sū.* may denote all these various objects of worship. But it is clear from *Sū.* 79 below that Nārada is of opinion that God alone is to be worshipped—a view strongly supported by Parāśara: आब्रह्मस्तम्बपर्यन्ताः जगदन्तर्व्यवस्थिताः । प्राणिनः कर्मजनितसंसारवशवर्तिनः । यतस्ततो न ते ध्याने ध्यानिनामुपकारकाः । अविद्यावशगाः सर्वे ते हि संसारगोचराः । पश्चादुद्भूतबोधास्ते ध्याने नवोपकारकाः । नैसर्गिको न वै बोधस्तेषामप्यन्यतोयतः ॥—No created being is an object of worship, because every creature down from Brahmā is within the region of rebirth, ignorance, and slavery to Karma. The implication behind such freedom in the choice of the Ideal of worship and at the same time restrictions laid down in respect thereof, seem to be that an aspirant must be meditating only on the divine perfections whatever may be his objects of worship—Avatāras or Symbols or God-men or Gurus. The choice of the word Bhagavān shows that to Nārada it is these qualities that matter and not the embodiments. But those who worship a human Guru should carefully exclude from thought all his limitation and imperfections due to Prārabdha and think only of his exalted spiritual states and divine excellences, as otherwise it may lead to spiritual loss and retrogression. They should always see God in the Guru and never his human failures.

Sutra 38. तु (but) in the *Sū*. shows that it is an answer to a possible objection, namely: when we know from actual experience that many of our independent efforts do not produce even worldly effects desired by us, unaided by outside help, how can we safely expect that spiritual Realization, which is so rare, can be had by personal endeavour alone? The answer is given in this and the following four aphorisms. Spiritual realization is primarily due to the Grace of God working through saints, but made available to us by our own effort.

[1] Great controversy has raged as to the relative importance of grace and self-effort in spiritual life. As a rule those who follow the path of knowledge are in favour of self-effort, while the followers of the path of devotion always advocate the necessity of grace. The latter have always felt grace of God at every step in their spiritual struggle. But even they agree that self-effort is also necessary for self-purification and for enabling grace to manifest itself and be effective. Sūtras 35-37 emphasize in what ways active and strenuous self-effort can be made to achieve the end. According to some Bhaktas even this self-effort is powerless as grace alone can give Realization. They say that self-effort is the result of grace which predisposes the heart to seek God. Several Vedic verses show that the Ṛṣis were familiar with the doctrine of grace. Vide *Ṛgv*. I. 156. 2; *Bṛh*. IV. 4. 24: *Kaṭh*. II. 22; *Muṇd*. III. 2. 3; *Śvet*. II. 6; V. 5; VI. 4, 11, 12; *Kauṣ*. III. 8; *Bsū*. II. 3. 41, 42; II. 1. 34; III. 4. 38; *Bg*. XVIII. 56, 58, 62; *Mbh*. XII. 340. 16, 17; XII. 337. 20 (These last two passages state that the revelation of God to man is the greatest of His boons to him, and that only he can see Nārayaṇa to whom He is gracious, and not he who relies on self-effort

The word मुख्यतः (primarily) deserves attention. Even though we agree with the words of *Bg.* VI. 43 that we

alone.) *Bhag*. II. 7. 42; III. 13. 49; VIII. 22. 16, 24; X. 80.6; etc. While insisting on the fact that grace alone can save man, the scriptures are also unanimous in declaring that the Lord has no partiality to his devotees, and that He showers his grace equally on all. In order to justify the fact that it is only a few who are actually benefited, the devotees fall back on the doctrine that even though the Lord's grace is equally available to all, through his own fault man does not take advantage of it. It is not the fault of the sun if one shutting up within a room does not get light; nor is it the fault of the fire if it warms only one who is near it. The sun does not remove the chilness of one away from it. One cannot level the charge that the wish-fulfilling celestial tree confers its bounty only upon those who approach it and ask for benefits. It is one's own Karma that enables one to secure divine grace. By making efforts in an improper direction man is deprived of divine grace; but when the obstacles on the path of grace are removed by fresh efforts in the right direction, he gets grace once again. Thus self-effort is still needed to remove the hindrances brought about by past deeds; but primarily it is the Lord's grace that saves and nothing else. The Bhakta's mind considers that even the pains and sufferings are messages from the Beloved and as such evidence of His grace. Just as the extreme school of Bhaktas would say that even self-effort is made possible only by the Lord's grace, the extreme school of Jñānins, on the other hand, would stress that grace is only a pious imagination of the emotional devotees. According to them, it is only the weak and mean-spirited that rely upon external help, throwing the burden of their own responsibilities on the shoulders of someone else. Man can make or mar himself without any external help, for he alone is the architect of his fortune. They say, no God can help anybody against himself; for, if it were otherwise, consistent with His gracious nature, God would have saved every sinner long ago. It would be small praise, if the omnipotence of God's grace could be thwarted by the frailities of man. *Vide*, Ātreya: *The Philosophy of Yogavāsiṣṭha*, pp. 126-133, T.P.H., Adyar. Saṅkara commenting on *Bsū.* II. 3. 41 emphasizes both—tad anugrāha-hetukenaiva vijñānena mokṣa-siddhir bhavitum arhati. Similarly Nārada too appears to have in view the necessity of cooperation between self-effort and divine grace. Saint Nammālvār is reported to have asked God why all men are not saved by His grace, and to have got the reply from the Lord that since man is endowed with a free will God would wait to see man's predeliction for Him. The saint, it is said, retorted that even this predeliction can be generated by the Lord Himself. After the Mahābhārata war Utaṅka met Srī Kṛṣṇa and took him to task for the huge may get a natural inclination towards, and taste for, a higher life as a result of our spiritual practices in a previous life, proper stimulus from outside is almost invariably necessary to stir up these latent tendencies. To many, this first spiritual awakening comes only through another perfected soul, a Guru. If we look at the history of various spiritual movements in the world, we see how every one of them was started under the soul-stirring spiritual inspiration of a man of realization, and how the spiritual

massacre, *Mbh*. XII. 53. When Kṛṣṇa defended himself by saying that he agreed to war only when he had found the utter impossibility of redeeming the Kauravas, Utaṅka retorted that as the Eternal Ruler of the hearts of men he could have even manipulated their minds. Kṛṣṇa replied that since they had their free will he could not coerce it and had to wait till of its own accord the predeliction for God evolved from it. 'The same all-merciful Being desires to call us to our origin, provided we have the happiness and wisdom not to flee from the arms of infinite goodness and mercy. . . . Though God designed in creating them to have them a free will by which they might choose between good and evil, He also resolved to create them in original justice that they might have reason to reproach themselves alone, if they forfeited eternal glory . . . Yes, my God, Thou art infinitely good. Thou only abandonest those who forsake Thee. Thou wouldst never withdraw Thy grace from us if we were not the first to flee from Thee and refuse Thee dominion of our hearts' —Francis de Sales : *Treatise on the Love of God*. Cf. also 'Ask and it shall be given you, seek and you shall find, knock and it shall be opened unto you' *Matthew*, VII. 7. Thus, although at first sight there is an irreconcilable opposition between the doctrine of self-effort, usually known as doctrine of free-will, and the doctrine of grace, writers on Bhakti everywhere have found no difficulty in reconciling both to their satisfaction. Some explain that the law of Karma is an aspect of grace, as the Omnipotent would otherwise be interfering with the individual's freedom; and He does not want to force the Jīva to do anything against its own likes and dislikes. Others say that grace is only one aspect of Karma; it is only right under the law of Karma, that good acts such as love of God and self-surrender must have their result, namely grace of God. So they treat grace as only an exception which proves the universality of the law of Karma. All accept both the doctrines and allow each its own sphere of influence.

fire in the organization is kept up by a succession of highly spiritual men. Even the Incaranations, prophets, and Messiahs had their first awakening from contact with such Gurus. Madhusūdanasarasvati takes Nārada's case as typical and gives the first place in spiritual life to the service of saints. The necessity for service of saints and sages is referred to in *Bg.* IV. 34, *Muṇd.* I. 2. 12 & 13; *Chānd.* IV. 9. 3, VI. 14. ; 2 and *Kath.* II. 8 & 9 and *Bhāg.* XI. 10. 5, also. It is this spiritual rebirth that is effected by the grace of a great soul, which makes one a Dvija or 'twice-born'. Manu goes to the extent of saying that such a Guru is superior even to one's natural father. Vide *Mnu.* II. 147 & 148.

One would do well therefore to be on the look out for a perfected soul and when one finds him to accept him as one's Guru and place oneself unreservedly under his influence and guidance. But it is quite possible for one to come under the spiritual influence of another without his being conscious of it and without any deliberate desire or intention on his part, nay, sometimes even in spite of his desire not to be so influenced. It is not seldom that we find that those who come to scoff remain to pray. This is due to the subtle influence which only the saints can exert on those who come in contact with them. Emerson speaks of this influence in his essay on 'Uses of Great Men' thus: 'It costs a beautiful person no exertion to paint her image on our eyes. It costs no more for the wise soul to convey his quality to other men . . . With the great our thoughts and manners become equally great. There needs but one wise man in a company and all are wise—so rapid is the contagion. . . . Great men are a collyrium to clear one's eyes of egotism. This is the key to the power of great men—their spirit diffuses itself.'

Bhāg. VIII. 5.32, V. 5. 2, and V. 12. 12 state that service at the feet of the great is the one means to final emancipation. In *Bhāg*. IV. 21. 39 Pṛthu exhorts his subjects to resort to the great souls, as by their worship alone the Lord is pleased. Bhagavān himself devotes an entire chapter (*Bhāg*. XI. 12) to describe the glories of such goodly company. Vide also *Bhāg*. XI. 2. 30; XI. 26. 31 & 32. The *Bṛhannāradīya purāṇa* IV. 33 & 37 says: Bhakti is born from contact with the devotees. Just as the sun dispels external darkness, the devotees dispel internal ignorance by their advice and teachings. The various steps by which this contact with the great souls leads to the highest Bhakti are stated in the *Bhaktirasāyana* I. 32 to 34. Association with holy men, leads to Bhakti through S'radhā or faith. The same is corroborated by Kapila in *Bhāg*. III 25. 25 to 27. Even the man who is prone to doubt comes to believe in the possibility and practicability of realization by coming face to face with a living embodiment of the scriptural teachings. Faith is forced upon even a sceptic. To sum up, holy company helps a man to free himself from temptations, gives him opportunities for hearing and learning about spiritual realities, creates faith even in a sceptic mind, and sustains one in all efforts directed towards realization.

The Siddha does not stand in need of anything for himself, because he has attained the highest that can be attained. He need not worry himself with the fate of others. But still his heart bleeds for his less fortunate brethren struggling in the ocean of Saṁsāra. It is indeed gracious on his part to undertake various activities merely for the good of the world. Often we see that these selfless souls are so very anxious to communicate the results of their realizations to others, that they actually go about in search of deserving disciples and help them in various ways to attain the same realization ; but people are not so anxious to come to them ! See *Tait.* I. 4. 2 and lives of Jesus, Buddha, Mohammed, and Rāmakṛṣṇa.

And who are these great souls ? 'I count him a great man', says Emerson, 'who inhabits a higher sphere of thought into which other men rise with labour and difficulty. He is great who is what he is from nature and who never reminds us of others.' 'Him I call a Mahātmā whose heart bleeds for the poor,' says Swāmi Vivekānanda. *Bg.* II. 55-72 ; XII. 13-20. *Bhāg.* III. 25. 21-24 ; V. 5. 2-3 ; XI. 2. 45-55 ; XI. 10. 5-7 ; XI. 11. 29-33 ; XI. 26. 27 ; *Vivekacūḍāmaṇi* 33, 37 & 38 ; and many other passages describe the nature of the Sādhus whom one may safely resort to for spiritual help. Swāmi Vivekānanda says that one should be very careful in one's choice of a Guru. He gives the qualifications of a proper Guru in his *Address on Bhakti-yoga* as sinlessness, unselfish, and knowing the spirit of the scriptures. Vedāntadeśika has beautifully summarized the qualifications of a proper Guru and the reason for worshipping him in his *Nyāsaviṁśati* in two beautiful verses thus : सिद्धं सत्सम्प्रदाये स्थिरधियमनघं श्रोत्रियं ब्रह्मनिष्ठं सत्वस्थं सत्यवाचं समयनियतया साधुवृत्त्या समेतम् । दम्भासूयादिमुक्तं जितविषयगणं दीर्घबन्धुं दयालुं स्खालित्ये शासितारं स्वपरहितपरं देशिकं भूष्णुरीप्सेत ॥ अज्ञानध्वान्तरोधादघपरिहरणादात्मसाम्यावहत्वात् जन्मप्रध्वंसिजन्मप्रदगरिमतया दिव्यदृष्टिप्रभावात् । निष्प्रत्यूहानृशंस्यादनियतरसतया नित्यशेषित्वयोगादाचार्यः सद्भिरप्रत्युपकरणधिया देववत् स्यादुपास्यः See also *Advayatārakopaniṣad* : आचार्यो वेदसम्पन्नो विष्णुभक्तो विमत्सरः । योगज्ञो योगनिष्ठश्च सदा योगात्मकः शुचिः । गुरुभक्तिसमायुक्तः पुरुषज्ञो विशेषतः ॥

The particle वा in the *Sū*. shows that the help that we receive from perfected souls is in the last analysis due only to the grace of God Himself. It is not meant to make God's grace an alternative to the grace of saints. For the devotees, who have surrendered themselves completely to the Lord, have no will of their own. They are but the instruments made use of by the Divine will to carry out Its own inscrutable purposes, which include the saving of deserving souls. Therefore what appears to be due to the grace of devotees may more properly be considered as due to the grace of God himself. Only two alternative explanations are given of the same phenomenon, the latter of which is truer than the first. This is made clear in the next three Sūtras.

(भगवत्कृपालेशः) God's mercy is infinite and is perpetually flowing towards mankind, and this help rendered to deserving souls through devotees, is only one of the many ways in which His grace manifests itself. God's grace manifests itself in various other ways also, according to Hindu theists. For instance, the very act of creation, at the beginning of a cycle, is for giving an opportunity to Jivas to struggle again to attain Him. Destruction of the world, at the end of the cycle, is to save them from themselves by depriving them, temporarily, of their instruments of doing evil, and to give them some rest from the incessant struggle in Saṁsāra. Promulgation of knowledge through the Veda, revealed to Brahma and other Ṛṣis, is to enable the Jivas to know and adopt the proper methods of realizing Him. He Himself comes down and takes human shape for teaching Dharma and for providing a realizable ideal for the Jivas, destroying obstacles in their way and enabling them to enjoy His company. The provision made in the divine scheme for cancellation of all previous Karmas as a result of continuous meditation is also another aspect of His grace. Gift of Buddhiyoga to those who meditate upon Him, gift of fruits even for unintentional good acts, help in difficulties, correction when the Bhakta gets conceited, making Himself available to man in various forms such as images, Pratikas, Vibhūtis, and the like, and mixing with persons who are very inferior to Him during His Incarnation, are other aspects of the grace described in devotional literature. The very inexorable law of Karma is only due to his grace; for He thereby gives ample freedom to individuals to work out their own salvation as they think best without external interference. In fact all the troubles and tribulations of Saṁsāra are meant only to wean those who go astray, from their evil ways, just as a loving parent puts obstacles in the way of his children ruining themselves. Thus, to the devotional mind every thing that happens is due to His infinite grace, and is meant only to bring the Jivas nearer and nearer to Him. The most important manifestation of His grace, however, is that inner urge for perfection that is present in every one of us, which makes us discontented with everything worldly and thus leads us higher and higher, step by step, until we reach the goal in the long run.

That after all it is the Lord's grace that saves us is clear from the life of many great Bhaktas like the Avadhūta described in *Bhāg.* IX. 7. 32. 35. The stimulus may be supplied not only by another human personality, but also by any phenomenon of nature. It is a universal law of nature that a deserving soul shall not suffer for want of help. 'As soon as the field is ready the seed must come. As soon as the soul wants religion, the transmitter of religious force must come. The seeking sinner meets the seeking saviour. When the power that attracts in the receiving soul is full and ripe, the power which answers to the attraction must come.' On the other hand, unless one is sufficiently ready, no power on earth can help one. It is not sufficient if the seed alone is good, the field also must be well-ploughed and manured before a good crop can be raised. Christ's parable of the sower (*Matt.* XIII. 3-9) and the saying 'Neither cast ye your pearls before swine (*Luke,* VII. 6)' illustrate this point. 'The speaker of religion must be wonderful', says *Kaṭh.* II. 7, 'so must the hearer be.' The seed need not come always in the form of a formal initiation from the teacher. The real teacher of everyone is his own Higher Self or

God (Cf. *Bhāg*. XI. 7. 20 ; 19. 43 :—आत्मनो गुरुरात्मैव पुरुषस्य विशेषतः । यत् प्रत्यक्षानुमानाभ्यां श्रेयोऽसावनुविन्दते । and also बन्धुर्गुरुरहं सखे । and *Bg*. VI. 5, उद्धरेदात्मनात्मानं नात्मानमवसादयेत्) The ordinary human teachers are only different conduit pipes carrying the spiritual inspiration from the same source which is God. If the disciple has made himself fit by self-effort, the Higher Self, always working for his betterment from inside, can save him even without the help of an external Guru or even with an inferior Guru. Śri Rāmakṛṣṇa remarks, 'God alone is the guide and Guru of the Universe. He who can himself approach God with sincerity, earnest prayer, and deep longing, needs no Guru. But such deep yearning of the soul is very rare ; hence the necessity for a Guru. When going to a strange country, one must abide by the directions of the guide who knowns the way. The broom, though a contemptible thing, removes the dust and dirt of the street.' Every human being who has helped us spiritually must be paid divine honours, see *Bhāg*. XI. 17. 27 ; XI. 18. 39 ; & XI. 27. 9, Manu also says : अल्पं वा बहु वा यस्य श्रुतस्योपकरोति यः । तमपीह गुरुं विद्यात् श्रुतोपक्रियया तया—II. 149. Even though one may get God's help through an inferior channel it is not always safe to worship such imperfect teachers as mere men forgetting the Divine in them. There is no danger in completely surrendering oneself to a Guru who is a man of perfect God-realization and implicitly obeying him. Such complete surrender to lesser teachers may not be always advisable. Their instructions and commands are better tested in the light of the teachings of the prophets, sages, and incarnations of the past, and time-old scriptures before they are accepted *in toto*. If there is conflict between the two it would be better to discuss the entire matter with the spiritual guide himself until one is convinced of the correctness of his instructions. So the *Yogakuṇḍalyupaniṣad*, 2. 2, says: शास्त्रं विनापि सम्बोद्धुं गुरवोऽपि न शक्नुयुः—Even the teachers cannot instruct perfectly without the help of the scripture. Since the suitableness of the Guru is to be understood by the disciple, the latter is the Guru of the Guru himself, says another Upaniṣad—गुरोर्योग्यत्वविज्ञाता त्वं ततोऽसि गुरोर्गुरुः । If even after such discussion with a teacher one feels convinced that the latter's directions are against the scriptures or Dharma as one has understood it, it is good they are not followed till one is convinced by further light being thrown on the problem. In such difficult situations one had better surrender to one's own conscience. Though Arjuna, like a true disciple, surrendered himself to S'rī Kṛṣṇa and was willing to be guided by him (*Bg*. II. 7), Kṛṣṇa after discussing the entire matter exhorts him (*Ib*. XVIII. 62) to use his own reason and discretion and follow him only if his teachings were found satisfactory after critical examination. The implicit obedience that is usually expected of a disciple is not to the human person through whom God helps, but God Himself, equally present in both, and Who alone is the real Teacher. If there is discrepancy it would be better to follow the Divine than the human Guru. But in spite of such freedom in thought and action the disciple is to serve the human Guru with all respect and love. Rāmānuja's repudiation of Yādavaprakās'a's interpretation of

Vedānta and Madhva's rejection of Acyutaprekṣa are classical examples which cannot otherwise be justified. Again in one's great admiration for one's Guru one should not imitate him in every respect. The true Guru instructs: Follow only the good deeds of ours—यान्यस्माकं सुचरितानि तानि सेवितव्यानि नो इतराणि, *Tait.* I. 11. 2. The Guru and the disciple being on different levels of spiritual evolution, what suits the former may not be safe or possible for the latter; hence the latter is only to do what the former allows and commands him to do. See how beautifully this point is explained by Śuka to Parikṣit in *Bhāg.* X. 33. 30—38. Manu also makes the point clear when he says, न चैवास्यानुकुर्वीत गतिभाषितचेष्टितम्। These warnings are absolutely necessary as many disciples are likely to copy blindly every action and behaviour of their teachers without thinking the least whether such copying would injure or benefit them. Again, since Paramātman alone is the true Guru, the human medium through which the Divine help reaches a spiritual aspirant may belong to any caste, sex, or age. Śaṅkara's *Manīṣāpañcaka* makes this point crystal clear—जाग्रत्स्वप्नसुषुप्तिषु स्फुटतरा या संविदुज्जृम्भते या ब्रह्मादिपिपीलिकान्ततनुषु प्रोता जगत्साक्षिणी। सैवाहं न च दृश्यवस्त्विति दृढप्रज्ञास्ति यस्यापि चेच्चण्डालोऽस्तु स तु द्विजोऽस्तु गुरुरित्येषा मनीषा मम॥ He who has the firm realization that his Self is the pure Consciousness which permeates all creation, he is my Guru whether he be a Brāhmaṇa or a Caṇḍāla—this is my conviction. Sages are born, says *Bhāradvāja-pariśiṣṭa* II. 44, in all wombs; one should not search for the caste, clan, and the rest regarding these souls who have realized the Lord of their souls—किमप्यत्राभिजायन्ते योगिनः सर्वयोनिषु । प्रत्यक्षितात्मनाथानां नैषां चिन्त्यं कुलादिकम् । Manu also says: श्रद्दधानः शुभां विद्यामाददीतावरादपि । *Vide*, *Mnu*. II. 238-241. Examples also are not wanting. The Avadhūta Dattātreya is reported to have accepted a fowler and Piṅgalā, the prostitute, as Upagurus (Cf., *Bhāg*. XI. 7. 34). The life of Rāmānuja reveals how eager he was to get initiation into the holy word from Kāñcipūrṇa, and how he honoured as divine incarnations Nammālvār, Tiruppāṇālvār, and others. Again as the real Guru is God Himself and as He works through various agencies, there is no harm in taking instructions from various teachers in so far as they are helpful and not mutually conflicting. S'rī Rāmānuja learned Vedānta from Yādavaprakās'a, received Pañcasaṁskāras and Dvaya from Mahāpūrṇa, Tirumantra from Goṣṭhipūrṇa, Caramopāya from Araiyār, *Tiruvaymozhi* from Mālādhara, and Rāmāyaṇa from S'rī S'aila-purṇa; and after all he considered himself as the disciple of Yāmunācārya. S'rī Rāmakṛṣṇa also had different teachers who taught him different spiritual disciplines; but he considered the Divine Mother as his all in all. It is explicitly stated: नैकस्मात् गुरोर्ज्ञानं सुस्थिरं स्यात् सुपुष्कलम् *Bhag*. XI. 9. 31. Thus in our anxiety to be true to one Guru we should guard ourselves from falling into the fanaticism of discarding helpful light from other sources or of showing disrespect to other spiritual personalities; for all really great spiritual men belong to one authority and derive their power from one Divine Source. Disrespect to any one teacher is therefore disrespect to God Himself.

Sutra 39 administers a warning to the unwary and the lazy not to be misled by choosing an unsuitable spiritual guide to whose grace they are likely to leave everything. Such a danger is possible because inferior aspirants are often unwilling to undertake strenuous spiritual practices by themselves. And men of true spiritual enlightenment are very rare, दुर्लभ as the *Sū.* puts it. It is only one in a thousand, says *Bg.* VII. 3, that struggles for spiritual realization, and even among such aspirants only one in a thousand realizes the Divine in truth. Apart from the paucity of great souls, other circumstances like distance, illness, poverty, and opposition of relatives and friends add to the difficulty of approaching a perfect guide. Besides there is yet another difficulty: just as there is the chance of being duped by a false spiritual guide, so also there is the likelihood of failing to recognize a really worthy spiritual guide even after coming into contact with him ; for great souls generally hide their greatness ; and unless one has earned by one's own effort and sincerity the fitness to receive their grace it will be impossible to recognize them. The behaviour of such perfect souls may even repel the careless aspirant by its queerness, as stated in *Sū.* 6 and *Bhāg.* XI. 2. 40 ; XI. 18. 29 as well as *Bsū.* III. 4. 50. It is in view of these obstacles that contact with perfectly illumined souls is said to accrue only from the religious merit earned by strenuous endeavour in the present life or previous ones. This is hinted in *Bg.* VII. 28 and *Kaṭh.* III. 14. The lazy and indolent have therefore no chance ; for contact with perfect souls is the outcome of earnest spiritual struggle. अगम्य in the text implies the subtle and incomprehensible nature of the contact with a perfect Guru. It is only seldom that a perfect Guru accepts someone as a disciple and gives him spiritual training. In many cases a true sense of humility would not allow him to assume the role of a teacher, unless there is the Command from God to do such work. The influence that they shed on the disciple when he is accepted is subtle and incomprehensible whether the latter may know it or not. 'It costs a beautiful person no exertion to paint his image on our eyes. It costs no more for the wise soul to convey his quality to other men. With the great, others' thoughts and manners become equally great. There needs but one wise man in a company and all are wise. Great men are a collyrium to clear one's eyes of egotism ; this is the key to the power of great men, their power diffuses itself '. This unconscious and unintentional conversion of one mind by another is something mysterious. Men are surprised when an extremely wicked man is suddenly transformed into a good citizen for no apparent reason. Such happenings result from this subtle influence of saints. Sometimes this influence is transmitted through their literature. The spiritual waves set up by a saintly soul often travel along distances of time and space to receive a proper centre where they are amplified. There are also instances of people being influenced by a look or touch of perfect souls. The textual word अमोघ again suggests that it is unerring and infallible in effect. Once we come into contact with a saint as a result of our past merits, our minds are irresistibly pulled higher and higher, by something like a spiritual gravitation, towards the centre of all attraction, namely, God. Though this influence may not be consciously felt in the beginning, one subjected to it cannot help becoming a devotee of the Lord in the long run. Thus the effect of saintly contact is unerring even if the transformation brought about in the aspirant is slow and gradual.

Sutra 40 suggests that one need not, however, despair of getting a proper Guru. The guiding Power of Providence would take a genuine Guru to a proper spiritual aspirant. History has recorded several such incidents in which without any previous knowledge a great Guru has favoured a fit disciple. Even if the disciple is not able to recognize the worth of the Guru, the latter, who is an instrument and abode of God, easily finds out and favours the disciple. It is truly the grace of God that brings this about. It is this Power of the Lord to liberate bound souls that is described as Vidyāmāyā or Gurus'akti. 'Some designate this Divine Power as the liberating wisdom. Others, O Mother, as the Ether, others as Bliss, others as Māyā, and yet others as the Universe—but we consider Thee as the infinite Divine mercy taking shape as Guru'—विद्यां परां कतिचिदम्बरमम्ब केचित् आनन्दमेव कतिचित् कतिचिच्च मायाम् । त्वां विश्वमाहुरपरे वयमामनाम साक्षादपारकरुणां गुरुमूर्तिमेव ॥ *Ambāstuti*, 27. It is thus this Divine Power in the aspirant that makes him restless and sincerely active in his search for a Guru. It is again the same Divine Power that makes the saint restless to work for the liberation of others. Thus the

Guru and the disciple are brought together by the Divine behind in a mysterious way when the time is ripe.

Sutra 41. We are all one in God, being His diverse manifestations. He is in the living and non-living matter, in saint and sinner. He is not partial to anybody; His grace is available to all without any distinction. It is His grace that works at the heart of all when the urge for higher and higher perfection is felt. It is the wrong movement on the part of man that obstructs grace working to its logical end. Spiritual growth becomes natural and easy when man's aspiration for perfection is steady and powerful and when he willingly surrenders his whole being to the inflow of grace. Man intrudes in and impedes the path of grace by his own ignorance and inadvertence. The causes that obstruct grace are the same as नामापराध (dishonouring Divine Name) described in Vaiṣṇava texts and ज्ञानानुत्पत्तिकारण (hindrances to the dawn of Knowledge) listed in *Sūtasaṁhitā* III. 6.

Sutra 42. तत् (that) in the *Sū*. refers to renunciation and loving service described in *Sū*. 35-37, as well as the grace of God and godmen that inevitably manifests itself in their wake. Divine grace is already with us; we have only to allow its free play in us by surrendering ourselves to the Divine completely; it will then guide us to our natural birth-right with the aid of external stimulus, or without it. External helps are only secondary; they may not work unless the primary condition of an unconditional and sincere acceptance of the guiding Divine Voice is fully recognized, and acted up to, by a complete surrender of individuality and egoistic impulses. This abdication of the conditioned self or ego is what is to be effected by spiritual practices. This is what is called Prapatti or Nyāsayoga, which when once affected the whole of Nature will supply the external help and stimulus; for Nature is not in reality different from God to whose grace the aspirant has surrendered himself. By strenuously applying oneself to the practice of the instructions in *Sūs.* 35-42 one is sure to get divine help and inspiration. Spiritual impulse, as from a Guru, comes to such a seeker from the whole Nature, which he sees instinct with God, the truest and best Guru. The best aspirant is of the type of the Avadhūta described in *Bhāg.* XI. 8.9.

Sutra 43. God being in all creatures and everything, it must be conceded that wicked and evil persons as well as objects that excite sordid passions also are not apart from God. But one should not resort to such persons and objects. Though it is true that God dwells in every place, says Śrī Rāmakṛṣṇa, yet every place is not fit to be visited by a man. One kind of water may be used for washing our feet, another for ablution, and a third for drinking, while there are still others unfit even to be touched. The Deity Nārāyaṇa broods over the water, but every kind of water is not fit for drinking. An aspirant cannot afford to be careless about his surroundings and associations. दृष्टिं ज्ञानमयीं कृत्वा पश्येत् ब्रह्ममयं जगत्—acquiring the sight of realization one should see the whole world as God alone, says the Upaniṣad. But before realization, that is, while one is still an aspirant in the early stages of spiritual practice, one should not trust oneself in the midst of temptations, taking shelter under the trite maxim 'all is Brahman'. Every object and event that stimulates lower passions must be carefully shunned. Only when one finds it unavoidable, one may summon one's resources to visualize God even at the heart of evil. For example, a man or woman, engaged in spiritual practices when compelled, in the course of performing unavoidable duty amidst the opposite sex, may ward off undesirable thoughts by trying to see in the other sex embodiments of the Divine. The Tantric scriptures advise them to see S'iva or Rāma in all males and Pārvati or Sitā in all females. The Mahopaniṣad says: आदौ शमदमदमप्रायैः गुणैः शिष्यं विशोधयेत्। पश्चात्सर्वमिदं ब्रह्म शुद्धस्त्वमिति बोधयेत्॥ अज्ञस्यार्धप्रबुद्धस्य सर्वं ब्रह्मेति यो वदेत्। महानरकजालेषु स तेन विनियोजितः॥ प्रबुद्धबुद्धेः प्रक्षीणभोगेच्छस्य निराशिषः। नास्त्यविद्यामलमिति प्राज्ञस्तूपदिशेद्गुरुः॥ First the teacher will test the disciple and see that he has absolute moral purity: then only the instruction that the 'Divine Reality is everything' should be imparted. If this doctrine is taught to an ignorant or half-awakened man he is only sent to horrible hell. One who is intellectually awakened and free from cravings for pleasures and has no anxiety for future, is alone fit to be told the truth that there is in reality not a second either in the shape of evil or Nescience.

Sutra 44. *Bg*. II. 62, 63 and *Bhāg*. XI. 14. 27-30 form an apt commentary to this *Sū*. स्मृतिभ्रंश refers to forgetfulness of one's object in life as well as one's duty. Essentially it is the same as Pramāda condemned in the *Sanatsujātīya* (*Mbh*. VI. 40-5). S'aṅkara says:

विषयाभिमुखं दृष्ट्वा विद्वांसमपि विस्मृतिः। विक्षेपयति धीदोषैः योषा जारमिव प्रियम्।—Oblivion distracts even a learned man through the wrong intellectual propensities as a woman does her dear paramour, whenever he hankers for sense pleasures, *Vivekacūdāmaṇi*, 323; also, लक्ष्यच्युतं चेद्यदि चित्तमीषद्बहिर्मुखं सन्निपतेत्ततस्ततः। प्रमादतः प्रच्युतकेलिकन्दुकः सोपानपङ्क्तौ पतितो यथातथा। If, through want of vigilance, the mind deviates an iota from its aim by extravertion, then like a ball dropped on the first rung of the stairs falls down and down, *ib.* 325. बुद्धिनाश or loss of discrimination refers to the inability to distinguish between truth and falsehood, good and bad, and the rest. Some texts read सर्वनाश also, which means total ruin, *Vide Bg.* XVI. 21.

Sutra 45. In the beginning propensities for lust, anger, and the like may be easily checked; but once agitated into a storm through evil company, they become like a veritable ocean hard to be crossed. Just as a father who has in mind the future greatness of his children calls them back when they run away into the unprotected open in all directions, so also an aspirant should from the beginning always keep the senses under the control of the intellect and remain calm and contented. —इन्द्रियाणि प्रमाथीनि बुध्या संयम्य यत्नतः। सर्वतो निष्पतिष्णूनि पिता बालानिवात्मजान्। तानि सर्वाणि सन्धाय मनःषष्ठानि मेधया। आत्मतृप्त इवासीत बहुचिन्त्यमाचिन्तयन्। *Mbh.* XII.

Sutra 46. In this and the immediately following four aphorisms Nārada points out that all spiritual practices dealt with in the eight aphorisms just preceding must inevitably lead to love of God before they can confer Release. *S'sū*. 98 points out that the cycle of transmigration and all evil thereof are due to want of Bhakti and not lack of Jñāna, संसृतिरेषामभक्तिः स्यात्, नाज्ञानात् कारणासिद्धेः। *Adhr*. says: भक्तिर्जनित्री ज्ञानस्य भक्तिर्मोक्षप्रदायिनी। भक्तिहीनेन यत् किञ्चित् कृतं सर्वमसत्समम्। VI. 7. 67, तस्मात् त्वद्भक्तिहीनानां कल्पकोटिशतैरपि। न मुक्तिशङ्कां विज्ञानशङ्का नैव सुखं तथा। I. 7. 41. Bhakti is the parent of knowledge and liberation; devoid of devotion everything done is futile; and one who has no devotion cannot hope for happiness even after ages. In the present Book of Aphorisms Jñāna and Dharma also are pressed to serve as auxiliaries to Bhakti. On a careful study of the various schools of spiritual discipline we find a great similiarity in the exercises prescribed; the difference is only in the emphasis laid on certain aspects. There can be really no question of superiority or inferiority; nor can there be any question of priority or posteriority in respect of the practices like Jñāna, Bhakti, and Karma. Superiority or inferiority, if at all admissible, will rest entirely on the particular seekers and the temperament, capacity, and opportunities they possess. Various writers on Bhakti prescribe different acts and processes such as Japā, Pūjā, Kīrtana, Praṇāma, and the like, to take the aspirant to the goal. On the strength of *S'sū*. 62 and similar other authorities and by one's own reasoning one may say that each aspirant is free to take up such of these acts and methods as would suit his taste and convenience. The various practices cannot be divided into water-tight compartments; for each one shades off into the other. Each one may lead to the goal, because each one, developed to the fullest extent, epitomizes all the rest. For an exhaustive list of such spiritual practices one may look up in *Bhāg*. XI. 19. 20-24 ; XI. 3. 21-31 ; *Bg*. IX and XII ; *Adhr*. III. 9. 47-49 : etc. In *Śrī Caitanyacaritāmṛta* II. 18, Śrī Caitanya expounds to Rāmānanda the following steps : 1. स्वधर्माचरण (*Vp*. III, 8. 9.) 2. कृष्णार्पण (*Bg*. IX. 27) ; 3. स्वधर्मत्याग (*Bg*. XVIII. 66 and *Bhāg*. XI. 11. 32) ; 4. ज्ञानमिश्रभक्ति (*Bg*. XVIII. 54) ; 5. ज्ञानशून्यभक्ति (*Bhāg*. X. 14. 3) ; 6. प्रेमभक्ति *Padyāvalī* नानोपचारकृतपूजनमार्त्तबन्धोः प्रेम्णैव भक्तहृदयं सुखविद्रुतं स्यात । यावत् क्षुदस्ति जठरे जरठा पिपासा तावत सुखाय भवते ननु भक्ष्यपेये ॥ ; 7. दास्यप्रेम (*Bhāg*. IX. 5. 16) ; 8. सख्यप्रेम (*Bhāg*. X. 12. 11) ; 9. वात्सल्यप्रेम (*Bhāg*. X. 8. 46) ; 10. कान्ताभाव (*Bhāg*. X. 47. 60, X. 32. 2, X. 32. 22, etc.) ; 11. राधाप्रेम (*Bhāg*. X. 30. 28, etc). Performance of one's duties as dedication to the Lord, dedication of actions and their results to God, giving up of one's duties, love mixed with knowledge, love devoid of knowledge, Divine Love, devotion of a servant to the master, love of a parent to the child, devotion of a wife to her husband, and devotion of a mistress to her paramour—these are the divisions according to this school. Another classification is : सतां कृपा महत्सेवा श्रद्धा गुरुपदाश्रयः । भजनेषु स्पृहा भक्तिरनर्थापगमस्ततः ॥ निष्ठारुचिरथासक्ती रतिः प्रेमाथ दर्शनम् । हरेर्माधुर्यानुभव इत्यर्थाश्चतुर्दश ॥ The steps to realization according to *Bhaktirasāyana*, 32-34, are प्रथमं महतां सेवा तद्दयापात्रता ततः । श्रद्धाथ तेषां धर्मेषु ततो हरिगुणश्रुतिः ॥ ततो रत्यङ्कुरोत्पत्तिः स्वरूपाधिगतिस्ततः । प्रेमवृद्धिः परानन्दे तस्याथ स्फुरणं ततः ॥ भगवद्धर्मनिष्ठातः स्वस्मिंस्तद्गुणशालिता । प्रेम्णोऽथ

परमा काष्ठेत्युदिता भक्तिभूमिका: । *Bhaktirasāmṛtasindhu* gives various stages consisting of श्रद्धा, सङ्ग, भजनक्रिया, अनर्थनिवृत्ति, निष्ठारुचि, आसक्ति, भाव, and प्रेम । Besides these classifications we also meet in Bengal Vaiṣṇavism पूर्वराग, मिलन, सम्भोग, विरह, and भावसम्मिलन. The *Yogavāsiṣṭha* as well as *Varāha Upd.* 4. 1-16 describe the seven steps or Bhūmikās as शुभेछा, विचारणा, तनुमानसी, सत्वापत्ति, असंसक्ति, पदार्थभावना, and तुरीयगा—*i.e.* (*a*) consciousness of one's ignorance and desire to know the truth through scripture and holy company, having shunned worldly life, (*b*) virtuous life following from the distaste for sensuous life and right endeavour, (*c*) lightness of mind resulting from dispassion, (*d*) ability to abide in the true self, (*e*) detachment from the material world, (*f*) the realization that wordly objects are ephemeral and unreal, (*g*) the final stage in which all distinctions are negated in the one experience of Identity (*Yogv.* III. 118. 3-16). Vasiṣṭha gives two other classifications in VI. 120 1-8 and VI. 126. 4-13. The Jain scriptures point out fourteen stages or Guṇasthānas between the life of an ordinary man and the perfected Kevalin. In the Mahāyāna Buddhism ten Pāramitas are mentioned which are to be gone through before one attains the state of a Bodhisattva. Saint Augustine describes seven steps to realization : Fear of God, reverent study of the divine revelations, love of God and fellow-men, steadfast self-discipline, cleansing of the soul, enlightenment of the soul, and bliss. St. Teresa also speaks of the seven steps : Recollection, quiet, union, ecstasy, rapture, the pain of God, and ritual marriage. The three stages of spiritual endeavour chalked out by the Neo-platonists are purgation, illumination, and ecstasy. The mystic Richard of St. Victor speaks of the dilation of the mind, elevation of the mind, and ecstasy. Another mystic of Spain, Jacopone da Todi, divides the spiritual path into self-conquest, loving intuition, and union. Bearing in mind all these divisions of the spiritual way devised by various sects of spiritual seekers we shall now see what Nārada has to offer. He begins with the giving up of all contact with objects of senses such as are likely to inflame passions and allure the aspirant away from his path, and through twelve stages he takes the seeker up to the love of God which alone is the cure for bondage and suffering.

Just as a man hankering after health has to be away from unsuitable food, surroundings, and activities, so the seeker after perfection and liberation must place himself in a situation in which he is not exposed to temptations and injurious influences. Again just as one desiring a strong and agile body has to attend a gymnasium and exercise his body under expert guidance, so also a genuine aspirant after spirituality shall have to resort to a perfect spiritual guide and endeavour in the light of his instructions and example, with reverence for him and readiness to serve him. A disciple, no sooner he comes into contact with a perfect soul, than will be willing to commit everything he possesses to the service of the Guru, and thus free himself from the sense of proprietorship and possession. Christ advised his disciples to go and sell all they possessed, give to the poor, and follow him. To swim across the ocean of transmigration one would find it much easy with as few encumbrances as possible. The weight of possession and clinging for it can easily be got rid of by surrendering oneself and one's possessions to the Guru and devoting all one's effects for his service. The Guru, on his part, shall consider all property as belonging to God and would spend all, without any self-interest, in the service of God, His devotees, and the suffering creation. An enthusiastic aspirant may thus cut himself away from belongings and domestic bondages, feeling like Thoreau that all property is theft, or like Tolstoy that riches are smeared with the blood of the poor. Such an aspirant will look upon the whole creation as one family and will be contented with the least creature comforts compatible with the spiritual practices he has to do. The service of the Guru (महानुभावसेवा) is very important for the attainment of wisdom. यथा खनन् खनित्रेण नरो वार्यधिगच्छति । तथा गुरुगतां विद्यां शुश्रूषुरधिगच्छति । Only one who serves the spiritual guide comes to possess the wisdom that is lived and taught by him, just as only he who digs with a spade gets water, *Mnu.* II. 218. महत्सेवां द्वारमाहुर्विमुक्तेः तमोद्वारं योषितां सङ्गिसङ्गम् । महान्तस्ते समचित्ताः प्रशान्ताः विमन्यवः सुहृदः साधवो ये ॥ ये वा मयीशे कृतसौहृदार्थाः जनेषु देहंभरवार्तिकेषु । गृहेषु जायात्मजरातिमत्सु न प्रीतियुक्ता यावदर्थाश्च लोके ॥ The portal to liberation lies through the service of great saints; the company of those who are given up to women leads to darkness. Who are the spiritually great? Those who are equanimous, calm, free from anger, friendly, and noble; who have dedicated their love and possessions to the Lord; who are not fond of selfish society, kinsmen, and home; and who are satisfied with least material things, *Bhāg*. V. 5. 2, 3. *Vide* also *Bg*. IV. 34.

Sutra 47. Freeing oneself of all distractions and bondages one has to meditate upon the blissful form of the Lord in one's own heart with utmost absorption. By such uninterrupted meditation in a secluded place for a long time the various complexes in the mind are removed and supreme detachment or Vairagya is attained (*Ysū*. I. 15, 16). The aspirant is no more subjected to egoistic impulses, and he becomes free from the effects of the Guṇas of Nature; he even transcends Sattva. Such a stage is called Paravairāgya. At this stage all desires vanish; for desires arise only as long as one is subjected to the effects of the Guṇas. The Bhakta has no care even for his personal needs; the Lord arranges for what is required for his life on earth (*Bg*. IX. 22) so that he need not have any worry on that score. (Cf. the words of Christ, *Matt*. VI. 24-34.) The lives of godmen like Sri Rāmakṛṣṇa show that they never were anxious about creature comforts, all their needs being fulfilled by providence.

Sutra 48. Karma-tyāga here has reference to all activities prompted by self-interest. When a person is once convinced of the divine promise (*Bg*. IX. 22) that the Lord Himself takes care of the devotee, he has no more need to undertake any work for his own sake. But life is not possible without some kind of activity, देहवान् नह्यकर्मकृत् *Bhāg*. VI. 1. 44 and *Bg*. III. 5; XVIII. 11. So, all activities that are prompted by

Nature and cannot be avoided, he does in a spirit of detachment. He therefore, is not disturbed when the activity does not produce the usual results. For he knows that his duty is only to do the work and not to expect any fruit thereof, *Bg.* II. 47; XVIII. 9; etc. He dedicates the results of all his actions at the feet of the Lord as directed in *Bg.* IX. 27; XVIII. 56; etc. By such dedication the Bhakta becomes free from the effects of meritorious deeds as well as sinful acts, and all pleasure and pain resulting from the gain or loss of the results of activities, do not affect him in the least, *Bg.* II. 56, 57; IX. 28; XII. 13—19; XIV. 24, 25; etc. The word संन्यस्यति denotes dedication as well as renunciation; the former applies to selfless activities and the latter to selfish ones, *Bg.* XVIII. 2-6. In *Sū.* 62 Nārada points out that selfless activities must be continued. Such a Bhakta is beyond the effects of the Guṇas: for being immersed in the remembrance of God, he is no more affected by pain, *Vp.* I. 17. 36, 39; and wordly activities which he has left far behind have no more attraction for him.

Sutra 49. By 'Veda' we are to understand here the ritualistic portion of the Veda. The Vedic teachers recognize the legitimate place of rituals and ceremonials in the early stages of religious life; they are very careful to remind us also that a time comes when the aspirant has to outgrow these, *Vide Bg.* II. 42-45 as well as *Bhāg*. I. 5. 15, 17; II. 2. 2; II. 3. 10; V. 5. 15-17; V. 18. 26; VI. 3. 25; XI. 3. 25, 44-46; XI. 5. 11; XI. 6. 11; XI. 12. 18-20; XI. 23. 46. The substance of these passages is that the S'āstras are meant to lead man to God-realization, and that the work prescribed by the Veda must be done only if it helps that end. If the Karmakāṇḍa or rituals are understood as leading to sense enjoyment here or hereafter, it is far better to give up Karma rather than get entangled further. The Vedas purport to help spiritual progress and not hinder it. The scripture enjoins duties on Sāttvika, Rājasika, and Tāmasika aspirants. A Bhakta should take only such practices as will help him and leave the rest ; his choice must be based on one principle : whether a particular act leads to the renunciation of ego and remembrance of God. If the act is conducive to it, he must adopt it as his own duty or Svadharma, *Bg.* III. 35; XVIII. 47; etc. Only those Vedic acts which thus form Svadharma should be practised ; and that involves the rejection of all other rites and ceremonials. This is one kind of Vedasannyāsa. Even those acts enjoined by the Veda and form one's Svadharma should be dedicated to God and performed in the spirit of worship, *Bg.* XVIII. 46. This is a second kind of Vedasannyāsa where sannyāsa has the sense of dedication. There is a third variety in which all rituals and observances fall off of themselves when the goal is reached. The man of realization does not stand in need of the rituals prescribed by the Vedas (*Bsū.* III. 4. 25, 26) ; but they may be undertaken in earlier stages as a means, just as a horse is made use of to take us to a friend's house. The moment we reach the destination, the horse will be left at the gate and will not be taken inside the house. A boat is useful to take us across a river, but when we reach the opposite bank we have to get down and walk away leaving the boat. Aphorisms 48 and 49 refer to the practices of a man still on the ascent; and this should be distinguished from the practice of one who has reached the goal mentioned in aphorisms 4-8. These *Sūtras* may be read along with *Sūtras* 8-14 on the one hand, and *Sūtras* 61, 62, and 76 on the other. अविच्छिन्नानुराग (unintermittent love) refers to the dawning of the hankering after God and God alone. The term केवलम् suggests that the love that arises at this stage is never satisfied until God is realized and that it is not diluted with desires of any other kind such as pleasures of earth and heaven. This love is the Mukhyabhakti which is the immediate practice leading to Parabhakti.

Sutra 50 shows that the अनुराग referred to in the previous aphorism is only the highest rung in the ladder of spiritual striving and not the attainment of perfection itself. It is the only means that will take the aspirant across transmigration, and will enable him after realization, to help others in reaching the goal which he himself has gained. In setting forth the various practices required for attaining the goal of the Bhakta, Nārada practically follows in the above aphorisms the order given in *Bg.* XVIII. 51-54.

Sutra 51. In the chapter beginning with this aphorism Nārada describes the characteristics of devotion in so far as they are capable of being observed and noted down. The distinction between the secondary variety and primary variety of Bhakti is also pointed out with special reference to the dynamic nature of Bhakti in general. It concludes with the exhortation that the aspirant should not rest satisfied until the Mukhyabhakti, which expresses itself in loyal service, is attained. In describing the ladder of Bhakti (*Sūtras* 34-50) Nārada has been particularly insisting on undiluted devotion as the final step to which all self-effort must lead. The question arises now: what is the test by which one can be sure that various steps have led to this consummation? The author of the aphorisms first of all points out that it is impossible for anyone to give an adequate account of this devotion so as to enable one to identify it when it manifests itself; for an inner experience of this kind defies all analysis and description. Nevertheless, it will be extremely easy to recognize it when one reaches that stage; for it is self-evident and needs no external proof. One who demands a description of this kind of devotion before-hand is like the child requesting the mother to call up from sleep when it is hungry. The mother of that child would say that hunger itself will wake up the child; Nārada would similarly say that devotion itself will make one acquainted with what it really is. The word प्रेम used in this aphorism refers to that devotion which is the last stage of devotion and not the Paramaprema mentioned in *Sū.* 2, which is nothing but Parabhakti or the goal of the Bhakta's realization. The word 'parama' makes it clear. Every verbal description has its own limitations. It can never represent the object itself exactly; it must necessarily be coloured by the defects of the observed, and subjected to the limitations of language and other factors. If such are the handicaps in representing concrete objects, much more would be the difficulty in reporting an inner experience like devotion to God by means of words. The intellectual equipment necessary for such introspection and description is all too rare. He who has the necessary intellectual power and command of language has often no experience of such devotion. Even if one is fortunate enough to have the experience and possesses the necessary mental capacity and training, the moment the searchlight of the intellect is focussed on the experience, it vanishes or becomes wholly coloured by the previous contents of the mind ; and it is not possible then to study the experience critically in its naked simplicity. A third man like the psychologist of religion who pretends to give such a description, being an utter stranger to the experience itself, has to depend upon the secondary evidence afforded by the, not un-often, uncritical observations and analysis of the mystics or devotees ; or he has to rely merely on the physical effects visible on the devotee as the Behaviouristic school of psychology does. In either case the account of devotion as given by psychologists of religion like Leuba, is quite unreliable and untrue. This point is now illustrated by an analogy.

Sutra 52. The dumb man too has the pleasures of the palate ; only vocal defects prevent him from describing his delight. None should be so foolish as to think that the joy of devotion is a chimera because it cannot be precisely described. Like the dumb man's joy which can be only felt by him, the experience of love of God also can be only felt within; it cannot be described. 'Does one who had been to Delhi,' asks S'rī Rāmakṛṣṇa, 'go about boasting of it? Does a gentleman ever tell us that he is a gentleman?' The very presence of divine love makes itself felt in the aspirant and even in those who come into contact with him.

Sutra 53. The moment the conditions are favourable and the mind becomes sufficiently pure as a result of the discipline prescribed before, the experience of Mukhya-bhakti comes automatically by the grace of the Lord and makes itself felt by the devotee. This shows the intimate relation that exists between the various preliminary spiritual practices and devotion which forms the last rung of the ladder. Nārada who is both a Jñānin and a Bhakta is in a peculiarly favourable position to proclaim to the world the reality of the experience of such devotion although he accepts his inability to do full justice to an attempt at its description. He thus boldly challenges the uncritical opinion of psychologists like Leuba, who may often be tempted to relegate such experience to the category of hallucination and hysteria, which are forms of mental disease often caused by over-wrought nerves or repression. Since these psychologists have not sufficiently purified their minds by cleansing it of the dirt of egotism, they could not have the first-hand experience, and are therefore unreliable and dangerous guides for the spiritual aspirant. It will be evident from the next aphorism why psychologists make such mistakes and why the experience itself is indescribable.

Sutra 54. गुणरहितम् (devoid of attributes). We can grasp with the mind and describe in language an object only through its characteristic properties and tendencies to action. Devotion or Prema, being devoid of these, eludes description. No particular characteristic can be predicated as typical of a Bhakta, for all such marks can be found associated with various other emotions also. The experience of devotion is one and indivisible, Avicchinna. All the powers of the mind are so unified and integrated that it is not possible for the mind to work compartmentally. Intellect, emotion, and will are always in harmony and they never work, the one suppressing the other. The logical and analytical faculty of the intellect is kept in abeyance at the time of the experience of devotion, and hence it is impossible to describe it. Again, devotion is a subjective experience, an Anubhava, which cannot be observed by another person; and hence, too, it defies description by anybody except the subject who experiences it. The professional psychologist, having no sufficient spiritual training, cannot have the inner experience itself. Unless the conditions needed for the manifestation of devotion are fulfilled in a psychologist he cannot have the power to describe devotion actually. Because devotion is very elusive, it is qualified as subtle, sukṣma. The moment one tries to cognize it as an object, the experience itself vanishes or becomes coloured by the previous contents of the mind. प्रतिक्षणवर्धमान (expanding every moment); this description is significant, for ordinary emotions are dependent on certain external causes and objects, and are therefore transitory. With the removal of the cause, the emotion that is produced by it also vanishes. One also becomes satiated in a short time by sense enjoyments. But as devotion is Ahaitukī, *i.e.* independent of causes, and its content being a perennial fountain of eternal bliss, it becomes more and more enjoyable as it deepens and strengthens in course of time. One can never become satiated with devotion and so devotion is something that can be enjoyed for all time.

Sutra 55 shows how devotion works up to the highest spiritual realization, which consists in seeing God in everything and loving and serving Him in all beings. An aspirant who has developed this devotion by undergoing the discipline mentioned above (*Sūs.* 46-49) sees the whole world as a manifestation of the God of love; and every one of the activities of such a devotee, physical as well as mental, will be an expression of his devotion to God. Such a Bhakta's entire life becomes one Yajña. He thinks of nothing else, he talks of nothing else, he sees and hears nothing else. Every activity that proceeds from him, nay his whole being, will be redolent with the sweetness of love (vide *Sū.* 36, 37). This is how the general purification of the emotions through devotion affects the mind as a whole, so that the intellectual powers also are purified along with the emotions, and it becomes so easy and natural for the Bhakta to attain the same stage of vision reached by the Jñānin through the intellect. In fact this stage of Bhakti in which the mind always sees only the Beloved everywhere is considered to be the final stage by many devotees, although it is only the penultimate stage according to Nārada; and so many of the definitions of Bhakti given from the standpoint of Jñāna refer only to this stage, for example S'aṅkara's definition of Bhakti as continuous meditation in the *Vivekacūdāmaṇi*. Rāmānuja also actually identifies Bhakti with continuous meditation of this sort in his commentary on *Bsū*. I. 1. एवं ध्रुवानुस्मृतिरेव भक्तिशब्देनाभिधीयते, उपासना पर्यायत्वात् भक्तिशब्दस्य । Bodhāyana says in his Vṛtti: वेदनमुपासनं स्यात् तद्विषये श्रवणात् । Rāmānuja, however, refers to a still higher stage of devotion in his independent treatises, based upon the teachings and realizations of the Ālvārs. S'aṅkara in his commentary on *Bg*. XVIII. 55 identifies Bhakti with Jñānaniṣṭhā. सेयं ज्ञाननिष्ठा आर्तादिभक्तित्रयापेक्षया परा चतुर्थी भक्तिरित्युक्ता । तया परया भक्त्या भगवन्तं तत्वतोऽभिजानाति । यदनन्तरमेवेश्वरक्षेत्रज्ञभेद-बुद्धिरशेषतो निवर्तते । अतः ज्ञाननिष्ठालक्षणया भक्त्या मामभिजानाति इति वचनं न विरुध्यते । S'aṅkara's designation of Jñānaniṣṭhā as Parabhakti is not acceptable to Nārada from the standpoint of Bhaktis'āstra; Nārada would reserve the term Parabhakti not to denote the penultimate stage as S'aṅkara does, but to the stage after the attainment of realization, where even the difference between the lover and the Beloved vanishes completely. Yamunācarya's definition of Parabhakti as Dars'ana also refers to this stage, although according to Nārada Parabhakti is the highest. This *Sū*. reminds of *Bg*. VI. 30 and *Chānd*. VII. 2. 41.

Sutra 56. It is the inherent nature of the soul to love God; but the vision of the soul is clouded by the ego manifesting in multifarious ways. As an aspirant makes progress in spiritual practices the barriers set by the ego are broken down gradually, and the intrinsic attraction of the soul for God becomes more and more pronounced. As the aspirant's love for God percolates the mind, which is full of complexes, it appears to be coloured by the qualities of the mind. Thus during the stage of practice it takes various aspects. These aspects of Bhakti are called Gauṇabhakti; for they are associated with the Guṇas or qualities of the mind. This Gauṇabhakti which culminates in Mukhyabhakti, which is one continuous unobstructed stream of love for God, is classified in two ways in this *Sūtra*. The first classification is based upon the traditional division of the mental qualities and dispositions into Tamas, Rajas, and Sattva, given in *Bg*. XIV, XVII, XVIII. When the religious emotion filters down through a mind that is Tāmasika in nature, the devotion also is of a Tāmasika type and may be characterized as such; so also Bhakti becomes Sāttvika or Rājasika in the same manner. As this differentiation is based on the qualities of the mind, found in association with religious devotion, which in itself is pure and simple, these three expressions of Bhakti are called Gaunabhakti as distinguished from Mukhyabhakti which is devotion bereft of all taint, see *Bg*. XIV. 26; XVIII. 54; etc. The second classification is based on the difference in the motives that impel the Bhakta, *Bg*. VII. 16. Of the four varieties of devotees mentioned in *Bg*. the first three are varieties of Gauṇabhakti, and the fourth denotes Mukhyabhakti in which the devotee loves God, and God alone, and that for the sake of love as is clear from *Bg.* VII. 17-19. The Gauṇabhaktas are here classified into three groups according to their attitude and outlook and what fulfilment they seek through devotion to the Lord. The evils which these seekers want to conquer by resorting to God are three; namely, sin, pain, and error resulting from the improper functioning of volition, emotion, and cognition. When an aspirant is moved by the sense of sin he is an Arthārthin; when moved by the sense of misery he is an Ārta; and when impelled by the sense of error he is a Jñānin, according to the predominance of volition, emotion, or cognition. In the Tāmasika stage of mental development the devotee does not often know clearly either the means or the goal. He is too lazy and indolent and prone to rely too much upon mere habit and external helps given by mere custom and tradition. Unmeaning slavery to rituals, dependence on priest-craft, fanaticism, faith in the magical power of incantations and mystical formulas, fear of evil powers which are sought to be propitiated by burnt offerings and animal sacrifices, resorting to occult methods in injuring others—these are among the signs of a Tāmasika devotee. Rājasika devotion is associated with extremely selfish desires and worldly ambitions, and the consequent incessant activity to gain fame and power for oneself. These types of devotees seek God only as a means to gain their own selfish ends. The Purāṇas are replete with examples illustrating this kind of devotion; the staggering austerities of demons and Titans, Tāraka, Hiraṇyakaśipu, Rāvaṇa, and the rest are vividly described in the Purāṇas. Rājasika-bhakti is found also sometimes in organized churches that aim practically at the conservation of power, prestige, and prosperity for their own sect rather than realization of God. In the Sattvika type of devotion, God is loved for His own sake; the goal and means are perceived by a Sāttvika Bhakta clearly and intelligently, and enthusiastic effort is made by him to realize the goal in the face of all ob structions, *Bhāg.* III. 29. 8-10. We may explain the three kinds of devotion expressed by the terms Ārta, Jijñāsu, and Arthārthin in a different and significant way. The underlying motive of Artabhakti is to get rid of the misery of birth and death and to enjoy infinite bliss. In the devotion of a Jijñāsu the underlying motive is to have the highest knowledge of the Reality behind the phenomenal appearances by knowing which every thing else becomes known. The Bhakta who is an Arthārthin wishes to achieve the divine kingdom on earth. These three types represent the longing to realize the three aspects of Divine reality, namely bliss, consciousness, and being. In fact the apparently threefold quest leads to the same God. We may cite as example of the first Buddha who was moved by the miseries of the world. The Upaniṣadic sages are examples of the second type; for they always endeavoured to realize the highest knowledge of Truth. The Jewish Prophets as well as Christ and Mohammed are the representatives of the third group, for they were moved by the sense of sin and were seekers after righteousness of God.

Sutra 57. The word 'S'reya' stands for Mukhya-bhakti which matures into Parabhakti. Devotion of the Sāttvika type is nearer to Mukhyabhakti, for the former merges into the latter. Similarly Mukhyabhakti is nearer to Parabhakti as it slides into it. Devotional practices raise the mind from Tamas to Rajas and from Rajas to Sattva. Similarly the devotion of an Ārta is nearest to Mukhya-bhakti, that of Jijñāsu comes next in order, and that of an Arthārthin lowest in order. Righteousness which the Arthārthin seeks is valuable only in so far as it is required for Jñāna, which itself is only a means of Release from trans-migratory existence and the miseries attendant on it. It is only a person who has a divine discontent with every worldly prospect that never rests satisfied with anything less than the supreme divine Realization. Again the misery of separation from the Beloved is an aspect of Bhakti which is considered as directly leading to that permanent one-pointed love known as Mukhyabhakti. This gradation is made only from the standpoint of the Bhaktis'āstra, which has a special leaning towards Love of God as Supreme Bliss. The Jñānayogin may equally be right if he advocates the supremacy of that Bhakti which is characteristic of the Jijñāsu and the Karma-Yogin of the Bhakti characteristic of the Arthārthin, each from his own standpoint. The word 'sukṛtinaḥ' in *Bg.* qualifying all these refers to the fact that all of them have, reached the Sāttvika stage ; and it would be very difficult to consider one above the others except on the ground of individual temperament, or view-point of a particular discipline.

Sutra 58. Though the religious experience of devotion cannot easily be scrutinized or described (*Sū.* 51), it is easily realizable through the practices mentioned above and recognizable when it is engendered. There is none who has not had experience of love towards something or somebody at some time or other. When this natural love of the world is directed towards God, after strengthening and purifying it, it is called Bhakti. So it is not very difficult to achieve or recognize it when it comes, as any person is quite familiar with the emotion of love itself in some form or other.

Sutra 59 gives another reason why Bhakti is easily recognizable. Unlike any other new object, the reality of which cannot easily be recognized, love does not require some other proof to recognize it ; for it is self-evident. It does not require a second person to prove to one whether one is happy or miserable ; nor is it necessary to apply any inference to know it. Any amount of argument cannot convince one against one's own experience. Direct experience is the primary and infallible means of all valid knowledge. The doubt, however, may arise as to how a Bhakta can possess perfect peace when every moment he has to be anxious about the welfare of the world, if not of himself. For we find all great devotees of the Lord eager to save the world from sin and misery. The answer for this doubt is now given.

Sutra 61. The devotee of the Lord may be intensely active for bringing about the welfare of the world; but it is not at all the result of his worry over the miseries in the world; but because he feels a great joy in serving the world, for he sees the whole world as a manifestation of God. Since the devotee knows very well that the Lord is the creator, ordainer, and master of the universe, and that He is always gracious and powerful enough to bring about its true good, he is not in the least anxious about the world. And surely God does not stand in need of any help from his devotees. Though the Lord is omniscient and all merciful, in order to continue his sport of this universe he puts his creatures in such situations in which they may solicit His protection, engage themselves in His service. सर्वज्ञोऽपीह सर्वेशः सदा कारुणिकोऽपि सन्। संसारतन्त्रवाहित्वाद रक्षापेक्षामपेक्षते। The Lord therefore only gladly gives an opportunity to his devotees to enjoy themselves in serving Him and His creatures. The true devotee's altruistic activities and sympathies do not cause any worry for him; he is not actually peaceless because of the thought of evil and misery in the world.

Sutra 62. The Bhakta does not develop a stony heart or become anti-social because he has come to possess one-pointed love for God. There is nothing which necessitates his forsaking good work for others. He can and will be active; for though he has nothing to achieve for himself he is impelled by love to work for the sake of his Beloved Lord. The Bhakta gives up only the attachment for the fruits of actions and not the fruits themselves; therefore every activity will be undertaken by him for the benefit of society. Thus the disinterested acts, advocated in the *Bg.* and performed by the Bhakta, does not mean aimless activity like that of a lunatic; they are work consciously done with a definite purpose. The distinction is only this, namely, that the purpose or aim kept in view is not at all self-regarding. This shows the dynamic character of Bhakti as conceived by Nārada.

Sutra 63. Even though a spiritual aspirant may perform acts of social service without attachment to the fruits thereof, it is not safe for him to engage himself in those activities which would compel him to mix with the opposite sex freely or consort him with atheists or entangle him in the meshes of worldly riches. Contact with these is so dangerous that a strict warning is ministered in this aphorism not even to hear or read about them. Even through hearing stories about these a person aspiring after spirituality may become deflected from his proper course—may become interested in these, and be gradually tempted to give up the service of the Lord and run after worldly pursuit. It is therefore necessary for a modern seeker of divine love to be careful to keep away from novels and dramas, pictures and songs, and other pronographic forms of art, woven round sexual passion, from biograpnies of industrial and commercial magnates, and from the life and works of atheists and materialists. The insistence of Nārada on this point is re-stated in a summary way by S'rī Rāmakṛṣṇa recently in his well-known phrase कामिनीकाञ्चनत्याग। Hence those who take to good work as a spiritual discipline will have to take sufficient precautions against sexual temptations, self-aggrandizement, and lapse into atheism. The religious aspirant ought to examine his motive well when he feels anxious to help a member of the opposite sex all on a sudden fallen into distress; or when he has the desire to acquire money for relieving the sufferings of the poor. Nor should he be anxious to read the writings of atheists, however well-written they might be, even if it be for guidance in serving the world. For in all these there is the danger of fall. Even if a Bhakta is above all temptations, it is better on his part to submit himself to these wholesome restrictions in order that he may set by his own life an example to the world which he wants to serve and direct in the path of devotion. When these spiritual practices have led a man to the stage of Mukhyabhakti, it is safer for him to become a formal Sannyāsin by taking orders. It is only very few that can remain householders and still continue at the height reached by a Mukhyabhakta. Surrounded by the worldly temptation amidst which he has to live, the emotion of love roused to its highest pitch is likely to be diverted into low channels, if he still continues in the company of the other sex. This is the rationale of Manu's dictum that in solitude one should not occupy the same seat with the opposite sex, even if they are one's relatives. The senses are powerful enough to drag away even a wise man. A devotee should apply the rule in actual practice. अविद्वांसमलं लोके विद्वांसमपि वा पुनः। प्रमदाह्युत्पथं नेतुं कामक्रोधवशानुगम्॥ मात्रा स्वस्रा दुहित्रा वा न विविक्तासनो भवेत्। बलवानिन्द्रियग्रामो विद्वांसमपि कर्षति॥ *Mnu*. II. 214, 215. Sexual union forges the fetters of the heart both of man and woman; from that proceeds all delusion based on ego instinct and craving for possessions—पुंसःस्त्रिया मिथुनीभावमेतं तयोर्मिथो हृदयग्रन्थिमाहुः। अतो गृहक्षेत्रसुताप्तवित्तैर्जनस्य मोहोऽयमहं ममेति ॥ *Bhāg.* V. 5. 8. Not only the company of the other sex must be avoided, but even those who are given to sexuality also must be shunned—न तथास्य भवेन्मोहो बन्धश्चान्यप्रसङ्गतः। योषित्संगाद्यथापुंसो तथा तत्सङ्गिसङ्गतः ॥ स्त्रीणां स्त्रीसंगिनां सङ्गं त्यक्त्वा दूरत आत्मवान्। क्षेमे विविक्त आसीनश्चिन्तयेन्मामतन्द्रितः ॥ Vide *Bhāg.* III. 31. 32-42; XI. 14. 29, 30; XI. 26. 3. If an aspirant has really reached the stage of Mukhyabhakti, it is not at all hard for him to give up all domestic ties and the company of the opposite sex. When that kind of spiritual eminence is reached, if the aspirant has been an unmarried youth, he never thinks of marriage; and if he is already married, he shall have no more sexual contact with his partner. Strict Brahmacarya is a condition precedent to high spiritual life. S'rī S'aṅkara also stresses this point in his *Bhāṣya* on *Chānd.* 5. 10. 1; VIII. 4. 2; *Mund.* III. 2. 4-6; *Ait.* I; etc. The tradition established through the life of S'aṅkara, Rāmānuja, Caitanya, and other great teachers also supports this principle. Although one does not become a formal Sannyāsin, absolute chastity is to be observed even if one remains a householder, *Bhāg.* XI. 17. 40-58. Every true devotee, though living at home, has been a Sannyāsin in spirit and has observed the rule of Kāmakāñcana-tyāga. It is perfectly clear from the aphorism in question that Brahmacarya is not only mere refraining from sexual act, but a complete rejection of all act, thought, word, or sight directly or indirectly associated with sex. The *Kaṭharudropaniṣad*, 8, 9, says: दर्शनं स्पर्शनं केलिः कीर्तनं गुह्यभाषणम् । सङ्कल्पोऽध्यवसायश्च:क्रियानिर्वृत्तिरेव च । एतन्मैथुनमष्टाङ्गं प्रवदन्ति मनीषिणः । विपरीतं ब्रह्मचर्यमनुष्ठेयं मुमुक्षुभिः ॥ S'aṅkara defines it as स्त्रीविषयतृष्णात्याग: (*Chānd.* VIII. 4. 2) and Rāmānuja as योषित्सु भोग्यता बुद्धियुक्तेक्षणादिरहितत्वम् *Bg.* XVII. 13. Yogiyājñavalkya has: कायेन मनसा वाचा सर्वावस्थासु सर्वदा । सर्वत्र मैथुनत्यागो ब्रह्मचर्यं प्रचक्षते । St. Ignatius writes: 'They that are carnal cannot do spiritual things; neither can they who are spiritual do carnal things, just as faith is incapable of the deeds of infidelity and infidelity of the deeds of faith.' Christ said: 'Every one that looketh on a woman to lust after her hath committed adultery with her already in his heart,' *Matt.* 5. 28. Saint Augustine says: 'By continency verily are we bound up and brought back into One, Whence we were dissipated into many,' *Confessions*, X.

Sutra 64. When a devotee of the Lord is engaged in good work of an altruistic kind, there is likelihood of his vanity and egotism being roused as a result of his own estimation of his achievements as high or great. He is therefore warned to curb such feelings by nipping them in the bud. Better such activities are given up if one cannot avoid pride and vanity. Even when a man offers help to the needy, he should consider himself only serving the Lord, and should therefore be grateful to the recipient foı having given him an opportunity to have the joy of service. If the aspirant cultivates this attitude, he can easily escape pride and vanity, which are usually found in ordinary philanthropic activities.

Nārada includes by the word आदि (etc.) all the vices warned against in *Bg*. XVI., as Āsurīsampat.

Sutra 65. It is very difficult to destroy completely selfish instincts and impulses all at once. Forcible repression is not advisable as it would lead to injurious results. Therefore gradual sublimation is the process suitable to conquer the instincts. One method of achieving this end is to be always conscious of the fact that all the activities of the aspirant are only to serve the Lord Himself. Therefore whenever feelings of anger, vanity, and the like, are roused they should at once be recognized; and then they should be carefully directed towards the Lord Himself. The rising of remorse will at once quell all undesirable feelings, and gradually the baser passions and impulses will be rendered impossible. A still safer course is to make use of these passions themselves helpful in the practice of devotion towards God. Anger may be directed towards the obstacles to Bhakti; it will then take the shape of renunciation and dispassion. Pride may be entertained in association with the feeling that the aspirant is powerful enough to resist all temptations, being conscious of the fact that he is a child of the Lord. Even this pride is not laudable, for the Lord destroys the pride of everyone of his devotees. An epithet of the Lord is Darpahā or destroyer of pride. This type of pride, however, is not so bad as worldly pride, for it would gradually wear out as devotion reaches its perfection. This pride, namely, 'I am the servant of the Lord' would take the form of self-respect, which would prevent one from doing wrong.

In this way the sting may be removed from all the passions that are possibly roused in the course of a man's conduct in society.

Sutra 66. When the love of the devotee expresses itself in actual life in the form of various kinds of service or Kainkarya, the spirit of the devotee should be that of a loyal servant or a devoted wife. Just as a loyal servant or devoted wife does not expect any return or even gratitude from the master or the husband for all the services that are rendered as a mere offering of love, similarly the devotee sees only God in every creature, and all his social activities will therefore take the form of an offering of pure love to God without any mercenary motive, or even recognition from Him. He loves because he cannot help loving God, and he serves because his love must find an outlet in service. In the spiritual realm the real master and servant are those who are mutually attracted by intrinsic excellences and not by contract for securing some selfish end—स वै स्वामी स वै भृत्यो गुणलुब्धौ न कामुकौ, *Bhāg.* VII. 10. 6. This is the force of the word नित्य (permanent) in the terms नित्यदास्य and नित्यकान्ताभजन in the *Sū.* A true servant is a servant for all the time and a true wife is a wife for all the time. Such service is the test of the purest love, and therefore it must be cultivated carefully. One should not be satisfied with the Gauṇa varieties of Bhakti described in *Sū.* 56, but should transcend them. It is this Gauṇabhakti that is meant by the word त्रिरूप.

Sutra 67. The fifth and the last chapter begins with this *Sū.* Up to this point we have seen that according to this Gospel all spiritual endeavour is for the purification of the emotions through the cultivation of undiluted, one-pointed, incessant, stream of love for the blessed feet of the Lord similar to the love of a servant or wife. We have also hinted before that this is the highest stage of spiritual effort; it naturally and gradually ripens into the manifestation of the natural glory and perfection of the Ātman. A description of one who has attained to this stage of devotion known as Mukhyabhakti is given in this chapter. The word मुख्य or primary distinguishes the devotion of this supreme stage from the Gauṇa or secondary devotion mentioned in *Sū.* 56. One is called a Bhāgavata and a Sant when one has attained to this absolute stage of devotion—यदैकान्त्यं गता विष्णौ भगवत्यात्मभावने । तद्वैष्णवा भागवताः सन्त इत्यभिधीयते—Bhāradvāja. The devotion of these devotees has transcended the Gauṇa forms and therefore is not tinged with any worldliness or selfishness. They do not yearn even for Mukti; they do not love God as a means to an end, *Bhāg.* XI. 14. 14. etc.

Sutra 68. The conversation referred to in the *Sū.* is not confined to mere talk on God. Every one of their activities, the least of their movements, conscious or unconscious, their entire life, are eloquent of the surge of divine love within and proclaim it to the world. Devotees always like to talk of their Beloved to other devotees like themselves. But that does not mean that they while away all their time in mere talk with their equals. Their interest will lie more in redeeming the sinners and evil-doers, and for this purpose they will always be eager to teach and preach, so that all may become sharers in the bliss of devotion and love, which they themselves enjoy. But they are not like ordinary teachers and preachers, who are conscious of their superiority. These Bhaktas consider themselves only as servants when they teach or preach; they only see God in their disciples and only serve Him. They deem themselves blessed because they have thereby got an opportunity to serve the Lord in that form. This is also included in the eternal Dāsya mentioned in *Sū*. 66. The word पावयन्ति (purifies) is significant. The devotee does not consider himself superior to others in purity. When he consciously undertakes to purify others, it is in the spirit of a servant who ministers to the needs of his beloved master, or a mother who nurses her lunatic son, or even like a cow that licks away the dirt from the new-born calf. This he does in spite of the kicks and abuses he may get from the persons whom he attempts to serve. Very often such Bhaktas' presence itself is sufficient to purify others who come in contact with them. This capacity of the devotee to purify others is powerfully expressed by S'rī Kṛṣṇa when he says (*Bhāg*. XI. 14. 16) that he himself always takes care to follow his devotees wherever they go, so that he may purify himself by the dust of their holy feet. The dirt that the devotee removes is the dirt of ego and its various manifestations. Again, one devotee in a family unconsciously affects other members. Even those who oppose the true lover of God will have a change of mind later. It is easy for the members of a family who love one another to catch the contagion of devotion. कुलं पवित्रं जननी कृतार्था विश्वम्भरा पुण्यवती च तेन । अपारसच्चित्सुखसागरे सदा विलीयते यस्य मनःप्रचारः—The clan is hallowed, mother is made blessed, and the earth is rendered meritorious by that devotee whose entire mind has lost itself in the boundless ocean of Existence-Knowledge-Bliss. *Sūtasaṁhitā*, II. 20-45 ; also *Jīvanmuktiviveka*, page 133, published by T. P. H., Adyar. The *Adhr.* says : लोके त्वद्भक्तिनिरताः त्वद्धर्मामृतवर्षिणः । पुनन्ति लोकमखिलं किं पुनः स्वकुलोद्भवान् । I. 7. 43. It may also be noted that the idea underlying *Bsū.* IV. 1. 7 is the same. The greater the Bhakta is, the greater the orbit of his spiritual influence. The greatest of them are the light of the entire world. Even if they live the life of the recluse in caves, the spiritual waves set up by their devotion will spread over the whole world, and find an echo in all pure hearts ready to receive them. Vide *Bhāg.* IX. 9. 6 and XI. 14. 24.

Sutra 69. The word तीर्थं comes from the root तॄ and means 'that which enables a man to cross over an obstacle—such as a ford in a river'. Holy men, sacred places and objects, sanctifying qualities, all these are therefore called Tirtha. The scriptures therefore consider, compassion, truthfulness, and the rest as Tirtha. ज्ञानं तीर्थं क्षमा तीर्थं तीर्थमिन्द्रियनिग्रहः । सर्वभूतदया तीर्थं सत्यतीर्थं तथार्जवम् । दानं तीर्थं दमस्तीर्थं सन्तोषस्तीर्थमुच्यते । ब्रह्मचर्यं परं तीर्थमहिंसा तीर्थमुच्यते । अस्तेयमपरं तीर्थमद्रोहस्तीर्थमुच्यते । श्रद्धा तीर्थं धृतिस्तीर्थं तपस्तीर्थमुदाहृतम् । तीर्थानामपि तत्तीर्थं संशुद्धिर्मनसः परा । न जलाप्लुतदेहस्तु स्नात इत्यभिधीयते । स स्नातो यो दमस्नातः स तु शुद्धतमो मतः । यो लुब्धः पिशुनः क्रूरः नास्तिको विषयात्मकः । सर्वतीर्थेष्वपि स्नातः पापो मलिन एव च । न शरीरमलत्यागान्नरो भवति निर्मलः । मानसैस्तु मलैस्त्यक्तो

भवत्यत्यन्तनिर्मलः। विषयेष्वनिशं रागो मनसो मल उच्यते। तेष्वेव वीतरागत्वं निर्मलत्वमुदाहृतम्। चित्तमन्तर्गतं दुष्टं तीर्थस्नानैर्न शुध्यति। शतशोऽपि जलैर्धौतं सुराभाण्डमिवाशुचिः। दानमिज्या तपः शौचं तीर्थं वेदाः श्रुतं तथा। सर्वाण्येतानि तीर्थानि यस्य भावः सुनिर्मलः। निगृहीतेन्द्रियग्रामो यत्र यत्र वसेन्नरः। यत्र रागादिरहिता वासुदेवपरायणाः। वसन्ति पुण्यकर्माणस्तत्क्षेत्रमधिकं ततः। तस्मादेव महाभागाः वैष्णवा वीतकल्मषाः। पुनन्ति सकलं लोकं किं तीर्थमधिकं ततः। इतिहाससमुच्चये शुकानुशासनम्॥ The *Sātvatasaṁhitā* say: गंगादि तीर्थेषु वसन्ति मत्स्याः देवालये वृक्षसङ्घाश्च नित्यम्। भावोज्झितास्ते न फलं लभन्ते तीर्थैश्च देवायतनैश्च पुण्यैः॥ But in common parlance holy water and sacred places are considered Tīrtha. By resorting to them one becomes purified and free from sins, and is thus enabled to surmount mundane existence and its imperfections. Wherefrom do these derive their efficacy? It is only the association with saints and holy men that confers on them this sanctifying power. Those who know that these Tīrthas are linked with saints are reminded, by the law of association of ideas, of the pure love of these saints, and through them of God Himself. The thought of purity, thus engendered by these make them pure at least for the time being. If a man resorts to Tīrthas without any previous knowledge of their sacredness, no spiritual effect is produced. That Christians and Mohammedans do not derive any benefit out of pilgrimage to Vrindāvana, Kās'i, or Jagannāth, but derive benefit only by pilgrimage to Jerusalem or Mecca, and vice versa, show that these places do not have anything inherent in them which makes them holy. That is the reason why many people are not benefited by pilgrimages; for holy associations are not awakened in them. It is not the waters or idols of the place that really form the Tīrtha; but the saints who purify by mere sight by virtue of God residing in their hearts, *Bhāg*. X. 48. 31. Holy places are either the birth-place of some saints, or the place of their spiritual endeavour, or attainment of perfection, or ministration. Sometimes many holy men visit the holy places; that is why they are considered holy. Thus it is the saint that constitutes the real Tīrtha, *Bhāg*. IV. 30. 37; I. 13. 10; II. 19. 8. For the esoteric significance of Tīrtha see also *Mbh*. XIII. 108 and Madhva on *Bg*. III. 20. सुकर्मीकुर्वन्ति means 'makes deeds righteous'. It is only such actions as are characteristic of, advocated by, and taught through, the saints that are considered righteous by others, and fit to be followed. भक्तिहीनेन यत् किञ्चित् कृतं सर्वमसत्समम् —If devotion is wanting, all deeds are null and void, says *Adhr*. VI. 7. 66. Therefore it is these saints of God that are looked up to for guidance by others, *Bg*. III. 21. It is, again, these saints that set the standard of Dharma through example and precept, Vide, *Tait*. I. 10. 4; Āpastamba I. 1. 2; Gautama I. 1. 2; etc. So also the scriptures become authoritative (सच्छास्त्र) from the fact of their being a record of the experiences and teachings of saints and sages. It is this fact that distinguishes a scripture from an ordinary book, vide, *Sū*. 12, notes.

Sutra 71. The living parents rejoice in the end because their son will be honoured by the world after his attainment of realization. The departed ancestors who are considered to be in a heaven of their own, also rejoice on seeing such a worthy son being born in the family. The word पितृ is used in the S'āstras to denote not only living parents and the departed ancestors but also permanent demi-gods known by the name Agniṣvātta and others. Every man who is born is considered by the scriptures as owing a debt to the Gods and departed ancestors, and if he fails to discharge these debts all his spiritual practices will be in vain. But if a son becomes a devotee of God, there is no more debt for him to any body; see *Bhāg*. XI. 5. 41, 42; *Us'anaḥsaṁhita* I. 37. Not only the Gods do not get angry with him, but they rejoice; for all worship which the aspirant undertakes in the beginning, whether of Devas or of Pitṛs, is primarily meant to lead him to this final stage. When they find a descendant of theirs attaining to the goal, they naturally rejoice. 'He, who has given up all his ordinary duties, says the scriptures, 'and surrendered himself, body and soul to the one refuge of all, that is God, the giver of Mukti, is not a debtor to Devas, Ṛṣis, Pitṛs, and others.' Also, 'As by watering the roots of a tree the whole tree is satisfied, as by satisfying Prāṇa all Indriyas are satisfied, so also by worship of God all others are worshipped.' 'The parents are elated and the grandfathers dance' because within their family is born a saint who will save them also.

The various Devas or minor deities being all included in the one Supreme God, they too derive satisfaction when the devotee loves and worships the one and only God. In fact the various Gods are all only symbols of the one God and are not different from Him. So there is not only no harm in giving up the worship of these minor deities, but it is the duty of all to give their whole heart and soul only to the one God. Vide, *Bg*. XVIII. 65; IX. 22, 25; VII. 21 to 23; IV. 11; etc. The demigods are often described as virtuous souls who have come to the celestial regions to enjoy the results of their religious merit earned on the earth, and who come down again to the earth when their term is over. So when they see a real devotee in this world and find how he has saved himself by devotion and renunciation, they also feel glad; for they get an example of winning everlasting bliss through devotion to God. Naturally then, they must dance finding a possibility of higher bliss. The demigods are often troubled by Asuras, and when they find a real devotee being born on earth, they are quite sure that their salvation is near, because wherever the devotees are, there God must also be. There is a common misunderstanding that these demigods get jealous when they find any man becoming spiritual, and that they put obstacles in his way of God-realization. Stories describing such obstruction from the demigods like Indra, which we find in the Purāṇas, must not be taken as referring to a sincere devotee's spiritual struggles. They relate only to those who are doing sacrifices and other ritualistic practices in expectation of heaven. They do not and cannot ever touch a sincere devotee, for God is always at hand to help His devotee. To substantiate this there are very many illustrations in the Purāṇas, like the story of Ambarīṣa. No doubt some obstacles are found by sincere spiritual aspirants also, but they are provided by God Himself, so that the devotee may grow stronger by such opposition. A mother may throw her child into the water so that it may learn to swim, but will never allow it to drown itself!

The earth gets a saviour. Only a real saint can save the world. All others are interested only in seeing that the world caters to their own self-aggrandizement and enjoyment. They never have the welfare of the world at heart. Their interest in the world is like that of a butcher in his kid or the peasant in his cattle. It is only the loving service of the selfless saints that really leads human beings to their destination, *viz.*, the footstool of God, far away from the troubles and tribulations of this worldly life and death. From the poetic and mythological standpoint of the Purāṇas, the earth or Bhūdevī is one of the wives of Viṣṇu, or God. When virtue subsides and vice prevails, she is said to be feeling as if she is deserted by her Lord and protector. When some saint takes his birth in this world, he must necessarily be followed by God himself and so Bhūdevī may be poetically described as regaining her Lord and protector, whenever devotees appear on earth. Thus according to this Sūtra, the devotee satisfies the denizens of all the three worlds.

Sutra 72. With the advent of Divine illumination, says S'rī Rāmakṛṣṇa, all distinctions of caste vanish. In spite of the reproach of exclusiveness based on caste and custom levelled against Hinduism, it will have to be admitted that the religion of Vedānta according to its accredited interpreters has always considered that distinctions based on caste or birth as mere social accidents or adjustments having no true or ultimate value in spiritual life. Even the priestly order of society which considered itself to be second to none in high-birth and eminence have always bowed down and admitted the spiritual greatness of godmen and illumined souls irrespective of their birth and parentage. That is how Vis'vāmitra, Vyāsa, Kavaṣa, Jābāla, Mahidāsa, S'rī Rāma, S'abari, S'rī Kṛṣṇa, Nammālvār, Nanda, Kannappar, Tukārām, and a host of other spiritual luminaries of varying magnitue, though they were not born of Brahmin parentage, have compelled worship and divine honour from all posterity. The priestly order was always willing to sit at the feet of spiritual or intellectual eminence and learn the greatest of truths. This healthy outlook was present from the Vedic times, and it has made Hinduism a living religion for all time. In the Upaniṣadic and Epic periods we see many cases where caste has not been a bar for teaching or learning spiritual truths. The spirit of Buddhism is clear from the following verses from *Lalitavistara*, a work of the 3rd century A.D. जातिं भवान् पृच्छति शाक्यभिक्षुष्वन्तर्गतांस्तेषु गुणान् न चेति। अतो भवान् जातिमदावलेपात् आत्मानमन्यांश्च हिनस्ति मोहात् ॥ आवाहकालेऽथ विवाहकाले जातेः परीक्षा न तु धर्मकाले। धर्मक्रियायां हि गुणा निमित्ताः गुणाश्च जातिं न विचारयन्ति ॥ यद्युच्चकुलीनगता दोषा गर्हां प्रयान्ति लोकेऽस्मिन्। कथमिव नीचजनगता गुणा न सत्कारमर्हन्ति? ॥ चित्तवशेन हि पुंसां कलेबरं निन्द्यतेऽथ सत्क्रियते। शाक्यश्रमणमनांसि च शुद्धान्यच्चर्यास्यतः शाक्याः ॥ यदि गुणपरिवर्जितो द्विजातिः पतित इति प्रथितोऽपि यात्यवज्ञाम्। स तु निधनकुलोद्भवोऽपि जन्तुः शुभगुणयुक्त इति प्रणम्य पूज्यः ॥ These verses are the answer given to a Brahmin who questioned the caste of the Buddhist monks : 'You enquire of the caste of monks, and do not want to know of their qualities ! Sir, you are deluded and therefore you injure yourself as well as others. This signifies insolence born of caste-pride. Caste may be a subject of inspection and investigation for marriage or invitation, but not in religious matters. Spiritual endeavour demands no condition except mental qualities, and these do not depend on birth. If the vices of a person born of high caste merit censure, how is it that the excellence of a man of low caste does not merit honour ? Man is honoured or despised because of his mind : so these monks of excellent character deserve respect, because they have good qualities.' This spirit of Mahāyāna Buddhism was absorbed into Vaiṣṇavism and strengthened by the Vedic philosophy. The *Bhāradvājaparis'iṣṭā* says : न जातिभेदं न कुलं न लिङ्गं न गुणक्रिया: । न देशकालौ नावस्थां योगो ह्ययमपेक्षते ॥ ब्राह्मणैः क्षत्रियैर्वैश्यै: शूद्रै: स्त्रीभिस्तथापरैः । यथार्हमर्च्य: सेव्यश्च नित्यं सर्वेश्वरो हरि: ॥ न परीक्ष्य वयो वन्द्याः नारायणपरायणा: । अपिस्युर्हीनजन्मानो मान्या निम्नेन चेतसा ॥ *Garudapurāṇa* says : भक्तिरष्टविधा ह्येषा यस्मिन् म्लेच्छोऽपि वर्तते । स विप्रेन्द्रो मुनिः श्रीमान् स यति: स च पण्डितः ॥ Again *Bhāradvājasamhitā* says : प्रत्यक्षितात्मनाथानां नैषां चिन्त्यं कुलादिकम् ॥ The discipline of surrender to the Lord, or Bhaktiyoga, does not demand the special qualifications of caste, birth, clan, sex, qualities, work, time, place, and stage of life. Every day the Lord of the universe must be served and worshipped according to one's ability by all—Brāhmaṇas, Kṣatriyas, Vais'yas, S'ūdras, and others. The devotees of the Lord should not be examined in respect of their age and the like, before one pays one's respect to them; with an attitude of service they should be revered even if they belong to low caste. He who has the eight-fold devotion, indeed, is an excellent Brahmin, a sage, a shining soul, a hermit, and a wise man, even if he be a foreigner. Do not enquire about the family etc. of one who has realized God. The paragon of devotees, Prahlāda says: 'I consider an outcaste who has dedicated his thought, word, deed, wealth, possessions, and life to God, far superior to a Brahmin endowed with the twelve well-known traits, but has not the inclination for the Lotus Feet of the Lord; because the former, by his utter self-surrender, elevates and sanctifies the whole family, whereas the latter, conceited as he is in his virtues, does not even purify himself: what to speak of others!' विप्राद् द्विषट्गुणयुतादरविन्दनाभपादारविन्दविमुखात् श्वपचं वरिष्ठम्। मन्ये तदर्पितमनोवचनेहितार्थप्राणं पुनाति सकुलं न तु भूरिमानः *Bhāg.* VII. 9. 10; see also *Bhāg.* III. 33. 6, 7; XI. 14. 21; etc. *Adhr.* says: पुंस्त्वे स्त्रीत्वे विशेषो वा जातिनामाश्रमादयः। न कारणं मद्भजने भक्तिरेव हि कारणम् III. 10. 20. S'rī Kṛṣṇa's words in *Mbh.* XIII: न शूद्रा भगवद्भक्ताः विप्रा भागवताः स्मृताः। सर्ववर्णेषु ते शूद्रा ये ह्यभक्ता जनार्दने ॥ चण्डालं मम भक्तं वा नावमन्येत बुद्धिमान्। योऽवमन्येत मूढात्मा रौरवं नरकं व्रजेत्।—Devotees of the Lord are not S'ūdras; S'ūdras are they who have no faith in the Lord whichever be their caste. A wise man should not slight even an outcaste if he is devoted to the Lord; he who looks down upon him will fall into hell. Thus it does not behove us to make a distinction between one devotee and another. And these devotees also do not feel any distinction between man and man, *Bg.* V. 18; *Bhāg.* XI. 29. 14. They see the same God everywhere.

Sutra 73 gives the reason why there is no such distinction. Bhaktas are equal in the sight of God, because their devotion is the same in spite of apparent physical or social differences; they all belong to one group. To every Bhakta all the creatures in the universe are the children of God, or God Himself, and as such he sees them with an eye of equality.

Sutra 74. Those who have attained to this stage of devotion never cares to enter into a controversy about God, or His devotees, or other spiritual matters. They have so completely destroyed their egotism that there is no possibility for them to hanker after name or fame by scoring victory over an opponent in a religious controversy. They themselves do not stand in need of any support from reason either; for their faith is based upon direct actual experience. Vain disputation has therefore no place in their life. If any controversialist challenges them for discussion they do not take up the gauntlet.

Sutra 75. It is quite possible to look upon the very same truth from different standpoints; and views taken do change as observers' angles of vision, capacities, and tendencies change. Two apparently contradictory views may not be really contradictory at all, and may be reconciled from a higher viewpoint. Hence there is no sense in one's trying to controvert another's views, honestly and sincerely believed in. It behoves a real saint therefore not to unsettle the honest and sincere views of another ; he ought only to allow him opportunity to follow what he considers right, *Bg*. III. 26, 29. Again, convincing reasons may be given to support two diametrically opposed views. Therefore it does not follow that a view is true because it has support from reason. What one man considers well established by reason can easily be shaken by another more intelligent man. As we often see in law courts, two lawyers taking opposite sides, try to prove their contention, based on the same evidence. Reason may thus be used in proving even a false thing to be true. Therefore it is often an unreliable guide. Again, what appears as reasonable at one time may appear quite unreasonable when we gather more experience. Thus no one view based on mere reasoning can be considered true once for all, for there is always a possibility of its again being proved by better reason or further observation, to be untrue. The history of science provides with many examples of exploded theories, which were all once considered as well established through reason. Moreover when the intention is to secure victory over an opponent and not to establish truth, the chances are that one may be carried away from truth ; and truth may even be thrown overboard in the zeal to get victory. The *Sū*. reminds us of *Bsū*. II. 1. 11 and *Kaṭh*. II. 2. 9, which also speak of the unreliability of Tarka or logic. For the real place of reason in spiritual life vide *supra*, pp. 122,123.

Sutra 76. In using the term भक्तिशास्त्र the author might have had in mind the ancient text books on Bhakti such as *Bg*., *Bhāg*., *Npāñ*., etc. The modern adherent of the Bhakti Path may however add to this list such comparatively later devotional literature as the songs of the Ālvārs and Nāyanārs of South India, of the Mahārāṣtra saints like Jñānesvar, Tukārām, and Rāmdās, of the North Indian saints like Tulsidās, Mīrābāī, and Kabīr. Apart from such outpourings of the hearts of saints, we have also the special treatises on Bhakti such as *S'su.*, the *Bhaktirasāyana*, the *Bhaktirasāmṛtasindhu*, etc. The works of S'aṅkara, Rāmānuja, Madhva, Vallabha, Nimbārka, and Gaurāṅga are also fit to be read by a devotee. The qualification of the word S'āstra by the word Bhakti shows that in the eyes of Nārada books exclusively dealing with Jñāna, Karma, or Yoga are naturally not relished by a Bhakta, as they are not helpful to him in his love of God. We may add also that a modern devotee does not dabble in such literature as the publications of the Rationalistic Press Association, and books on religion written by modern Psychologists. The Bhaktas mind has reached a stage where it can tolerate nothing but love, and he therefore takes care to read only such books as will feed and nourish his intense love for God. Reflection or मनन is mentioned to show that even in the study of devtional literature, the Bhakta does not swallow everything that the books apparently say. Like the bee interested only in the honey, the Bhakta takes only the essence and rejects everything else. Everything that goes against the spirit of love, he naturally avoids, and he is always sufficiently awake to detect poetic exaggerations. He does not also fall into the common error of unintelligently copying other great men. *Bhāg.* XII. 13. 8, insists upon the necessity for such reflection on the teachings of scritpures. The *Skp.* also in ch. IV, Vaiṣṇavakhaṇda, *Bhāgavatamāhātmya*, goes to the extent of saying that the real *Bhāgavata* consists of only such passages of the text as describe the sweetness of Bhagavān and which are helpful in rousing and keeping up devotion to His Blessed Feet, and that therefore a sincere student should be devoted to reflection and careful scrutiny of the teachings of the scripture. *Bhāg.* XI. 8. 10 compares the Bhakta to the bee. It is to denote this intelligent use of reason in aid of devotion that the word **मनन** is used in this Sūtra as opposed to **वाद** in *Sū.* 74 ; the former is never given up at any stage of spiritual life, whereas the latter is never undertaken by the Bhaktas. **तदुद्बोधककर्म** means practices that rouse devotion. As in the selection of texts for study, the Bhakta is very careful also in the adoption of spiritual practices referred to in the books. Only spiritual practices specially understood as conducive to devotion, are continued in this stage. These practices are known as **भागवतधर्म** or practices meant to create and sustain love of God, and they are described in detail in the Purāṇas and Āgamas. Vide, *Bhāg.* VII. 5. 23 and 24 ; IX. 4 ; XI. 3. 21 to 31 ; XI. 19. 20 to 24 ; *Bg.* IX, XII, etc.

This *Sūtra* must be read as a supplement to *Sū.* 12 & 14 on the one hand, and *Sū.* 49 & 62 on the other. While *Sūtras* 12 & 14 refer to the Bhakta's attitude to study and spiritual practices, as well as social service, even after realization of the highest Truth, the latter two refer to his attitude towards the same before the dawn of love. The present *Sū.* deals with the same attitude during the stage of Mukhyabhakti. When all these *Sūs.* are read together, it will be clear how, according to Nārada, a Bhakta does not give up his spiritual practices or social service at any stage either before or after realization. The Bhakta's life is an intensely dynamic one, whether his activities are for himself or for the sake of others. Much similarity also will be noticed with regard to the activities of the Bhakta in all stages. This will be explained by the fact that it is the characteristics of the perfect man that a spiritual aspirant has to cultivate voluntarily by self-effort. S'aṅkara points out this in his *Bhāṣya* on *Bg.* II. 55.

Sutra 77 gives us the reason why the Bhakta continues his practices even after Bhakti has been already roused. Being free from all incentives for work, which keep an ordinary man healthily engaged, time may hang heavily on him ; and if he discontinues his practices and becomes idle mentally or physically, Satan might easily find a loop-hole to enter and work in him mischief. The downward pull of Tamas, like the natural action of gravity, might drag even a Bhakta down from the height he has attained, if he does not constantly and vigilantly exert himself to keep up his spiritual balance characteristic of Sattva. Like the brass vessel, mind may automatically become impure again, if it is not cleansed every day. The Bhakta therefore does not allow himself to be caught by Tamas even for half a second ; he scrupulously keeps his body and mind alert with the help of such activities as are conducive to devotion.

No man is ever safe until he attains Parabhakti (cf. *Bhāg.* XI. 2. 53) after the attainment of which every moment spent in forgetfulness of God, or free from spiritual activity, is deemed grave waste of time.

Sutra 78 shows the necessity for discrimination and reflection in the choice of spiritual practices as mentioned in *Sū.* 76. It also shows in what direction and for what reasons the aspirant should use such discretion. The Bhakta is not free from the necessity of preserving his character. No doubt he must have had sufficient training in character even before he reached the stage of Mukhyabhakti, but as he still continues to live an active life even in this stage, he has to be careful not to offend any of the moral virtues in the choice of activities. Moral virtues can never be transcended even in spiritual practices or social service. The elements which go to form character are designated as Yama and Niyama. They are also regarded as constituting the real spiritual worth of a man, and so they are designated as Daivisampat in *Bg.* XVI. Only a few of these practices are referred to in the *Sū.* by name, but the rest also are to be understood by the word 'ādi'.

Amongst the moral virtues अहिंसा or non-violence occupies the first place. Vide *Vyāsa-bhāṣya* on *Ysū* II. 30. Non-violence is practice of active abstention from using or abetting or approving force, in thought, word or deed, by oneself or through agents, intentionally or through carelessness or wanton negligence, so as to cause harm to others. It does not include the discipline enforced on a disciple, or the brakes put by moral law on wrong-doing, or the benevolent force used for the good of another, for example, by a doctor on a patient. Nor does it include any pain that is caused to another, if such pain is caused in the discharge of one's supreme duty to conscience and God. The general rule of non-violence laid down by the Vedas as मा हिंस्यात् सर्वभूतानि is unconditional and absolute ; the ritualists and Smṛtikāras have hedged it in with so many conditions and exceptions that the rule becomes a mere mockery in the practices followed by the ritualists. No doubt many of these conditions and exceptions are sane and necessary in the case of ordinary people who follow the Karmamārga, or of those lay men who have no higher spiritual aspirations. But to those who have devoted their whole life to spiritual realization and who have given their heart and soul to God, such exceptions are not applicable. Thus the Bhakta has so much love for God and His creatures that under no circumstances and conditions will his heart agree to harm another. This is the force of *Ysū.* II. 31. The *Bṛhanmanu* says thus : हिंसा चैव न कर्तव्या वैधहिंसा तु राजसी । ब्राह्मणैः सा न कर्तव्या यतस्ते सात्विका मताः ॥ *Mbh.* XII. 265. 4 to 9 corroborate this. The *Bhāg.* supports it in XI. 21. 29 & 30. Vijñānabhikṣu, in his *Bhāṣya* on *Sāṅkhyasūtra* I. 6, says expressly that there is no authority for circumscribing Ahiṁsā so as to make Vedic sacrifices an exception. It will thus be seen that as the Bhakta understands the scriptures intelligently, he does not undertake such practices as involve the taking of animal life even though they may apparently have the sanction of the Vedas. He understands all such practices, as the Vedic sacrifice, not as sanctioning the taking of innocent life, but as symbolic of the burning of one's own animality in the fire of divine love. Those who, therefore, like to continue the Vedic sacrifices will do it only symbolically, using sometimes a vegetable, or an animal made of dough, for such sacrifices, in place of live animals. Cf. *Mbh.* XII. 265. 10 & 11.

The next positive virtue is सत्य or truthfulness; truth is God, and so the Bhakta cannot go against it. The many exceptions mentioned in the scriptures are only meant for lay men, and in actual practice they only provide a safety valve by which to escape from the duty of veracity. The devotee of God does not accept such exceptions nor does he take advantage of them to bypass his duty. He cannot dupe anybody by making a false representation. He sees God in everybody and to dupe anybody will be as good as duping God Himself. He knows that God who is in his own heart knows the truth even before the speaker thinks of duping another. Compare S'akuntala's words to Dușșanta in *Mbh.* I. 74. 28, 29. एकोऽहमस्मीति च मन्यसे त्वं न हृच्छयं वेत्ति मुनिं पुराणम् । यो वेदिता कर्मण: पापकस्य यस्यान्तिके त्वं व्रजिनं करोषि । मन्यसे पापकं कृत्वा न कश्चिद्वेत्ति मामिति । विदन्ति चैनं देवाश्च यश्चैवान्तरपूरुष:
Cf. also the story of Devas'arman and his disciple Vipula in *Mbh.* XIII. 43, where the Guru tells his disciple that every one of our actions done in secret are all noted by time in the form of day and night and seasons. न मां कश्चिद्विजानाति इति कृत्वा न विश्वसेत् । नरो रहसि पापात्मा पापकं कर्म वै द्विज । कुर्वाणं हि नरं कर्म पापं रहसि सर्वदा । पश्यन्ति ऋतवश्चापि तथा दिननिशेप्युत । अहोरात्रं विजानाति ऋतवश्चापि नित्यश: । पुरुषे पापकं कर्म

शुभं वाशुभमेव च । The rule adopted by true Bhaktas is mentioned by S'iva to Devī in *Mbh.* XIII. 144. 19. आत्महेतोः परार्थे वा नर्महास्याश्रयात्तथा । ये मृषा न वदन्तीह ते नरा स्वर्गगामिनः । The devotee's interest in truth is not confined to mere veracity alone. He is interested in practising the highest Truth of the presence of God as the one underlying reality of the universe and knowing everything else as untrue. When he reads scriptures, therefore, he takes delight in reading only such books and such passages as insist upon the ultimate reality of God and God alone, and which lead to a distaste for all worldly pleasures. He undertakes only such practices as enable him to see and love and serve all beings alike as the abode of God. Cf. Bhagavān's definition of Truth as समदर्शन in *Bhāg.* XI. 19. 37. Cf. also *Ibid.* XI. 2. 41, XI. 29. 14 and *Bg.* V. 18.

As ordinarily understood शौच or purity is of two kinds: Bāhya or external and Āntara or internal. The Bhakta does not stand in need of all the rules of external purity laid down by the Smṛtis. He is interested, not in ceremonial purity, but the purity of the mind itself. The dirt that makes the mind impure is the dirt of ego and its appurtenances such as Tamas and Rajas. Anything that helps to keep the mind free from the ego, the Bhakta eagerly adopts. One most important practice leading to such purity is non-attachment. Cf. Bhagavān's definition of S'oucam in *Bhāg.* XI. 19. 38 and XI. 22. 15; कर्मस्वसङ्गमः शौचम्; कर्मशुद्धिर्मदर्पणम् । Other means of internal cleanliness are referred to in *Garudap.* ch. 110. सत्यशौचं मनःशौचं शौचमिन्द्रियनिग्रहः । सर्वभूतदयाशौचं

जलशौचं तु पञ्चमम् । Another list of purity is given by Bṛhaspati: अभक्ष्यपरिहारं च संसर्गश्चाप्यनिन्दितैः । स्वधर्मे च व्यवस्थानं शौचमेतत्प्रकीर्तितम् । Rāmānuja defines it in his *Bhāṣya* on *Bg.* XVIII. 3 as बाह्यान्तःकरणानां कृत्ययोग्यता—fitness of the various internal and external instruments for the due discharge of their functions. Most probably, however, in the eyes of the Bhakta, the most purifying agency is God Himself and remembrance and service of Him. अपवित्रः पवित्रो वा सर्वावस्थां गतोऽपि वा । यः स्मरेत्पुण्डरीकाक्षं स बाह्याभ्यन्तरः शुचिः ॥ Cf. Also *Bhāg.* XII. 12. 46, XI. 14. 21; *Nṛsiṁhap.* 59. 46; *Vp.* II. 6. 29 to 34, III. 7. 35, VI. 7. 10 etc., all of which speak of the purifying effect of the Bhāgavata-dharmas. Cf. also *Ssū.* 59.

The *Sāṇḍilyopaniṣad* defines दया or compassion: दया नामसर्वभूतेषु सर्वत्रानुग्रहः । The *Padp.* says: यत्नादपि परक्लेशं हर्तुं यद् हृदि जायते । इच्छा भूमिसुरश्रेष्ठ सा दया परिकीर्तिता । The *Mātsp.* describes it as आत्मवत्सर्वभूतेषु यो हिताय च शुभाय च । वर्तते सततं हृष्टः क्रिया ह्येषा दया स्मृता । In *Kāśītatvam* it is defined as: परे वा बन्धुवर्गे वा मित्रे द्वेष्टरि वा सदा । आत्मवद्वर्तितव्यं हि दयैषा परिकीर्तिता । The *Saṁkṣepaśārīraka* also says: एतदेव हि दयालुलक्षणं यद्विनेयजनबुद्धिवर्धनम् । From a careful perusal of the above definitions, it becomes quite clear that Dayā is active benevolence which is the positive expression of love, as Ahiṁsā is the negative expression of it. These two form the obverse and reverse of the same coin. The love of the Bhakta does not remain satisfied with mere abstinence from injury; his heart gladly goes out even to his enemies and eagerly searches for an opportunity to do some good to them. Since he sees

God in every being, he is free from all superiority complex that characterizes an ordinary kind man. His kindness is not limited to particular persons, places, times, or other conditions; it is universal. It is this compassion that makes him restlessly active in redeeming sinners with missionary zeal, and it is this that makes him a God in the eyes of the people. Cf. *Bhāg.* III. 27. 8 which speaks of the compassion of the Bhakta. The *Vivekacūḍāmaṇi* speaks of him as अहेतुकदयासिन्धुः। While even God's grace is proportionate to one's deserts, the saint's grace does not depend upon one's deserts. Vide, *Bhāg*. XI. 2. 5 and 6.

आस्तिकस्य means faith in spiritual realities. In S'āṇḍilyopaniṣad it is defined thus: आस्तिक्यं नाम वेदोक्तधर्माधर्मेषु विश्वासः। In defining a नास्तिक *Mnu*. II. 11 says नास्तिको वेदनिन्दकः। The terms नास्तिक and आस्तिक are defined by Bhimācārya as परलोकाद्यस्तितत्ववादी and वेदमार्गमननुरुन्धानः, respectively. Consistent with this definition he speaks of Sāṅkhyas and Advaitins as Nāstikas—मायावादी वेदान्त्यपि नास्तिक एवपर्यवसाने सम्पद्यते। Kumārila also considers the Sāṅkhya, Yoga, Pāñcarātra, and Pās'upata systems as being opposed to the Veda (*Tantravārtika* I. 3. 4.) S'aṅkara himself says in his *Bhāṣya* on *Bg*. XVIII. 42. अस्तिक्यं श्रद्धानता परमार्थेष्वागमार्थेषु। Rāmānuja defines आस्तिक्य as वैदिकार्थस्य कृत्स्नस्य सत्यतानिश्चयः। A persual of these views shows to us that these definitions are only partial and sectarian. If we accept these definitions, many devotees like the Advaitic Bhaktas and Christian and Sufi mystics will have to be left out as Nāstikas. Many of the Āḷvārs and Nāyanārs of South India would not fare better as they are also followers of the Āgamas more than of the Vedas. Many of the followers of the six systems of philosophy including their promulgators like Kapila and Jaimini, who do not give any place to God in their systems, will have to be left out. We have therefore to take the word in a more liberal sense. The common characteristic of all Bhaktas is not faith in this or that scripture or Paraloka, but their intense faith in God and the redeeming power of love. Even the extreme Buddhist of Hīnayāna sect as well as the Jainas who profess to be atheists are not Nāstikas except in a very technical sense. They are all believers in the possibility of the transcendence of human miseries of Saṁsāra, which is the aim of all religions. If we agree to consider the test of Āstikya to be the faith in final redemption, whether it be through self-effort or through God's grace or through the grace of great men, all the great devotees and mystics of the world are characterized by this Āstikya.

Sutra 79 also shows how the intelligent understanding of scriptures, mentioned in *Sū.* 76, affects worship. We have already pointed out in the notes on *Sū.* 37 some of the implications of the worship of Bhagavān. The insistence that only Bhagavān is to be worshipped has got two more implications: First, the Mukhya-bhakta has outgrown the necessity for any props to his Bhakti, and so all lower forms of worship which might have been very helpful and beneficial in the early stages of his ascent, gradually fall away of their own accord. Among these come sacrifices, image worship, pilgrimages, and such other religious observances. His heart naturally turns to God. Even if he does not give up external worship lest he should set a bad example to people who look up to him for guidance, he knows their symbolic character, and his heart's love is given only to the Blessed Lord, who appears to him in his true form even through these symbols. Thus we must note the difference between the attitudes of ordinary men worshipping in temples and great devotees like Rāmānuja and Gaurāṅga, though all are found to behave similarly in external worship. This gradual transformation in mental outlook is referred to in all our devotional scriptures which prescribe the necessity for such growth. See *Bhāg.* III. 29. 21 to 34, XI. 2. 45 to 55. Vide also *Sivap.*, *Vāyusaṁhitā*, XVIII. 101 and 102 and *Maitryupaniṣad*, II. 21 and 26, and *Yogavāsiṣṭha* V. 43. 26. The *Mahānirvāṇatantra* says: बालक्रीडनवत्सर्वे नामरूपादिकल्पनम् । विहाय ब्रह्मनिष्ठो यः स मुक्तो नात्र संशयः । मृच्छिलाधातुदार्वादिमूर्तावीश्वरबुद्धयः । क्लिश्यन्तस्तपसा ज्ञानं विना मुक्तिं न यान्ति ते । उत्तमो ब्रह्मसद्भावो ध्यानभावस्तु मध्यमः । अधमस्तोत्रपाठादि बहिःपूजाधमाधमा । So also the *Jñānasaṅkalinī* says अग्नौ क्रियावतो देवो हृदि देवो मनीषिणाम् । प्रतिमास्वल्पबुद्धीनां ज्ञानिनां सर्वतः शिवः । The *Uttaragītā* has: अग्निर्देवो द्विजातीनां मुनीनां हृदि दैवतम् । प्रतिमास्वल्पबुद्धीनां [illegible]त्र विदितात्मनाम् ।

The second implication is that, however fanatical he might have been in the earlier stages in showing his love to his favourite deity by hating all others, the moment he rises to the stage of Mukhyabhakti, the aspirant understands that all the different paths described in the various scriptures refer to the same Bhagavān only, whom he had been worshipping. This recognition cures him of all fanaticism. If such fanaticism remains still, we may be sure that he has not reached Mukhyabhakti, in which the lover can detect his Beloved in whatever disguise He may appear before him. The Vedic Mantra एकं सद्विप्रा बहुधा वदन्ति *Ṛgv.* I. 164. 46 and similar other passages (for instance, *Bhāg.* I. 2.11 ; III. 32. 26-36 ; VIII. 12. 9 ; *Mudgalopaniṣad*, 3 ; *Mahopaniṣad*, 4. 45 ; *Annapūrṇopaniṣad*, 3, 19-24 ; and *Mahānārayaṇa*, XIII. 2) must have recorded the attitude of the Bhakta who has risen to this vision of unity. The Bhakta now finds out various passages in the scriptures emphazing the unity of God which had previously escaped his notice. In fact he now finds that the purpose of all so-called sectarian scriptures is only to lead him gradually to this non-sectarian stage. Cf. the following well-known verses: श्रीरामचन्द्रहरिशम्भुहरादिशब्दाः ब्रह्मैकमेव सकलाः प्रतिपादयन्ति । कुम्भो घटः कलश इत्यभिशस्यमानो नाणीयसीमपि भिदां भजते पदार्थः ॥ श्रीनाथे जानकीनाथे अभेदः परमात्मनि । तथापि मम सर्वस्वं रामः कमललोचनः ॥ महेश्वरे वा जगतामधीश्वरे जनार्दने वा जगदन्तरात्मनि । न वस्तुभेदप्रतिपत्तिरस्ति मे तथापि भक्तिः तरुणेन्दुशेखरे ॥ शैवा वयं न खलु तत्र विचारणीयं पञ्चाक्षरीजपपरा नितरां तथापि । चेतो मदीयमतसीकुसुमावतंसं स्मेराननं स्मरति गोपवधूकिशोरम् । These passages show the Bhakta's spiritual tolerance in spite of his predilection for his Iṣṭadevatā who has captured his heart. This recognition of unity again results in the Bhakta's directing his attention only to the qualities common to all the deities and considering the rest as unimportant super-impositions. God thus becomes to him only the Bhagavān or the possessor of all blessed qualities, and everything inconsistent with these qualities is rejected. The word सर्वभावेन (through every aspect of life) in the text suggests that in the life of the Bhakta, there are no compartments; in him there is no separation of sacred and secular activities. His whole life is one grand act of worship, each activity being prompted and supported by the fullness of his heart's devotion for Bhagavān. Such a Bhakta is free from all cares, निश्चिन्तत. Not only his activities but even his thoughts and feelings are expresssions of the predominant sentiment of love. Hence there is no possibility of any alien elements disturbing him. Practically, 'nis'cinta bhajana' refers to the complete concentration of the mind on God without a break at any time. This is denoted by the word Samādhi or Bhāva also. It is this kind of worship that is referred to in this *Sū.*

Sutra 80. As a result of such Samādhi, the Lord manifests himself in all His glory to the Bhakta's inner vision, not only in his own heart but in all beings, as a living presence, and not as mere ideas. He now feels that he is living in the same world as God, and this stage of consciousness is denoted by Sālokyamukti. Vide *Bhāg.* XI. 2. 41 & 45. He gradually finds himself in the constant company of the Lord when he comes to recognize various objects not merely as the abode of the Lord but as forms of the Lord Himself. This stage of consciousness is known as Sāmīpyamukti. The constant companionship of the Lord and unintermittent absorption in His divine glories gradually transforms the Bhakta into the likeness of the Lord Himself as mentioned in *Bhāg.* X. 29. 15. The *Bsū.* IV. 4. 17, however, qualifies this by pointing out that the Bhakta cannot acquire the qualities of being the creator, preserver, and destroyer of the world. This is the highest result of the meditation of Saguṇabrahman or Bhagavān according to S'aṅkara. This stage of spiritual attainment is known as Sārūpya. Ordinarily, Bhaktas reach this stage only. But this is not the highest stage of Mukti conceived by Advaitavedānta. Even in this stage, the Bhakta is separate from Bhagavān. The love, which brought him nearer and nearer to the Lord, would not have finished its function until there is no separation at all between the two. Even this duality is to be transcended through love. This final culmination is in the hands of the Lord alone and nothing but God's grace can effect it. Cf. *Kaṭh.* II. 2. 22. The Bhaktas do not have any desire except to serve the Lord and enjoy the sweetness of such service. Cf. *Bhāg.* III. 25. 34; III. 29. 13; XI. 14. 14; XI. 21. 34; etc. But the Lord in His infinite grace gives his devotee not only the three stages mentioned above, but the final stage of complete absorption in Him where all differences are wiped out once for all. (Vide notes on *Sū.* 4.) As S'rī Rāmakṛṣṇa says, 'One can attain the knowledge of Brahman, too, by following the path of Bhakti, God is all-powerful. He may give His devotee Brahmajñāna also, if He so wills. But the devotee generally doesn't seek the knowledge of the Absolute,' *The Gospel of Sri Ramakrishna*, p. 95. The part played by the

Lord in leading the devotee to various stages of realization is referred to in this *Sū.* Cf. *Bhāg.* V. 20. 27; III. 25. 36 and 40; I. 6. 17 and 18. This last stage is known as Sāyūjya or Ekatva. This is the culmination of Mukhyabhakti. That is why these Mukhyabhaktas are called Ekāntins by Nārada in *Sū.* 67. This stage of love is what is known as Parabhakti as described in the first chapter as Paramaprema and Amṛta. Many Bhaktas are afraid of intellectually conceiving this stage, as they think it is sacriligious to think of the possibility of man being really God Himself. Hence the misunderstanding of Advaita position by Bhaktas, who want to predicate intellectually an eternal difference between the Jīvātman and the Paramātman. But whether they like it or not, Bhagavān, out of His infinite grace, gives even this Sāyūjya to the Bhakta who has reached the highest stage. Nārada expressly refers to this stage in *Bhāg.* I. 6. 18 as his own personal experience. See *supra* pp. 42-45. Cf. also Nārada's description of the Bhaktas in *Bhag.* XI. 2. 22 where he expressly says that they found Bhagavān, the world, and their own Selves as one without any difference. Cf. also Svapneśvara's identification of Jīvanmukti and Parabhakti in his *Bhāṣya* on *Śsū.* 98, based upon *Vp.* I. 9. 59. Cf. also Śsū. 31, 85, and 93.

Sutra 81. Even after the realization of this oneness with the Lord, the Bhakta retains his individuality for some time more, until the Prārabdhakarma which gave rise to his last birth works itself out; or as long as God chooses to keep a little of this individuality so as to make him an instrument for His work of love. Cf. *Chānd.* VI. 14. 2 and *Bsū.* IV. 1. 15 and 19. The emotional equipment of the Bhakta, which has become part of his personality by constant practice of devotional discipline during early stages, and has left an indelible impressions on his being, continues to manifest itself throughout his life, as it is not in any way incompatible or opposed to his realization of oneness with the Lord. Although fully conscious of this oneness at every moment, he still loves the Lord and enjoys his sweetness and serves Him as long as he lives. It is the Mukhyabhakti, which is the highest manifestation of devotion attained before the Realization, that is carried into the remaining part of his life. Thus, to all appearance, Mukhyabhakti continues till the very end of a Bhakta's life. But we should not forget the great difference in outlook that is brought about by the Realization of oneness. The state of the Bhakta after the final realization is called Jīvanmukti by Jñānins and Parabhakti by Bhaktas. But as denoted by Vidyāraṇya and Svapnes'vara (see p. 50), there is no difference between Jīvanmukti and Parabhakti except in name. The difference between Mukhyabhakti and Parabhakti is so subtle that it escapes the notice of all except one who has had this experience of oneness. Nārada being one of those who have had both the experiences is in a position to point out this difference.

The Lord of his heart who had been such an entirely different and separate being from himself, the Bhakta now finds to be one with his own Higher Self. The object of his love now is not the personal God with an individuality of His own but the Absolute. The Bhakta now passes beyond all relativities of time, space, and causation, beyond the three Guṇas, beyond the three states of waking, dream, and deep sleep, even beyond the Tṛpuṭi or subject-object relationship, and realizes his oneness with the Lord whom he worships, and at the same time enjoys the sweetness of his loving relationship with Him. This experience of love is the highest experience of a Bhakta, superior even to the Mukhyabhakti. This is the significance of the first part of the *Sū*. The second part of it, which apparently is only a repetition of the first part, is meant to point out that, according to the Bhaktis'āstra and in the consciousness of the Bhakta, the Bhaktisādhana also is superior to all other Sādhanas such as Jñāna, Karma, and Yoga. This is emphasized in the following passages: भक्त्या विना ब्रह्मज्ञानं कदापि न जायते; सर्वोपायान् परित्यज्य भक्तिमाश्रय; भक्तिनिष्ठो भव, भक्तिनिष्ठो भव; भक्त्या सर्वे सिद्धय: सिध्यन्ति; भक्त्या असाध्यं न किञ्चिदस्ति—*Tripādvibhūtinārāyaṇopaniṣad*; अतस्त्वद्भक्तिसम्पन्ना मुक्ता एव न संशय: । त्वद्भक्त्यमृतहीनानां मोक्ष: स्वप्नेऽपि नो भवेत्—*Adhr*. III. 6. 35; न युज्यमानया भक्त्या भगवत्यखिलात्मनि । सदृशोऽस्ति शिव: पन्था योगिनां ब्रह्मसिद्धये—*Bhāg*. III. 25. 19; see also *Ib*. VII. 7. 50-52; X. 14: 4; XI. 2. 34; and XI. 14. 20; and *Brahmavaivarta*, Kṛṣṇakhaṇḍa 97. 8 and 9; and *Bg*. VI. 47: XII. 2; XVIII. 66.

Sutra 82 refers to the various important types of Bhakti. It does not mean that there are only these eleven types; there are possibilities of as many types as there are human relationships. Nārada points out that even if externally they appear as different, they are all manifestations of Love which in itself is only one. The difference in attitudes can only be attributed to tastes, preferences, and predilections due to the past Saṁskāras of the individuals, or to some inscrutable divine purpose to be worked out only in particular ways. Thus Nārada and Vyāsa are always found delighting themselves in singing the glories of the Lord, helping to convert others to a life of spirituality and love. The Gopīs of Brindāvan were naturally attracted by Kṛṣṇa's enchanting personal beauty, and they revelled in it. Ambarīṣa spent his whole life in worship, Prahlāda in remembrance, Hanumān in service. Uddhava and Arjuna had the attitude of friendship, Rukmiṇī and Satyabhāmā loved Him as a husband, and Kausalyā and Devakī as their son. Bali and Vibhīṣaṇa are supreme examples of complete self-surrender to the Lord; and the great Ṛṣis like Sanatkumāra and Yājñavalkya immersed themselves in His bliss. By this specification it is not meant to say that other attitudes were not found in their lives; what is meant to say is only that each one is characterized by a predominant attitude. The different attitudes may be found in the same person at different times, as in S'rī Rāmakṛṣṇa. The last attitude is a common characteristic of all Bhaktas, because it is in the very nature of intense love that it cannot bear separation; and Nārada has made this one of the supreme tests of devotion in *Sū.* 29, and Yāmunācārya calls it the highest manifestation of love, see p. 40 above. This stage of Love is typically manifested in Rādhā and the Gopīs when they were separated from Kṛṣṇa, and is glorified in the songs of the Ālvārs and the *Gītagovinda*.

Sutra 83. In this *Sū.* Nārada shows how his own teachings contained in this work have the sanction and corroboration of all the great paragons of Bhakti. Only a few of them are mentioned by name; we are to understand others also from the use of the word 'ādi'. There might be differences in emphasis in each one of these great Bhaktas, but in their realization and spiritual teachings they are all practically one. Some of the minor differences with regard to the characterization of Parabhakti Nārada himself has noted in *Sū.* 16 to 18 and 28 to 30. But with regard to Aparabhakti, there is no difference of opinion among them, so far as the teachings presented in this book are concerned. Some of these Bhaktas, whose names are quoted, have left their own writings, but many have only helped people by their example, and we have only got descriptions of their exemplary life in the devotional writings of the devotees who have left some literary records. Nārada therefore expects us to study the life and teachings of these Bhaktas as recorded in literature that has come down to us. We need not confine ourselves to the study of the lives of only Hindu Bhaktas. Even the life and writings of Christian and Sufi mystics as well as the doctrines of other religions will amply corroborate the teachings contained in Nārada's Sūtras. We have ourselves tried to indicate in our notes such corroborations. But Nārada expects us to follow his example in adopting only those teachings on which they are unanimous.

Kumāra, referred to in the *Sū.*, is Sanatkumāra, who was Nārada's Guru. In the *Brahmavaivarta*, S'rī Kṛṣṇakhaṇḍa, also he is reported to have obtained instruction from Sanatkumāra on the ultimate Truth. In the same book Sanatkumāra is said to be वैष्णवानामग्रणीः, the prince among Bhaktas, always repeating the Kṛṣṇa-mantra. He is also reported as repeating the Mantra: हरिःशरणम्. It is in the fitness of things that Nārada should head the list of Bhaktas with the name of his own Guru. Next in order comes his own S'iṣya *viz.* Vyāsa, whom he instructed to propagate the Bhakti-sāstra. It is Vyāsa who has popularised even the name of his Guru as well as the glories of Bhagavān, and the teachings on love through various books. S'uka comes third in the list as the mouthpiece of Vyāsa in promulgating the *Bhāg.* S'āṇdilya was an ancient Ṛṣi whose name comes in *Chānd.* III. 14. 4 as the promulgator of the S'āṇdilyavidyā. Many other S'āṇdilyas are also mentioned in *Bṛh.* II. 6. 1. etc. Which of them is referred to by Nārada is not clear. Anyhow the teachings of one S'āṇdilya on Bhakti have been systematized in the *Bhaktimīmāṁsā* which is now widely in use. It is a very important treatise on Bhakti. Whether Nārada refers to this book, we are not sure. Garga is an ancient Ṛṣi who is reported to have obtained knowledge of the 64 Vidyās from S'iva himself as a result of penance and worship, *Mbh.* XIII. 18. 38. He is also reported to have been the Ṛṣi who performed the Nāmakaraṇa ceremony of Śrī Kṛṣṇa. He is a great authority on Astrology. Garga's teaching is recorded in *Gargasaṁhitā.* A Brahmavādinī named Vācaknavī is mentioned in the *Bṛh.* as the daughter of Garga. Garga must have been a great Vedāntin as his daughter could have had no other Guru than her father; for according to Hārīta 20 to 23, women could study only in their own homes. Yama also says that nobody else should teach a girl. Another great Ṛṣi, Kunīgarga by name, is mentioned in Śalya Parva Ch. 52 as the father of a girl who spent her life in Tapas. We are not sure whether the two Gargas are the same. There was a great Ṛṣi called Viṣṇu who was a law-giver; but his name is not much associated with Bhakti. There was another Viṣṇusvāmin who was a great Bhakta but he lived in comparatively recent days and so could not have been thought of by Nārada. Perhaps the reference is to Viṣṇu in his Avatāra as Nārāyaṇa and Kṛṣṇa. In the Śāntiparva, Nārāyiṇīya section of the Mokṣadharma, we find Nārāyaṇa represented as a great pioneer of the Bhakti cult and as one of the teachers of Nārada himself. Hence there is every likelihood of Narada's referring to him as one of the Bhakti Ācāryas. Narada was a great Bhakta also of Kṛṣṇa, who was the first and foremost exponent of the doctrine of love for love's sake, and there would be propriety in Nārada's mentioning his name as an Ācārya of Bhakti. Perhaps he refers to them as Viṣṇu because they are both one, being the Avatāra of Viṣṇu. In many of the Purāṇas we find Visnu himself represented as discoursing on the Bhakti cult. So the reference may be directly to God Visnu himself. Kauṇḍinya is an ancient Ṛṣi and his name is mentioned in the *Bṛh.* geneology as the son of S'āṇḍilya, and so there is every likelihood of his having been a great Bhakta also. S'eṣa may be Saṅkarṣaṇa or Lakṣmaṇa or Ramanuja all of whom are considered as the Avatāra of Ananta. The reference could not be to Rāmānuja as he was later in point of time. Saṅkarṣaṇa was a great exponent of Bhakti according to the Bhāgavata cult, and he is even considered an Avatāra of Viṣṇu himself, being the second among the Vyūhas. His teachings can be gathered from the Āgamas and Purāṇas. The word S'eṣa is used as one of the names of Saṅkarṣaṇa or Baladeva in *Māgha* II. 68. The reference can also be to Lakṣmaṇa who was an exponent in his own life of Bhakti as fraternal love to God. This is one of the types not mentioned in the list given in *Sū.* 82. The glories of love as exemplified in the lives of Lakṣmaṇa, Hanūman, and Vibhiṣaṇa can be enjoyed by a study of the *Rāmāyana.* Although Hanumān is ordinarily considered as a monkey, the *Vālmīkirāmayaṇā* makes it clear that he was a man who had studied even the Vedas. See Book IV. Ch. 3. 28-34. Perhaps the people whom Rāma met in the forest were called Vānaras only because they were dwellers in the forest, or because they had the sign of the monkey on their banners as their insignia. It is something like speaking of the British Lion or German Eagle as representing the whole British people or Germans. Uddhava and Bali were well known Bhaktas who are referred to in

Bhāg. Āruṇi was a great Ṛṣi whose name is mentioned as a great knower of Brahman in *Chānd.* VI and *Bṛh.* III. His full name seems to have been, according to these texts, Uddālaki Āruṇi. The Ācārya Nimbārka also seems to have been known by the name of Ārunika: but surely the reference in the text cannot be to him, as he lived quite recently.

Sutra 84 is the last, and it forms a fitting conclusion to the whole discussion. The Upasaṁhāra naturally is consistent with the Upakrama. Just as we found that the text began with a few suggestive Sūtras which foreshadowed the whole ensuing discussion we are happy to find a beautiful recapitulation of the foregoing discussion in this last *Sū.* One should not take this *Sū.* lightly as a mere Phalas'ruti, like those met with usually at the end of many treatises, and treat it as a mere exaggeration of the benefits expected to be conferred by the study of the book. By a careful use of the words in this *Sū.*, Nārada suggests the whole contents of the book—the Adhikārin, Viṣaya, Sambandha, and Prayojana. To explain: The use of the vague relative pronoun suggests the catholicity of the Bhakti s'āstra which is open to all, irrespective of caste, creed, age, learning, sex, etc. Any man who is interested in the subject, who is able to understand the teachings, and who is earnestly willing to put it into practice is sure to be benefited by the study. By calling his book S'ivanus'āsana, Nārada suggests that his teaching is only an Anus'āsana about S'ivam; that as an Anus'āsana it is a teaching which follows or agrees with ('anu'=following) the teachings (s'āsana) of all Bhaktas, and that it deals with S'ivam or the Absolute mentioned in the *Mānd.* VII as शान्तं शिवमद्वैतम् । The word therefore is beautifully expressive of the subject-matter of the book and its universality and auspiciousness. The use of the word 'प्रेष्ठम्' suggests that the goal to be attained is supreme Bliss—through realization of oneness with the Absolute Ātman. See *Chānd.* VII. 23,24. *Bṛh.* I.4.8 : II. 4.4 ; IV. 3. 32 ; *Tait.* II. 81 ; *Bg.* IV. 20-22 ; V. 11. 17; etc. 'भक्तिमान्' indicates that the immediate and final means of such supreme realization is Bhakti or love of God. 'विश्वसिति' suggests the necessity of a conviction of the rational nature of the teaching, and 'श्रद्धत्ते' indicates the necessity of such conviction being followed by an earnest and sincere attempt to practise them. The separation of Vis'vāsa and S'raddhā into two elements also suggests the following difference between the two : Belief is mere intellectual conviction. Ordinarily it is based on mere habit, custom, or tradition ; or it may be based upon imagination, selfish ambition, or mere tastes and predilections. Such belief, no doubt, may be helpful sometimes in the early stages, but the belief or conviction that Nārada expects of his followers to develop is the one based upon a critical scrutiny of the teachings in the light of reason. The use of the word therefore suggests the willingness of the author to submit his book to rational inquiry and his readiness to allow his reader to use his discretion in accepting or rejecting any of his teachings as the reason and experience of the reader tells him. By adding on the word 'Sraddhatte' immediately after 'Viśvasiti' Nārada indicates his opinion that these intellectual convictions, however necessary they may be, must have the support of Śraddhā also. Śraddhā is conviction which has become dynamic, and involves not merely intellectual assent but readiness, sincerity, and earnestness to realize the highest Truth by actual practice of the teachings, when one is convinced of its rationality and utility. Śraddhā is not a mere partial response of the mind, but a total response of the whole mind to reality as reason presents it to the discriminating intellect. The intimate connection of Śraddha to Truth is suggested by its derivation from श्रत् which is one of the synonyms of Satya mentioned in Yāska's Nighaṇṭu. Thus the separation of Viśvāsa and Śraddha and the coupling of both together show that, unlike many people who find an opposition between reason and faith, Nārada holds that there is no such inherent opposition, and that reason and faith cooperate with each other in spiritual life. In this Nārada is in complete agreement with the great Acaryas, whether they are protagonists of Jñāna, or Bhakti, or Karma. Thus Śaṅkara the protagonist of Jñāna speaks of the necessity of Śraddhā in *Viveka-cūḍāmaṇi* 25. Yamunācārya, the champion of Bhakti, in declining to accept the assertion of an opponent, says in his *Siddhitraya*, 'All this teaching may carry weight with believers. We are not so credulous and so we require reason to convince us.' Tikācārya says in his *Nyāyasudha* I. 4, that even the Veda has to be understood in the light of reason. Śāṇḍilya expressly refers to the place of reason in *Ssu.* 27 and 28.

Manu also refers to the necessity of both reason and faith in matters of Dharma. Again the expression नारदप्रोक्तम् suggests the preliminary step of getting into touch with a perfect Guru like Nārada either directly or through books. Finally the word लभते suggests that the attainment of Supreme Bliss is not something which comes by mere self-effort, but is a gift from God, and thus it points to the element of Divine grace in spiritual realization. Thus the *Sū.* as a whole, is a beautiful recapitulation of the whole of Narada's teaching.

In this final aphorism, before he takes leave of the readers, Nārada blesses them so that they may have the grace of God, and through that grace realize Supreme Bliss, by gaining which there is no possibility of birth and suffering in Saṁsara.

'नमस्तुभ्यं भगवते निर्गुणाय गुणात्मने ।
केवलायाद्वितीयाय गुरवे ब्रह्मरूपिणे ॥
याऽहं ममास्ति यत्किञ्चिदिहलोके परत्र च ।
तत्सर्वं भवतो नाथ चरणेषु समर्पितम् ॥
पदे पदे यथा भक्तिः पादयोस्तव जायते ।
तथा कुरुष्व देवेश नाथस्त्वं नो यतः प्रभो ॥
पतिपुत्रसुहृद्भ्रातृपितृवन्मातृवद्धरिम् ।
ये ध्यायन्ति सदोद्युक्तास्तेभ्योऽपीह नमो नमः ॥'

Oṁ S'āntiḥ ! S'āntiḥ ! S'āntiḥ !

NOTE ON TRANSLITERATION

In this book Devanāgarī characters are transliterated according to the scheme adopted by the International Congress of Orientalists at Athens in 1912 and since then generally acknowledged to be the only rational and satisfactory one. In it the inconsistency, irregularity and redundancy of English spelling are ruled out: f, q, w, x and z are not called to use; one fixed value is given to each letter. Hence a, e, i and g always represent अ, ए, इ and ग respectively and never ए, इ, ऐ and ज् or other values which they have in English; t and d are always used for त् and द् only. One *tialde*, one accent, four macrons and ten dots (2 above, 8 below) are used to represent adequately and correctly all Sanskrit letters. *The letter C alone represents* च्. Since the natural function of h will be to make the aghoṣa ghoṣa (e.g. kh, ch, ṭh. th, ph, gh, jh, ḍh, dh bh), it would be an anomaly for a scientific scheme to use it in combinations like ch and sh for giving च् and ष् values; hence ch here is छ् and sh स्ह्. The vowel ऋ is represented by ṛ because ri, legitimate for रि only, is out of place, and the singular ṛi is an altogther objectionable distortion. The *tialde* over n represents ञ्, ñ. Accent mark over s gives श्, s'; dots above m and n give anusvāra (ं), ṁ and ङ्, ṅ, respectively. Dots below h and r give visarga (:), ḥ, and ऋ, ṛ, respectively. Dots below s, n, t and d give their corresponding cerebrals ष्, ण्, ट् and ड्, ṣ, ṇ, ṭ, and ḍ; and macrons over a, i, u and ṛ give ā, ī, ū, ṝ respectively. Macrons are not used to lengthen the quantity of e and o, because they always have the long quantity in Sanskrit. Sanskrit words are capitalized only where special distinctiveness is called for, as in the opening of a sentence, title of books, etc. The scheme of transliteration in full is as follows:

अ a, आ ā, इ i, ई ī, उ u, ऊ ū, ऋ ṛ, ॠ ṝ, ए e, ओ o, ऐ ai, औ au, ं ṁ, : ḥ, क् k, ख् kh, ग् g, घ् gh, ङ् ṅ, च् c, छ ch, ज् j, झ् jh, ञ् ñ, ट् ṭ, ठ् ṭh, ड् ḍ, ढ् ḍh, ण् ṇ, त् t, थ् th, द् d, ध् dh, न् n, प् p, फ् ph, ब् b, भ् bh, म् m, य् y, र् r, ल् l, व् v, श् s', ष् ṣ, स् s, ह् h.